The Politics of Peace

John H. Barton

The Politics of Peace
An Evaluation of Arms Control

Stanford University Press
Stanford, California
1981

Preface

I HAVE HAD three interrelated concerns in writing this book. The first is to attempt to define as precisely as possible what benefits arms control can bring. Arms control gained international respectability during the early 1960's. Before then, disarmament talks were generally perceived to be oriented primarily toward propaganda benefits. Since then, treaties such as the Limited Test Ban, the Non-Proliferation Treaty, and the SALT agreements have been negotiated. But the chances for future agreements appear to have collapsed with President Carter's withdrawal of the SALT II treaty early in 1980. Although the agreements have generally been honored, there is a real question whether the effort was worth its costs. More broadly, can arms control be any more effective than the elaborate structure of peace erected in the 1920's, which collapsed with the crises of the 1930's? And is arms control in any way relevant to the actual issues dividing East and West or North and South?

My second concern is that the dialogue between the proponents and the opponents of arms control is often weak, when any dialogue exists at all. The debate often seems to pit one set of preconceptions against another. Even scholarly articles frequently amount to little more than arguments based on prejudices, and these the reader may or may not share. Hence I wanted to examine the theoretical arguments underlying arms control and, to the extent possible, to take the analysis back to a set of ideas that might be acceptable to at least some on both sides of the issue.

Third, particularly after carrying out the analysis, I want to suggest a new agenda for arms control. Both the supporters and the critics of arms control generally agree that the intellectual framework developed in the 1950's that underlies the recent arms control effort is no longer adequate. That framework gave priority to U.S.-Soviet strategic nuclear issues, and tended to treat the two parties as united, rational actors able to enter bloodlessly into agreements that would bring mutual benefit. The negotiations, however, turned out to be anything but bloodless; they were marked by domestic struggles and an international politics of détente and special relationships that has now collapsed. My judgment is that the purely government-to-government approach, exemplified in the recent effort, is bound to be limited in its success. It is necessary to find ways to bring citizens more fully into the arms control process. I have made a number of suggestions in this direction in the hope that they can be helpful both during the current bleak period and perhaps in some future time of negotiations.

My basic analytic approach is to examine separately the political mechanisms underlying war and the political requirements for arms control. By combining these two examinations, it is possible to make a thoughtful estimate of the impact of an achievable arms control on the likelihood of war. This is the task of the first two-thirds of this book, the first third building the tools and the second third completing the analysis. Although I recognize that there are other goals of arms control, and I take into account the political influence of these other goals, I believe it reasonable to use the goal of preventing war as the central criterion for arms control. In the final portion of the book, I attempt to apply the analysis in order to define a new agenda for arms control. These aims are ambitious, and I have undoubtedly made many errors, for which I take full responsibility. Nevertheless, I hope that the book is developed carefully and accurately enough that it can stimulate others to criticize and revise my analysis and to consider my conclusions seriously.

I wish to thank many who joined in this effort, beginning with my students and colleagues in the Stanford Law School and the Stanford Arms Control Program, many of whom have contributed heavily to my thinking. Tom Shillinglaw, in particular, prepared a historical review of the legal doctrine of neutrality, and an outstanding group of law students helped me in understanding the possibilities of international nuclear organizations. Others who have worked with me on previous projects have provided particularly helpful criticism and insights. These include colleagues in the 1974 International Studies Association Panel on Arms Control, in the 1980's Nuclear Weapons Group of the Council on Foreign Relations, in the International Institute for Strategic Studies, and in the U.S.-Japan Working Group on International Security. Many of my friends have read drafts and provided criticism and encouragement. I wish to thank them all and must note special debts to Eric Stein, to Daniel Heradstveit, and to Larry Caldwell, who went beyond his role as a reviewer to offer enormous help in outlining the final editing. I wish further to thank Mary Carruth, who has cheerfully typed innumerable drafts. I must also note a special debt to my wife, who has consistently encouraged me in the effort and who suggested the title.

Finally, I wish to thank those who contributed financially. Travel to examine arms control policies in the developing world was supported by the Stanford Law School and the Stanford Center for International Studies. The Stanford Arms Control Group, under a grant from the Ford Foundation, supported half a year's leave for writing. The main revision was completed under a Rockefeller Foundation Conflict in International Relations Fellowship at the International Institute for Strategic Studies in 1976–77.

J.H.B.

Contents

1. Background: The Sources of War and Peace   1

2. The Initiation of War   15

3. International Law and Arms Control   44

4. Entry into Arms Control Agreements   67

5. The Impact of Contemporary Arms Control   105

6. Multilateral Techniques of Enforcing
   Arms Control   127

7. SALT and the Control of Bilateral
   Nuclear Deterrence   148

8. Regional Arms Control   175

9. Global Arms Control   200

10. Conclusions   219

     Notes   235

     Index   253

The Politics of Peace

1. Background: The Sources of War and Peace

Before we examine how man and his institutions shape war, we must briefly consider the nature of both. For assumptions about human nature and human institutions underlie any theory of war, and if the theory is to be persuasive, the assumptions must be made explicit.[1] Moreover, if peace is to be built, it is man and his institutions that must do the building.

HUMAN MOTIVATIONS: AGGRESSION AND AUTHORITY

Human aggression is probably relevant to war, but scientists are not agreed on what human aggression is.[2] Some believe aggression to be a genetically transmitted instinct, occurring inevitably in response to certain stimuli. Others argue that aggression is learned behavior, transmitted by culture. Still others see aggression as a psychological response to frustration. Each school of thought can point to experimental data that support its view; each school also finds some experimental data inexplicable. The debate is not inconsequential, for the choice of techniques for controlling aggression depends on which view is correct.

One way to resolve the question is to postulate several distinct genetically based mechanisms, some of which function in support of learned or frustration-derived aggressive behavior. The genetic theories do suggest, and some animals plainly exhibit, a number of different aggressive instincts. Each instinct must have a specific physiological mechanism—a chemical or neurological response, for example—corresponding to it, but only sketchy data on these mechanisms have so far been gathered. Each of the mechanisms must also confer evolutionary advantage by favoring the survival and reproduction of the species.

Territorial aggression, for example, is probably related to the benefits of spreading out to avoid pressure on limited resources such as food supply. When resources are significantly limited, evolution presumably favors those species that have a method of repelling each other. Other forms of aggression may help define a stable social order among the members of a group. The behavior of a higher-ranking member may be imitated by the lower-ranking members in a sort of learning process, with the leaders selected by an aggression system based on a series of individual combats. For these forms of aggression to benefit the species, the combats must not be mortal. These instincts typically operate through a ritualistic test of strength that terminates in a submissive gesture in which the loser exposes a vital area. But the winner is inhibited from actually killing the loser; death occurs only by accident or as a result of a struggle between two closely matched animals.

One could attempt to argue directly from these animal instincts to analogous behavior in man. For example, the relatively high crime rate among young men may be associated with inter-male aggression; and patriotism and the defense of the homeland may be associated with territorial aggression. Poetic and romantic views of war—the special fascination and horror of hand-to-hand combat, the concern that technology depersonalizes war, the sense that a soldier especially deserves his beloved's favors—suggest profound psychological roots. But one must be very careful about comparing aggression in humans and nonhumans, even with these limited parallels; human aggression is much more complex. In war, for example, instinctive aggression would often be counterproductive; the soldier, general, or national leader seeks to stay cool and use his skills rationally. And if humans have retained some aggressive instincts, they have probably also retained the associated inhibitions, which perhaps provide support for an ethics of self-restraint.

The evolutionary origins of authority and obedience have received less attention than those of aggression, but may be just as important an ingredient in war. Presumably, authority could evolve only in tandem with obedience. Neither seems likely to evolve except in highly social species, in which natural selection occurs among groups, as well as among individuals. Certain social insects exhibit obedience and authority mechanisms, for instance, and some primates show traits that appear directly relevant to man.

In one particularly provocative example of primate society, the animals live in small groups, almost extended families, numbering several males, a larger number of females, and the young. Ritual combats among the males create a dominance hierarchy headed by a leader whose authority all respect. This leadership structure probably helps the group defend itself. An aggressive attack on the leader by another male sometimes splits the group, probably helping to keep group size and spacing optimum in relation to the environment. This social system requires a form of nonlethal aggression, a pattern of leadership and obedience, and a mechanism to distinguish between the in-group and the out-group.[3]

This pattern from the primate world has striking parallels in human behavior. Human society incorporates a willingness on the part of its members to accept authority[4] and to be aggressive when so directed;[5] a process of in-group and out-group identification; and a tendency of individuals to band together when the group is threatened. Authority is in fact bestowed on a victor, as one might predict from the pattern. The identification of harm to an individual with harm to the group might also be expected, and is indeed often found in tribal law. And traditional warfare can even be seen as serving the survival functions of controlling population density and distributing scarce resources.[6]

Again, the parallels must be treated with care. Human instincts may differ from those of other primates, either because of evolutionary change or because of differences in ancestral social patterns. Although the evidence is unclear, prehistoric society may have been generally peaceful rather than warlike;[7] some traditional societies, such as those of the Eskimo, have no intertribal warfare, but only feuds and individual acts of aggression. Thus the elaborate primate pattern may not directly provide a biological basis for human warfare.

There is an important difference between man and other primates: man can generalize. He fights for many different reasons and in many different situations, and not simply at a signal from an instinct that depends on specific patterns of territory, opponent, and even time within the reproductive or seasonal cycle. In the context of war, man's instincts of aggression and obedience provide at most a biological potential for a range of behaviors that can reflect education, culture, or conscious decision. Within limits, man can break past an instinctive or learned role and develop new ideas that make it possible for him to assume new roles.[8]

Man's ability to generalize broadens his range of reasons for making war. He may fight to defend a nation, a religion, an ideology, or a notion of justice; and he may act in response to a feudal, national, or even international authority. He may limit his warlike actions out of revulsion for the suffering of others or out of an abstract ethical commitment. Conceivably, man's instincts have been left so far behind that war is almost entirely a cultural invention.[9] If so, it is a contagious invention; for when one group practices war, others must practice it as well.

Our current knowledge of human aggression, therefore, does not support the conclusion that war is an unpreventable product of innate instinct. To be sure, instinctive reactions sometimes influence war, as for example when a soldier reacts to the death of a comrade, or a leader reacts to a threat to his authority, or a population reacts to a particularly brutal form of conflict. Man's willingness to submit to authority, however, particularly the authority of a victor, may be more important than his aggression. This obedience, shaped by culture and ideology, is part of the foundation of both the nation-state and the law. Aggression and obedience can certainly influence human behavior, and probably can lead to war. But it is doubtful that these instincts make war inevitable. Whatever psychological effects these instincts may have are likely to be better understood at the level of human culture and allegiance than at the level of biological determinism.

GOVERNMENT AND NATIONALISM

Though war can involve individual aggression, it is by definition a group action, and typically an action of government. Indeed, government is often defined in terms of the monopoly of the right to use deadly force, save for the individual's right to use force in his own self-defense. The duty and right of group self-defense are regarded as belonging exclusively to the state, although perhaps theoretically delegated by the citizens.

Even though a government may have seized its power, the citizens' support of its authority to use force is more than simply an acquiescence in the seizure. The citizen usually believes the government holds its authority as of right, although various theories of government may limit that right. Thus the state's monopoly of force comes less from its ability to coerce than from its ability to enlist voluntary obedience, including the voluntary obedience of its police and military. Likewise, the citizen generally believes the state's use of force is ethical as well as legal. For centuries, personal moral beliefs have prohibited homicide except when it is authorized by the state in the exercise of a criminal or military sanction. Even people who disapprove of war or capital punishment view these government actions as fundamentally different from the unauthorized use of force by an individual.

A biological or psychological tendency may underlie obedience to government. Patriotic allegiance is readily given, especially in time of war, as the analogous primate behavior discussed in the previous section suggests. The primate model may thus shed light on government, as well as on war.[10] Also, obedience often seems to satisfy psychological desires not associated with aggression, such as the desire to avoid making difficult decisions by relying on authority instead.[11]

As I have argued, however, man operates at a level far beyond biological determinism when he creates and obeys a government. This is suggested by the vocabulary used in discussing government, which invokes legitimacy rather than instinct. The citizen's obedience is much more subtle than an obedience that is fundamentally psychological. Citizens sometimes withdraw their obedience and rebel. And they often think of the authority of the government as restricted. In the West, the traditional belief that government should be subject to law has given rise to many efforts to devise governments whose authority is limited in fact, as well as in theory. In the East, Imperial China tested government by whether it possessed the "mandate of heaven." Even governments that claim total power are not inevitably obeyed.

Nationalism, frequently and correctly cited as a barrier to peace, is a modern manifestation of the allegiance that citizens give to authority. Viewed historically, however, nationalism is not a simple glorification of the power of national government. Rather, it is a combination of several related forces, some of which reflect the limitations of allegiance, as well as its power.

One of these forces is a drive to transfer local and regional power to a centralized national level. This is the drive that created the nation-state system, which appears only infrequently in history. For the European nations that led the modern process, this transfer of power was well under way by the eighteenth century, effected at the elite level by arrangements that the central government imposed on or extracted from regional leaders in what later turned out to be one-sided bargains.[12] War was probably the most powerful factor in the centralizing drive; the emerging national leaders of Europe needed to increase their control in order to extract the financial and human resources needed to prosecute wars with other states. Thus the European nations grew up together to form an international system in which each nation was increasingly centralized as a defense against others. This force strengthened when newly centralized nations, such as France at the end of the eighteenth century and Germany at the beginning of the twentieth, became expansionist. As Japan and other nations entered this system, they responded by centralizing similarly.

A second form of nationalism followed, perhaps for domestic reasons. As government demands on the citizens mounted, the citizens understandably sought to increase their control over the governments, and the governments sought to increase the sense of national unity. This was the drive of mobilization: the awakening of individual citizens to a wide community of culture and responsibility. This mobilization, along with many other factors, contributed to democratic controls on government and to a widening of the franchise. Nationalism of this sort also tended to support the revision of frontiers to reflect cultural groupings. Thus, by the time the Austro-Hungarian Empire broke up in the twentieth century, nationalism had become a divisive force rather than a unifying one, fostering a separatism that supported local government against outside interference, as well as seeking to restrain government.

The centralizing and mobilizing phases of nationalism are necessarily telescoped in the new nations of the developing world.[13] Their leaders are striving to centralize their authority in the face of family, tribal, and regional loyalties; at the same time, the populations are becoming mobilized as a result of education and the example of the developed world. Political participation in these countries is too weak to help the central government solve problems and too strong to permit it to ignore its citizens. It was easy for the political elites of the developing world to base their independence movements on a separatist nationalism, but they have often turned to authoritarianism when confronted by domestic problems.

Whether nationalism in the developing world will become expansionist is less clear. The nationalism of these countries may aim more toward the goal of social justice than toward the goal of international power. And the external force impelling these new nations to unify is seldom the threat of war as it was in Europe; rather, it is in large measure a desire for economic growth. Nevertheless, it would be naive not to expect that some developing nations will follow the expansionist and totalitarian pattern of twentieth-century Germany; perhaps this will occur, as in Germany, following on success in development. It is likely that the developing areas will long be among the most unstable parts of the world, with most developing nations probably having difficulty in evolving mature, restrained governments. But demands for global justice can quickly turn into demands for local justice. The nationalism of the developing world contains the seeds of restraint, as well as the seeds of war.

FOREIGN POLICY

Traditionally, many of a government's foreign policy goals were independent of the interests of its citizens. Thus, in the dynastic politics of European royal houses, subject populations were little more than a source of wealth. Except when war loomed, foreign policy usually had little impact on the citizen; and until the advent of total war in the Napoleonic era, even war often left the citizen untouched.

Foreign policy was therefore left to governments. National legislatures respected the traditional confidentiality of defense and foreign policy matters, confining their attention to domestic issues. The executive could usually curtail any criticism by arguing a national security need or invoking the risk of upsetting a delicate balance of power. When legislatures did intervene, it was often in an excessively nationalistic way reminiscent of primate behavior. Political leaders seldom discussed foreign policy in domestic political campaigns, except as a way to demonstrate competence and provide reassurance to the people. As a result, foreign policy was usually left to a specialized establishment that cloaked itself with a claim of expertise and, like any bureaucracy, propagated the belief that its problems were special and beyond the competence of the average politician or citizen.

Foreign policy, therefore, tended to function independently of national politics. An important effect of this segregation of foreign policy has been the popularity in contemporary academic circles of the view that foreign relations are purely amoral and power-related. Foreign policy theory emphasized the rather abstract pursuit of "prestige" and power in order to achieve national goals in negotiations with other nations.[14] Foreign relations were indeed once hardly more than a game played by sovereigns. Few traditional political philosophers saw international relations as deserving much attention; most concentrated instead on domestic society. Moreover, international society and domestic society are so different that any political philosophy or ethics relevant to one would have to be radically modified to be relevant to the other. Efforts to base foreign policy on morality, for instance, have often proved naive or messianic, as with Woodrow Wilson's policies or the Crusades.[15]

Though the abstract, amoral view of foreign policy may no longer be empirically accurate, it can easily become a working assumption in a foreign office, and can even more easily be attributed to other nations' foreign offices. Within and between bureaucracies, the prophecy of amorality can be self-fulfilling. An example of this is the tendency to emphasize military aspects of foreign relations because military costs and benefits can always be calculated more persuasively than political costs and benefits. The result can be a pyramiding of strategic goals in which the military importance of one position derives from the military support it can give to another position. By way of illustration, South Africa derives strategic and political importance from oil routes that in turn derive importance from Middle Eastern politics and world energy problems. Great powers therefore concern themselves with South Africa in order to maintain a balance of power. Foreign policy often becomes an amoral game of accumulating power and influence, heavily shaped by military planning. Even though diplomacy seeks to avoid war, the game clearly risks war in a way that has little to do with nationalism.

In many respects this diplomatic pattern provides the basic components for the initiation of some wars. Right up to recent times, in spite of the development of total war, international diplomacy has remained in the control of the experts. But the pattern is now under severe attack and can be expected to change greatly during the next generation. Even in peacetime, foreign policy now affects citizens so directly that they are likely, if they have any political power at all, to seek a more important role in formulating it. International economic interdependence has created obvious examples of foreign affairs having a broad impact on the mass of citizens: the European Economic Community (EEC), the Organization of Petroleum Exporting Countries (OPEC), the multinational corporations. In areas such as economics and science, bureaucracies are losing their ability to segregate foreign policy from domestic policy.

In some cases this deepening interplay between domestic politics and international politics will simply make the diplomat's task of maintaining peace more difficult. In other cases it is likely to intensify citizens' efforts to restrict their government's ability to go to war. Today, legislatures often debate foreign policy issues such as international human rights and arms sales. This interpenetration of the politics of different nations is likely to produce its own pressures for reform. The assumption that foreign policy is amoral could change; nuclear arms and a growing concern for human rights might compel the world to give high priority to the institutional and philosophical tasks of restraining the international policies of governments.

THE MILITARY

Most societies appreciate the need to prepare for war, both to deter attack and to increase the chance of victory should war come. Because the task of preparing for war is so complex, almost all societies support some form of professional military. In feudal Europe, a professional military caste evolved. In the United States and other modern societies, taxes support a military consisting of hired professionals and short-term recruits. Only where defense is unimportant or where military technology is relatively accessible to the citizen do professional armed forces not emerge.

A warrior caste is likely to be accompanied by an elaborate ritual and a special ethics, as with the knight in feudal Europe, the samurai in feudal Japan, and the officer in eighteenth-century Prussia. This cultural pattern probably derives psychologically from the importance of defense and from the need to justify military action yet at the same time to prevent unnecessary death in combat. Perhaps it also helps maintain the military's loyalty to authority. It is a pattern characteristically found in eras of highly limited wars, when warfare resembles a game or ritual, with a symbolic outcome that affects relations between rulers but leaves most citizens indifferent. In a society that has a warrior caste, "militarism" has a clear meaning; and quite conceivably such a military culture directly encourages war.

Although the concept of a warrior caste still shapes some thinking about the role of the military, the composition of the military has changed drastically as war has changed. With the American and French revolutions, pressure grew for military forces to include as many able-bodied citizens as possible. Although in a few cases, such as Japan before the Second World War, a military philosophy may be espoused by a large portion of the nation, the discipline of citizen-soldiers tends to be based on national attitudes rather than on the military's special ethics. [16] One logical implication of the citizen-soldier idea is the Maoist concept of guerrilla warfare, in which the citizens and the army become essentially intermingled. Another implication is the expansion of stylized war into total war. The military and citizens together become a force for nearly total destruction. In neither the guerrilla pattern nor the total war pattern can the military remain a separate culture with its traditional cultural justification.

Militaries in both Communist and non-Communist nations appear to have responded by adopting one of two alternative models. In most of the developed world and in nations facing a serious likelihood of war, the military emphasizes its traditional task of preparation for war by training reserves and maintaining technological readiness. The military thus becomes a bureaucracy and a powerful pressure group, often allied with industry, that seeks new weapons and warns of the military risks in particular foreign policies. This model concentrates on the mobilization of resources, perhaps even at some cost to the ability to utilize those resources in combat.

According to the other model, typical in developing nations with little prospect of international war, the military assumes the role of guardian of domestic order and ultimate constitutional arbiter. Since the military is likely to be the most disciplined force in these countries and to hold the domestic balance of power, it is often tempted to intervene in political squabbles and impose its will. The particular goal of intervention may be to resist change as in Chile, to encourage development as in Brazil, or even to encourage revolutionary change as seems to have happened in Peru. In this model, the military is likely to orient itself toward reshaping the society, giving relatively little attention to preparation for war.

Military culture may vary radically from nation to nation, depending on recruitment patterns and on local traditions, [17] but even the most authoritarian contemporary military culture probably has little direct influence on the probability of war. Military advice, such as that offered to Hitler before the Second World War and that to American leaders before the Vietnam War, often opposes entry into a war, for the military is usually pessimistic in estimating the likely outcome of a war. Some military leaders may even fear war because it risks harm to the military machine; wars in Southeast Asia and Algeria may have aroused this fear in American and French military planners. Some militaries may regard war as a distraction from domestic concerns; perhaps for this reason the many military dictatorships in Latin America become involved in few international wars. The modern military only rarely hopes for war in the manner of traditional military castes.

Nevertheless, the modern military may encourage war indirectly. In Japan in the 1930's, for example, the military sought to lead the entire society into war preparation and to give a military color to an expansionist nationalism. More commonly, as in Germany before 1914, a martial patriotism and the development of industrial strength contribute to a national culture that directly encourages war. The most common indirect contribution to war is probably the maintenance of a large standing military force that enables political leaders to make war more easily. The presence of such a force may encourage an emphasis on war risks and strategic calculations that probably plays a role in causing war.

Thus today's militarism, like aggression, nationalism, and diplomacy, may contribute to war but does not itself explain why wars happen. However, although a relative optimism is possible about the future evolution of nationalism and diplomacy, the future evolution of the military appears problematic. The wide availability of nuclear weapons, which do not require a large force to develop and deliver, may cause the citizen army, dominant for the last two centuries, to be replaced by a small military elite, whose recruitment would not depend on national mobilization. The character of such a military is unpredictable. But it is plausible that if governments do not depend on citizen support for their military strength, they will find it easier to wage war.

2. The Initiation of War

ALL THE FACTORS discussed in the previous chapter interact to produce war in a striking variety of forms. The squabbles among Greek or Italian city-states differ radically from the imperial wars of Rome or China. And there are many other varieties of war: the onslaughts of Central Asian tribes against China, Europe, and the Islamic world; the colonial expansion of Europe into Africa, Asia, and the Americas; the stylized conflicts of European and Japanese feudalism; the religious crusades of Islam and Christianity.

Technological and economic factors explain some of this diversity. The limitations of military technology and the inability of rulers to pay for military forces, for example, sometimes kept war at a stylized level. This happened under European feudalism, when the castle was a reasonably effective defense against the knight and economics dictated both the number of knights in the field and the length of time they could serve.[1] Similarly, war in eighteenth-century Europe took certain forms because leaders were still too weak to extract the resources to pay for large armies. Training was expensive, and discipline was so poor that many armies forbade the rapid advance of troops because it facilitated desertion.[2]

In more recent times, however, political and social factors (which may indirectly reflect technology and economics) have probably predominated in shaping the character of war. The key factor is probably whether the general population or only the leaders are deeply interested in the outcome of the war.

This factor shapes both the nature of a war and the way a war begins.

One pattern of war, which I call the diplomatic pattern, reached a peak in the dynastic wars of the eighteenth century, wars that sprang from the politics of ruling houses. Since territorial changes were relatively unimportant to the general population, they were often determined by a form of military conflict in which civilians played little role. A sharp distinction between the civilian and the combatant could be maintained as a way to protect civilians. After a few battles, even indecisive ones, it was often possible for the leaders to draw the appropriate conclusions and, without further bloodshed, to negotiate a treaty providing for territorial adjustments.[3]

The eighteenth-century pattern, which still influences our ideas about diplomacy, changed drastically under the pressure of nationalism. Citizens gained an interest in who would govern them above the local level, and national leaders gained the ability to mobilize public support for their policies.[4] In the Napoleonic Wars, as in the two world wars of the twentieth century, nationalism enabled the government to utilize the entire population in war. The draft became the norm, and conscript soldiers could be trusted to carry out new tactics requiring independent initiative. The economic changes associated with nationalism gave governments the financial capacity to maintain an army in the field for long campaigns and to turn nations into arsenals of increasingly deadly and decisive technologies.[5] The coupling of war with morality became routine: the broad moral commitment to a military cause that had been seen before in the Crusades, in the Reformation, and at other exceptional times was now at the ready disposal of many national leaders for their own purposes.

Under these combined moral and technological pressures, war became total. Although lawyers and diplomats tried to preserve the distinction between civilians and combatants, this distinction was often ignored in such actions as strategic bombing and underground resistance warfare. The idea of calculating new frontiers on the basis of a few battles was discarded: even after the Second World War no peace treaty was drafted, the postwar status quo becoming the effective settlement. This was a type of war unlike the diplomatic pattern; it may be called popular or ideological war.

The rise of nationalism also made possible the revolutionary wars exemplified in France, the United States, Mexico, Russia, Spain, and China. In a dynastic era, a rebellion would typically involve only a coup d'état within a small group. But with nationalism, insurgent leaders, as well as governments, might seek and obtain the support of large portions of the national population, with the goal of modifying the nation's social structure.[6]

In much of today's world, the forces of nationalism and diplomacy are closely balanced; thus war can arise either from conflict between leaders of different nations or from conflict between national populations. Whichever way a war begins, it can grow into total war. With the vast expansion of military technology and wealth, conflicts between leaders can draw in entire populations and become much more devastating than the stylized dynastic wars of the eighteenth century. Popular conflicts can easily capture the support of the best-intentioned or the most ambitious leaders. It is this combination of mechanisms that makes the control of warfare so difficult today. Neither stronger government-imposed restraint nor balance-of-power diplomacy—the traditional means of preventing popular and leadership wars—can be relied on.

The dangers of nuclear weapons may encourage leaders to limit their use of conventional warfare so as to decrease the chance of escalation. Moreover, since much of the new military technology requires relatively little manpower, contemporary military forces may tend to resemble mercenaries or professional castes, rather than "nations in arms." On technical grounds, therefore, one might predict a move toward limited, stylized war. Perhaps a harbinger of this is the way the great powers have limited their conflicts to "proxy" wars in the developing world. But these conflicts are not limited in the destruction they bring to the nations in which they are fought. And perhaps even more seriously, all nations are subject to domestic political and ideological upheavals. The technical prerequisites for limiting war may be satisfied, but not the political prerequisites. Thus one can expect the potential for total war to endure. The world may have to learn new ways to prevent total war, whether it arises according to the popular or the diplomatic pattern.

EXAMPLES OF THE INITIATION OF WAR

The use of specific historical cases permits a more systematic analysis of the two mechanisms by which wars begin. In modern times, the Civil War in the United States is perhaps the clearest example of a major war that the people forced on their leaders. The First World War serves as a sharply contrasting example of how balance-of-power diplomacy can miscarry. Each has been well studied. Each is as close to a pure example as is likely to be found in an era in which the popular and governmental mechanisms are necessarily intertwined.

The Civil War. Historians have emphasized two general explanations for the American Civil War: the dispute over national unity that stemmed from the slavery issue, and the economic divergence between the North and the South. Both of these explanations involved broadly based rival political forces that were amenable to compromise for a generation and a half, but eventually dragged their leaders into war.

The slavery explanation, popular among historians immediately after the war and again in a postrevisionist period after the Second World War, emphasized two main issues that divided the North and the South: the future of slavery in the territories into which the nation was expanding, and the extent to which the North should cooperate with the slavery system by returning escaped slaves. In spite of the importance of slavery and its clear moral overtones, slavery itself was not the immediate focus of conflict. Until shortly before the war, relatively few in the North or the South favored the abolition of all slavery, let alone a position of social equality for blacks. Instead, the argument centered around related theoretical and practical political issues: the political and legal constraints on federal action for or against slavery; the supremacy of federal power over a state's right to nullify federal law or to secede; the balance of congressional voting power; and the future of the Union, the issue Lincoln stressed in his initial justification for the war.

The alternative explanation, preferred by many historians during the period just before the Second World War, rested on economic differences. The South was an "agrarian" society, based on plantation and small-holding agriculture, which looked culturally and economically to Europe. The North was a more industrialized society, desiring tariff protection that the South opposed. The West was agricultural, but not like the South; Westerners embodied frontier values and sought trade within the United States. The areas of potential conflict were manifold: tariff policy, competition between free labor and slavery, political rivalry between emerging Northern capitalists and Southern landowners.[7]

Though these economic differences were important, the major political disputes and compromises of the time were cast in terms of the slavery and nationalism issues. The first major confrontation after the Constitutional Convention of 1787 led to the Missouri Compromise of 1820, suggested by Henry Clay, a Southerner. Slavery had already been abolished in most Northern states, and the slave trade had legally ended in 1808. In 1819 there were eleven free states and eleven slave states; the proposed admission of Missouri would disrupt this balance. The compromise provided that the entry of Missouri as a slave state would be balanced by the entry of Maine as a free state, and that slavery would be excluded from the part of the Louisiana Purchase north of the Mason-Dixon Line.

The compromise bought time and set a clear pattern, but

that pattern proved to be of little help as new problems emerged. New tariff laws in 1828 and 1832 prompted South Carolina to attempt the nullification of federal law. The ensuing confrontation, complete with revenue cutters, was defused by compromise tariff legislation in 1833;[8] but nullification and secession were now added to the political agenda. At the same time, antislavery and abolitionist sentiment was building in the North.[9] This sentiment was complemented by another emerging Northern and Western attitude, this one favoring "squatter sovereignty" or "popular sovereignty," the principle that new territories should be entitled to decide for themselves whether they would be admitted as free or slave states. The new areas likely to become free states under any procedure, however, were rapidly outstripping the potential slave states and would soon qualify for admission.

By 1850 a new framework was needed. Henry Clay, working with Daniel Webster and Stephen Douglas from the North, developed one over eight months of congressional debate. The critical provisions, embodied in several bills and supported by different constituencies (that fact itself a sign of tension), were that California would come in as a free state, that the slavery question in the Mexican Cession would be decided by the territories themselves, and that a drastic new fugitive slave law would be enacted. Since a sectional balance could no longer be maintained in Congress, the fugitive slave law was presumably the quid pro quo for the South's acceptance of future imbalance. Some historians argue that this compromise may have prevented immediate secession; others point to the role of powerful economic interests in shaping the compromise and argue that there was no immediate danger of secession.[10]

It is undisputed, however, that the severe fugitive slave provisions of the compromise radicalized many in the North; and the North reacted even more strongly to the *Dred Scott* decision seven years later. In the meantime, in 1854 Senator Douglas rejected the compromise he had helped engineer only four years earlier, and introduced the Kansas-Nebraska

Act, which applied the principle of squatter sovereignty to an area north of the old Missouri Compromise line. Though Douglas's motives are controversial,[11] they certainly sprang more from an interest in sectional economic goals and popular sovereignty than from a desire to encourage slavery. Nevertheless, the new act further intensified Northern antislavery sentiment. Violence broke out in Kansas the following year as proslavery and antislavery forces struggled to dominate the territory.

The deepening Northern antislavery attitude contributed to the emergence of the Republican party, organized in 1854. And when the 1856 Republican presidential candidate carried all but five states in the North, it was the South's turn to be radicalized. Now Southerners talked more openly of secession and of their fear of a slave uprising encouraged by the North. Though this fear may have been unwarranted, growing out of a misperception of Northern politics and an overestimation of the plantation society's susceptibility to revolt, it was apparently strong;[12] and it understandably grew stronger after John Brown's raid on Harpers Ferry in 1859. In turn, President Buchanan's weakness and proslavery favoritism on the Kansas question exacerbated Northern feeling.

Thus the nation was deeply divided by the time Lincoln became president. Lincoln's opponents had argued that his election would mean war, but this was not the general view either in the North or in Congress.[13] President Buchanan reflected the majority opinion in his message of December 3, 1860, when he expressed the hope that secession and war could still be avoided and the belief that the execution of federal law by force was not the same as warfare.[14] Nevertheless, South Carolina adopted an Ordinance of Secession in December, and seven other states had followed by the end of January. But military action was so far limited. A federal relief expedition to Fort Sumter, South Carolina, failed on January 9.[15] The same month, Mississippi set up batteries at Vicksburg, temporarily disrupting river traffic.[16]

Northern public opinion now called for war, and nearly

a half-million men placed themselves at the disposal of state authorities and unofficial organizations.[17] Some leaders sought compromise, both in Congress and at a peace conference in February; but most leaders from the seceding areas refused to join in the effort.[18] The militant Republicans also rejected compromise,[19] and no new formula, like that of 1820 or 1850, was found that could unite even the moderates of both sides.

Lincoln, in his inaugural speech in March 1861, took a nuanced position. He promised to enforce the laws and refused to recognize the secession, but said he would not attack the South. This position was clearly popular in accepting the likelihood of war. Even though the war fever of January had faded somewhat, both politics and economics led the North to prefer forced union to the acceptance of secession.[20] Lincoln's first military action, which came a month after his inauguration, was part of a pattern designed to place the burden of aggression on the South. In response to an arguably exaggerated letter from the commander of Fort Sumter, who had apparently hoped his unit would be withdrawn,[21] Lincoln sent another relief mission. This action was widely interpreted as an act of war, although it left it to the South to fire the first shot.[22] Shortly after Sumter, the South commissioned privateers and effectively confiscated debts owed to Northerners.[23] Lincoln called for militia, and major land warfare began in July 1861.

This war clearly cannot be explained by "bad" motivations or by a breakdown of communication. Arms levels were relatively low when the war began. Although the Southern leaders were wrong in defending slavery, the leaders on both sides seemed essentially honorable in making the decisions that led toward war. Those who might be said to have wanted war—abolitionists in the North and "fire-eaters" in the South—were remote from any positions of official power, exercising their influence instead through direct popular appeal. Although Northern and Southern leaders may have misperceived each other's society, they kept in close touch and made many efforts at compromise.

The Civil War seems to reveal two societies evolving in fundamentally inconsistent directions, following two incompatible concepts of nationalism, with their leaders' efforts at compromise only reinforcing the drift toward conflict. Each compromise was designed to preserve a balance, and probably did keep the nation united in the short run; but it turned out in the long run that the compromises strengthened the hands of those most opposed to further compromise. Radicalization on one side encouraged radicalization on the other. The reaction to both the compromises and the increasing radicalization drove the two sides into a war that started almost without the participation of their political leaders.

The First World War. The events preceding the First World War were very different. Though popular sentiment and ideological differences played a role, diplomatic maneuvering played a much greater one.

When Germany was unified, with the clear destiny of becoming the most powerful nation in Europe, its chancellor, Otto von Bismarck, sought to build a stabilizing network of diplomatic relations. His settlement with Austria-Hungary in 1886 was relatively lenient, and he had avoided antagonizing either Great Britain or Russia during the unification wars. The cooperation with Great Britain appeared likely to continue, and the friendship with Russia was carefully extended into a working arrangement between Russia, Austria-Hungary, and Germany (the Dreikaiserbund).[24] Though Bismarck's settlement with France in 1871 was somewhat harsh, the German diplomatic pattern was generally peaceful, its alignments quite unlike those that were to generate war in little more than forty years.

During the 1870's Austria-Hungary and Russia became estranged over a series of crises in the Middle East. Bismarck, effectively forced to choose between the two, entered into a defensive alliance with Austria-Hungary in 1879. This agreement, between powers that had been at war only a little more than a decade earlier, was welcomed by the other major European nations. Following an incident with France, Italy also looked for allies; it joined Germany and Austria-Hungary in 1882 to complete the Triple Alliance, one of the contending groups in the world war. Bismarck's diplomacy did not stop there. Until his dismissal in 1890, he continued to build an elaborate network of conventions that seemed oriented toward preserving peace. Some of these conventions included Russia and Britain, and in other circumstances might have helped avoid the coming war in Europe.

At the same time that Bismarck's diplomacy was buttressing the European status quo, German economic progress was having a more profound impact on the world. Germany saw free trade as a system designed to bring prosperity to those countries that were already the economic leaders, principally Britain. The economy of unified Germany, by contrast, was built on a customs zone and on a protective tariff modeled after that of the United States. Germany judged that its future would lie with protection rather than free trade; therefore, it sought to establish a colonial system different from that of the British Empire. Germans would settle areas in which they could benefit from increased agricultural productivity and could also provide a market for German manufactures. The German colonial policy proved to have strategic consequences, since the obvious direction for seeking such areas, particularly in view of the Austrian alliance, was toward Africa and the Middle East. The 1889 Turkish concession to Germany for part of the Berlin-Baghdad railway was a logical step.[25]

Russia and England, naturally concerned by Germany's eastward thrust, felt impelled to create an opposing bloc. The first step in assembling such a bloc was cooperation between Russia and France. Both sensed a need for allies: Russia was left isolated after Germany's new link with Austria-Hungary, and France had not yet recovered from its disastrous 1870–71 war with Germany. Russia also desired French loans for the development of the Far East. And there were cultural ties between the two countries, including a French infatuation with things Russian and an enthusiastic reception for a French squadron at Kronstadt in 1891.[26] The two signed a military convention in 1893, oriented against attack by the Triple Alliance, and made it public in 1895.

Before England could enter into the Russian-French understanding, completing the Triple Entente, it had to reverse its diplomatic posture. Sir Edward Grey, the British foreign secretary, noted in 1911 that in the early 1890's he had thought of the Triple Alliance as a "solid quiet group" and of France and Russia as "the two restless powers."[27] The Russian-French understanding had met with disapproval in London. Nevertheless, a reversal came. England and Germany began to disagree over African frontier questions in the mid-1890's, and moved on to greater disagreements over the Middle East and South Africa. These disagreements were sharpened by a personal antagonism between the Prince of Wales, later Edward VII, and his nephew William II of Germany.[28]

German strategists, meanwhile, had begun to focus on the possibility of conflict with England. As early as 1897, the Kaiser had ordered the preparation of an operational study of war against England. Admiral Tirpitz's first great memorandum on taking office as minister of marine the same year said that "for Germany, the most dangerous naval enemy at the present time is England. It is also the enemy against which we most urgently require a certain measure of naval force as a political power factor."[29] Under these domestic pressures, and in response to specific disagreements with England over South Africa, Germany began a major naval construction program in 1898. England, believing itself seriously isolated, still sought accommodation with Germany; but it was consistently rebuffed. After considering alternative alliances,[30] England finally entered into a treaty with Japan in 1902, and into ententes with France in 1904 and Russia in 1907.

The opposing alliances were now essentially complete. Germany and England still cooperated to help settle conflicts over such matters as the partitioning of North Africa and the Balkan Wars of 1912 and 1913, but at the same time these conflicts created popular antagonism between France and Germany and between Russia and Austria-Hungary.[31] A similar antagonism between the English and German peoples grew under the pressure of the naval arms race.

The Balkan wars also heightened the tension between Serbia and Austria-Hungary over the disposition of Slavic groups within the Austro-Hungarian Empire. This empire had always been a collection of disparate groups; Hungary already had substantial autonomy. If Austria-Hungary gave Slavic groups a similar autonomy, Serbia might lose its role as a leader of the Slavs in the Balkans. Hence Serbia sought to break up the empire itself.

Thus, when the Archduke Ferdinand was murdered by Austrian Serbs at Sarajevo on June 28, 1914, Austria understandably felt the need to teach Serbia a lesson by making a strong military response. But it was not until July 23 that Austria-Hungary sent a deliberately unacceptable ultimatum to Belgrade. The character of the intervening negotiations and the role that Germany played in Austria's decision are not entirely clear. Count Tisza, the Hungarian prime minister, at first objected to any ultimatum that would provoke a general war; he could see no way the Hungarian aristocracy would survive such a war.[32] German influence was evidently important in Tisza's change of position, as well as in the decision of Count Berchtold, the Austrian foreign minister, to send the ultimatum.

Germany's intentions, however, are also unclear, in part because of Chancellor Bethmann-Hollweg's ambiguous character, and in part because there were several contending German positions. The more extreme wanted a war that would provide the opportunity to defeat England and create a new global order. The less extreme favored a defensive war that included annexationist goals. There was a general German belief that the balance of military and diplomatic power was swinging against Germany, and thus that an immediate war was in Germany's interest;[33] there were varying opinions on whether the local Serbian conflict would spread to draw in Russia or England. Those who sought a wider war probably also hoped to take advantage of a situation in which other nations would appear to be the aggressors.[34]

On July 30, after the Austro-Hungarian ultimatum, Russia mobilized to defend Serbia. Russia's action was understandable, though probably not inevitable. Russia was threatened strategically, for if Austria-Hungary were to conquer Serbia, Germany would have a line of allies into the Middle East. Within Russia, which was beset by political and social unrest, military and pan-Slavic forces were eager for war. Moreover, the French ambassador may have encouraged Russia to mobilize.[35]

After the Austro-Hungarian ultimatum and the Russian mobilization, the outbreak of war seemed automatic. Russia refused to halt its mobilization, despite Germany's request that it do so. Germany and France then mobilized nearly simultaneously on August 1. Germany, threatened by the possibility of a two-front war and restricted by its military planning to preemptive action, attacked on the Western front. When Germany violated Belgian neutrality on August 4, the British government gained the political support it needed to honor the entente arrangements; Britain entered the war on August 5, 1914.

Admittedly, there were underlying economic and popular forces at work; but it is nearly impossible to review this history and not conclude that the war grew out of a miscarriage at the diplomatic level. National leaders, constantly concerned with strategic military positions, built a structure of alliances designed to prevent war. The structure succeeded in maintaining peace through several disputes. But when the crucial test came, each foreign office, under little public pressure, took the deliberate power-oriented decisions that led step by step to war. The alliances that had been set up to prevent war became mechanisms for expanding the conflict into a war that struck many in its generation as pointless.

The two examples of the Civil War and the First World War illustrate the radical differences between the popular and diplomatic mechanisms by which wars begin. These mechanisms deserve separate analysis.

THE POPULAR MECHANISM

In the popular mechanism, it is the conflict between the political cultures of the two sides that ultimately leads to war. Political culture may be defined as the philosophical and practical beliefs that influence the way political problems are met.[36] These beliefs, which are not always explicitly recognized, influence the choice of the problems to be taken seriously and the character of the answers to be given. In the case of the Civil War, some of these beliefs related to the future of slavery, the role of the state and federal governments, and the intentions of the opposing side. It is easy to find current examples, such as the differing ways the Israeli and Palestinian peoples perceive each other and the future of the region. These beliefs are transmitted by a variety of institutions, including education and the news media. They change with time, in rough response to the insights gained from experience. Leaders, who are themselves influenced by such beliefs, may affect their people's beliefs, but they are limited in their ability to manipulate the citizenry. The belief pattern may vary among different political groups. But often, especially in a prewar situation, the pattern is widely enough shared among politically active persons that one can reasonably speak of a single political culture.

A disagreement between political cultures is not sufficient to create war; it is also necessary for military action to become legitimate in at least one of the two opposing cultures. Unless the use of force represents a moral imperative, it cannot overcome the normal inhibitions against force that were discussed in the first chapter. Sometimes the moral imperative comes from ethics itself; the ethics compels war, instead of restraining it. Thus, in the Crusades, religion commanded its own propagation by war. Today, some Marxist theories advocate force to bring about the dictatorship of the proletariat. An ethical opposition to colonialism is often made the justification for wars of decolonization. And nearly every culture approves of the use of force to defend against invasion.

Less direct—and much less easily understood—factors sometimes seem to help a political culture give legitimacy to the use of force. Major cultural change may create doubt about established ethical norms that oppose war. Thus, at the turn of the century, Japan mimicked Western imperialist ideas and sought to participate in carving up China. These ideas ran against Japanese traditions; the nation might not have pursued an imperialist policy had these traditions not already been upset by the impact of the West. Similarly, the depression of the 1930's interrupted a course of economic development in Japan that had raised individual expectations. Military service offered an alternative to unemployment. And more significantly, the society became what a writer generally sympathetic to Japan calls a "defense state," rife with secret societies and patriotic organizations, in which even religion was manipulated to encourage militancy.[37]

In a process that is equally unclear, a newly acquired national strength often seems to be followed by expansionism. The centralization of France was followed by the Napoleonic Wars, the unification of Germany by the two world wars, the modernization of Japan by its turn-of-the-century wars and the Second World War, the growth of American strength by the Spanish-American War. Part of this process may be a national belief that the country deserves increased external recognition and prestige.[38] For example, many Germans believed that their nation had been treated unjustly in the settlement at Versailles. This perception, perhaps offset in the

1920's by the memory of the First World War, undoubtedly contributed to the outbreak of the Second World War in the 1930's. Japan's desire to demonstrate its equality with the West was probably a factor in Japanese imperialism. A more direct part of the process may be that the possession of a capability creates a psychological tendency to use it, as seems to have happened in the Spanish-American war and in the Napoleonic expansionism following on the discovery of the citizen army. Bellicosity often comes on the heels of strength; together with the effects of rapid cultural change, the process suggests that some of the more successful developing nations are likely to become involved in war.

The cultural changes that legitimize war may also be deliberately stimulated by leaders or groups. The Church, for example, encouraged the Crusades. Governments may support militant groups or liberation movements in other nations; and terrorist groups often deliberately attempt to destroy moderate forces and generate a climate of fear to their own benefit.

As two political cultures evolve in different directions, points of conflict may develop: slavery and tariffs before the Civil War; religion and the relation between church and state in the Reformation. Then, new processes may come into play. Efforts at accommodation may help create militant groups on each side, and militancy on one side may provoke greater militancy on the other. Early on, groups that anticipate conflict may emerge and call for military preparation, as the naval groups in Germany did before the First World War. Such groups can exert a pressure that makes effective compromise more difficult.

If the differences continue to grow, even the moderates on each side may come to mistrust the potential enemy, seeing it as unreasonable and increasingly radical.[39] And if this happens, the militant position can begin to take over the center. Fear makes it easier to misinterpret the other side. Attempts to settle the conflict, like those of the peace movements during the Cold War, may come to be viewed as traitorous. Some militant ideologists are likely to endorse violence, as Luther did during the Reformation and the abolitionists before the Civil War. Militant groups, or governments under pressure from militants, may then undertake limited acts of violence. These acts encourage further violence on both sides,[40] and eventually governments and statesmen find themselves helpless to prevent war. The war tends to become as total as technology allows.

This process is not inevitable. The cultures may evolve in directions that help settle the conflict. Compromises may succeed in strengthening moderate constituencies and weakening militant ones. The fear of war may help populations, as well as governments, to curb responses that would have been automatic in an earlier age. Moreover, even in popular warfare the element of leadership may still be a prerequisite for large scale violence. Perhaps the leader provides a symbolic focus for popular feeling; sustained violence without a leader is rare. Lincoln's taking office was an important trigger of the Civil War. Riots without leadership are likely to be short-lived; and terrorist groups without allied political leaders can create a climate of insecurity but do little more.

Popular war arises by mechanisms that seem likely to persist. In a few regions, such as southern Africa and the Middle East, ethnic antagonism could lead to war. The demands of the developing world for economic justice might generate conflict in other areas. Perhaps more likely, the accompanying rivalry between traditional rulers and new national elites that frequently arises in the developing world could produce both civil and international conflict. Still more likely, economic growth in some countries might produce the dynamism that could lead to conflict with their neighbors.

The likelihood of a popular war depends only indirectly on the levels and characteristics of the weapons involved. This kind of war can begin without prior calculation of arms balances and even when the arms on both sides are at a very low level. The Civil War and conflicts in the Middle East, for example, support the folk wisdom that people will fight with sticks and stones (or terrorist guns and explosives) if they do not have more powerful arms.[41]

The prevention of popular war must therefore rest on strategies broader than arms control. The most important and most difficult strategies rely on diplomacy and thoughtful compromise to avoid the creation of militaristic or expansionist cultures. The lack of justice in relations between the developed and underdeveloped world could threaten world peace, just as the lack of justice in the Versailles settlement did. The concessions that might be helpful are not easily made, however, and concession can shade into appeasement. Moreover, it is hard to visualize how, say, Soviet or Mongol expansionism could ever have been prevented. Nevertheless, the strategies employed at the diplomatic and political level are the most relevant to preventing the emergence of militaristic cultures. Arms control can play only a secondary role, though it can make the first expansionist steps more difficult and less rewarding. Had post-Versailles Germany and post-Meiji Japan failed in their first expansionist ventures, they might not have continued in their course.

At the level of political culture, the main task in preventing war is to encourage the cultures to evolve in directions that give war a very low legitimacy. Thus the mutual trust between the United States and England reflects the shared belief that military conflict would be absurd, and also a pattern of reciprocal confidence that neither would take serious advantage of the other. Less effectively, the Catholic-Protestant enmity of the Reformation was resolved by the concept of the nation-state, symbolized in the settlement of Westphalia; the cultures evolved toward the toleration of religious differences between nations. In the most successful of the reconciliations following the Second World War, France and Germany established economic, military, and political bonds. Indeed, there came to be so many links between subgroups across the

French-German border as to make conflict along strictly national lines unlikely. Such links, which inherently weaken the national governments, probably secure the peace more effectively than an agreement to disagree like the Treaty of Westphalia.

In comparison, the effect of regulating arms levels and characteristics is quite limited. The weapons owned by one culture may affect another culture's perception of it. The nature and quantity of armaments may affect the destructiveness of any war that does occur. Arms control may sometimes also be the only strategy available, for other approaches may not be politically feasible. For example, building cultural restraints or links between cultures is likely to be politically difficult in countries where nationalism is being used as a mobilization device to aid development. In such a situation, arms control might at least be able to remove some grounds for conflict or help prevent the escalation of a conflict to the nuclear level. Further, arms control could play an important role in dampening the expansionist fervor in a successfully developing nation.

THE DIPLOMATIC MECHANISM

Though popular conflict may become the prevailing pattern of war in the developing world, diplomatic failure is still the most important source of war worldwide. The diplomatic mechanism is quite different from the popular mechanism, even though it would be easy to present an artificial description of diplomatic escalation exactly parallel to the escalation of a popular conflict. In the last days before some wars, for example, the psychology of political leaders might resemble the process of intensifying militance seen in popular escalation.

The diplomatic process is more elaborate. It rests on the assumption that war is possible, an assumption that becomes institutionalized in the form of strategic calculations, military preparations, and alliances. These actions make war the focus of expert attention, and at the same time create new points of potential conflict. Most specific differences between nations are settled peacefully, even though—or perhaps because—the threat of war is always present in the various negotiations. But sometimes this process fails to resolve a dispute because diplomats underestimate the power and commitment of a rising nation or overestimate another nation's political ability to make a concession. War results. And sometimes a nation starts a war quite deliberately because its leaders judge war to be the best way to improve the nation's power position.[42]

The background: strategic calculation and diplomacy. Diplomacy is preeminently a tool of peace, a means of resolving disputes without war. The task in explaining diplomatic war is to examine how this tool can instead produce war. Since diplomats recognize, wisely, that war is possible, each nation is compelled to analyze its strategic position in the light of possible wars and to work to protect that position. Thus there arises a new set of foreign policy goals, often described in this book as strategic goals, that are pursued only for their strategic benefits, and not for any intrinsic benefit. For example, Germany's movement into the Middle East before the First World War was taken by Russia as a threat that went far beyond the direct economic or political value that Russia attached to the region. As on a chessboard, each strategic goal creates in turn new strategic goals and new areas of conflict. This process is shaped by the character of armaments, by economics, and by expectations of the form a war will take, as well as by geography. Points of great strategic importance at one time may lose that importance at another.

It is not easy to evaluate strategic interests. One result of this, as pointed out in the preceding chapter, is that strategic planning is likely to become the province of an elite. Such an elite, like the German naval planners before the First World War, tends to become a constituency for the improvement of the nation's strategic position, its biases defining the expected shape of a war. Of particular importance, the elite's strategic calculations will focus on the specific nations with which conflict seems most likely. Since no nation can ignore another's strategic plans or armaments, the assumptions of each nation's strategists feed the strategists of other nations.

These assumptions probably underlie the concept in diplomacy of friendship or distance between nations. Bismarck moved "away" from Russia and "toward" Austria-Hungary in 1879; England and Germany slowly moved "apart." In each case, a constellation of relationships rested on the relative friendliness or unfriendliness of different pairs of nations. The reality corresponding to this political distance is a set of perceptions each nation has of the others, particularly the perceptions that the leaders and the strategic elites have concerning the risks of conflict or the likelihood of support. The attitudes of the leaders, the bureaucracies, and the public, and the inertia of these attitudes, may even make it likely that a pair of nations allied or opposed on one issue will be allied or opposed on other issues as well. These perceptions naturally feed into new strategic calculations, for they affect the alignments during a war and the reliability of alliances. Nations deliberately seek to influence these perceptions and to cultivate the friendship of other nations by means of arms deals, trade concessions, and other diplomatic devices.

In addition, diplomacy routinely involves the use of military forces in ways not normally expected to give rise to war. Some examples of this are the deployment of naval forces to "show the flag"; military reconnaissance and intelligence collection; military assistance to other nations; and short-term unopposed military intervention. The nature of military diplomacy has varied with time and circumstances. Gunboat diplomacy was once common. Intelligence organizations meddle more in Caribbean politics than in Western European politics. More support is given to private armies and guerrilla organizations in Africa and the Middle East than in Latin America. These differences reflect a mixture of practical considerations and tacit international understandings. It is understood that the transgression of certain norms, such as those that governed the Cold War or the nineteenth-century exploitation of Africa, might encourage retaliation and risk war.

Sometimes military action of this type can be a helpful ingredient in a diplomacy that leads to peace. At the same time, however, such action gives military power a relevance and a standing in the diplomatic process that can lower a decision maker's psychological inhibitions against the use of force and make the resort to force easier. Moreover, decision makers often view military action as essentially continuous with nonmilitary diplomacy; and they can usually authorize limited use of the military without obtaining legislative or popular consent. The effective decision-making power for such action often lies well below the highest political level. Thus intelligence collection, minor military probing like the American and Soviet harassment of each other's navies, and the support of insurgent and counterinsurgent groups tend to become routinely authorized at low levels of government. As this happens, the interests served by the actions may become those of a component of the bureaucracy rather than those of the nation.

Before we look at the escalation process, we may find it useful to note some of the ways in which the characteristics of armaments and the limitations on them can affect the diplomatic background of war. First, arms restrictions can be designed to permit opposing strategic requirements to be met in a more compatible and stable fashion. For instance, an agreement not to deploy military forces in an area such as Antarctica can help avoid conflict over strategic positions in that area. Second, if offensive weapons can be defined and made weaker relative to defensive ones, each nation can define its strategic requirements more narrowly, which decreases the risk of war. Third, arms control can lower the level of quasi-military activity. Thus, if the United States and the

Soviet Union withdraw their naval forces from the Indian Ocean, they can no longer show the flag in that area; this too might decrease the risk of war. The traditional use of a buffer zone of neutral states between two powerful nations is analogous; by giving warning of an attack, it helped reduce the military requirements on each side. It also reduced quasi-military contacts and the consequent risk of a confrontation between the two powers.

Even without arms control, the level of quasi-military activity can be reduced. The rules of mutual restraint governing military diplomacy do change; indeed, part of diplomacy is an effort to persuade other diplomats that one set of rules is better than another. The Kellogg-Briand Pact of 1928, which would have prohibited war, is an example of such an effort; but it clearly diverged too widely from the prevailing diplomatic norms to be successful. The growing consensus against the introduction of nuclear weapons into a conventional war may prove more successful. Similar rules might evolve against other forms of military diplomacy, such as threatening to use nuclear weapons and assisting terrorist groups.

Prestige and escalation. On occasion the strategists of two countries will become particularly concerned with the balance of power between their countries, leading to a pattern of escalation somewhat like that of popular warfare. Each nation's bureaucracy, assisted by a stream of intelligence reports and military evaluations, may institutionalize the other nation as the enemy. Military buildups and quasi-military actions may then become important forms of interaction between the countries. Military contingency plans, like the Schlieffen plan before the First World War, can shape each decision maker's perception of likely opponents. Each side's arms increase may be noted by the other side and used as an argument for a counterbalancing increase. Political leaders may become especially sensitive—and even paranoid—about the challenge of the particular opponent. It becomes easy to err in evaluating the opponent's actions,[43] seeing bad faith though the actions may have been taken innocently or defensively. A rivalry of this sort may turn into a process of reciprocal escalation that parallels the more emotional escalation of mass attitudes preceding a popular war.

When leaders of two nations are so highly polarized, it is relatively easy for a specific disagreement to lead to a dangerous general crisis. But a prior polarization is not essential to war, which can come unexpectedly. And if there is a polarization, the precipitating crisis may be a staged event, provoked intentionally by one side out of a belief that war is inevitable and that the power balance will be more favorable if the war occurs sooner rather than later. The strategists think well ahead, and may choose to fight a war some years before political differences seem to make war inevitable. Usually, however, neither side wants war, and the crisis is met by negotiation. But sometimes, even then, negotiation fails and war occurs; typically, the war is a result of threats and ultimatums made during the negotiations.

The problem in negotiation is that no one can confidently predict the outcome; in trying to obtain a beneficial outcome, either side may push the other too far. The result of the bargaining is likely to reflect both the relative need of the participants for a negotiated solution and the relative prestige of the participants. Generally, the nation that is more afraid of failure in the negotiations is the more ready to compromise, and is therefore likely to lose more in the compromise. Prestige, though a less tangible factor, reflects a nation's power, its willingness to use it, and its fairness in using it. Relative prestige affects each nation's assessment of the outcome of a prospective war, and also each nation's psychological willingness to regard concessions as acceptable.

This role of prestige in negotiations is part of the reason national prestige is so important to diplomats. They fear, for example, that if they yield too readily in one compromise, their nation will lose prestige and suffer in future compromises. And they are correct: being too submissive is sometimes as dangerous as being too aggressive. A show of weakness, such as that at Munich, can encourage subsequent, more exorbitant demands. When monarchs practiced dynastic diplomacy, prestige could be considered analogous to an animal pecking order. The analogy is perhaps still relevant. Among leaders, at least, prestige is a psychological phenomenon; and an unstated principle underlying public explanations of compromises is that it is easier to justify making a concession to a stronger power than to a weaker one.

When relative levels of prestige are well recognized, war is less likely, because the outcome of negotiations is predictable and concessions are more politically acceptable. The danger of war is great when prestige levels are in doubt or are changing too rapidly to be generally recognized. Traditionally, these dangerous times were associated with a succession crisis or a civil war.[44] More recently, this danger has arisen from a failure to recognize the growth of a new nation's power and dynamism. Much of recent European history, for example, has centered on the question of defining a place for Germany. The future may be shaped by the similar task of finding a place for the emerging great powers of the developing world.

Negotiation is not a purely verbal process. A nation may act to create a fait accompli designed to limit the responses available to the opponent; this is a familiar goal of the stronger forms of military diplomacy. A nation may make threats as a way to demonstrate its increased commitment and to pressure an opponent into making concessions in order to avoid war. The two sides can then enter into a dialogue like that displayed in the Cuban missile crisis. Probably, physical actions count for more in the dialogue than words; a fait accompli, for example, usually shifts to the opponent the difficult burden of changing the status quo. But there is a psychological aspect of this dialogue in which words are important: when one side issues threats, it risks its prestige, makes it harder for it to back down, and perhaps demonstrates its will to use greater force.[45]

At each step of the negotiations, a nation is faced with the choice of accepting the status quo, taking military action, or attempting a new step to induce the opponent to accept other terms. Absolute inaction is unlikely; a nation fears the consequent loss of prestige. Nevertheless, there may be ways—sometimes deliberately created by a wise opponent—in which a nation can accept the status quo with a minimal loss of prestige. Sometimes, also, a nation may find a way to resist the opponent's pressure without either escalating or losing prestige. The Berlin airlift of 1948, for example, demonstrated the American commitment to Berlin and circumvented the Soviet blockade without escalating the conflict militarily. Eventually the USSR was free to open land communications without losing prestige itself. At a more violent level, retaliation, as in the recurrent raids in the Middle East, may be used to protect prestige and to discourage further hostile action without seriously risking war. In still another pattern, when both sides are more eager to end a crisis than to win the point, they may submit a dispute to the United Nations or some other neutral decision-making body.

At the other extreme, a nation will sometimes reject continued dialogue in favor of immediate full-scale military action. In such a decision, the key questions are generally military ones. Thus, in the Middle East crisis of 1967, the tactical advantages of surprise undoubtedly figured in Israel's decision to make a preemptive attack; and the military rigidity of the Schlieffen plan influenced German diplomacy at the beginning of the First World War. As already suggested, a military attack may sometimes be carefully premeditated and executed in the absence of a crisis in order to gain the benefits of surprise; Egypt initiated the war in 1973 as a logical consequence of the failure of diplomacy months earlier. This pattern of deliberate attack with either diplomacy at an impasse or military victory expected is one of the most common ways that wars begin in the twentieth century.

In most crises, however, a nation tries to take steps on its own designed to force concessions from an opponent without starting a war. This coercive diplomacy, exemplified in Cuba in 1962, is perhaps typical of the nuclear era. In its most elaborate form, it combines a threat to use military force, enough use of force to show that the threat is to be taken seriously, and a signal to the opponent indicating what concession is desired. The coercing nation may ultimately be prepared to lose the point at issue, perhaps because the costs of a decisive battle are viewed as too great; but it still considers the point important enough to threaten war. Such an effort cannot succeed unless the opponent prefers to lose the point rather than go to war.[46] Each side wants to keep the level of danger high enough that the opponent will give in, but not so high that war will break out. Each side must manage its forces well, to avoid giving an inadvertent signal that war has begun.[47]

Usually, one side or the other will give in, but the game is risky and can lead to war. This kind of negotiation requires a high level of rationality in evaluating the opponent's commitments and goals, rationality that may evaporate in a crisis. Misestimations of commitments and misreadings of signals were evident, for example, in the German-Russian diplomacy preceding the First World War and in the Russian-Czech relations preceding Russia's invasion in 1968. Each side must also depend on the rationality of its opponent; this dependence is perhaps a source of the sense of loss of control over events that leaders frequently note in a crisis. Whether the opponent will back down depends on its own perception of the relative levels of prestige. Thus the practitioner of coercive diplomacy in a sense places himself at the mercy of his opponent's judgment. During the crisis itself the opponent may become unexpectedly reluctant to compromise; its national goals may change, making certain concessions unacceptable, or its sense that it is on the defensive may trigger a psychological need to hold firm. And in at least one case, that of the American intervention in Vietnam, the military actions designed to demonstrate credibility became a war in themselves.[48]

A further risk is that leaders, though perhaps seeking only to explain their actions, may inadvertently mobilize public opinion, thus binding their own hands and encouraging a parallel popular escalation. The two kinds of escalation can easily reinforce each other as military diplomacy evokes a mass reaction and public opinion reduces the leaders' options. The domestic pressure can upset a leader's attempts to compromise and lead to renewed tension; or at the other extreme, it can compel a strategically unwise concession that may make a later crisis more dangerous. Accordingly, many diplomats fear the influence of public opinion on foreign policy—for public opinion does not necessarily support the diplomatic actions they consider wise for strategic or bargaining purposes.

In summary, diplomacy seeks to resolve conflicts, but does so under the assumption that war is possible. Diplomats must ensure the protection of strategic interests, and must look after their nation's prestige because that prestige helps settle conflicts favorably and peaceably. But the escalation process that diplomacy uses for settling conflict almost necessarily involves the threat or use of quasi-military activity and even of war. In this process, leaders respond more or less rationally to the balance of interests present and to the military alternatives available. Thus nations will sometimes resort to deliberate war, and sometimes stumble into it because of a mistake in the escalation process. Diplomacy usually resolves crises peacefully. But a high probability of war will persist in a world of independent states that have seriously conflicting goals and that keep themselves prepared for war.

There are several factors, besides a high level of disagreement, that make war likely. One is doubt about the international prestige order; when nations challenge the order, the chance of war rises. A particularly important example of this effect is that rapidly changing arms levels favor war. Another factor is the misperception between nations of each other's goals or military capabilities. Thus cultural differences and rapidly changing military technology are likely to favor war. Finally, the unpredictability of leadership, as when national decision making oscillates between popular and elite control, favors war. These factors were not a force in nineteenth-century Europe, nor have they had a major impact on the nuclear standoff between the United States and the USSR. Thus these two examples, often used to demonstrate the desirable inevitability of balance-of-power diplomacy, rest on a particularly fortunate combination of circumstances. In contrast, in many areas of the developing world, these factors are much more likely to produce diplomatic war. Though diplomatic maneuvering may be inevitable, the world would choose badly to rely on it to bring peace in the future.

It is impossible to limit the role of diplomatic maneuvering without a major change in the character of international politics. But there are ways to make diplomacy safer. One is to de-emphasize prestige, or at least to improve the way it is evaluated and adjusted. Personal contact and communication among diplomats and leaders, which are clearly increasing, may serve these ends. Public scrutiny may help make diplomats less conscious of prestige; though public input can be risky in a crisis, its long-term impact may be favorable. Economic factors or status and voting power in international organizations might become more important in prestige than military factors. And arms control can certainly play a role. It can, for example, be designed to discourage rapid military buildups or to encourage the exchange of military data in order to reduce the risk of a disparity between a nation's military capability and its level of prestige.

Another approach is to attempt to make the bargaining process itself—and the possible attendant escalation of conflict—less dangerous. Presumably, diplomatic communication can be improved; and many techniques for mediating and settling conflicts might be applied more widely. These techniques can be particularly helpful in relieving the adverse short-term effects of public opinion on foreign policy. The role for arms control in this area is to make it easier to predict the outcome of a war, and to shape the military options available to decision makers so as to decrease the seriousness of each escalatory step and to allow more time for negotiation.

3. International Law and Arms Control

Arms control agreements, usually embodied in treaties, are a part of international law, and thus reflect the mechanisms by which international law is created and enforced. For this reason, it is important here to examine international law in general, which has sought to restrain war for much longer than arms control, and to consider why arms control is currently receiving much more attention than the more traditional forms of international law.

International law is indeed law, in a rather broad sense. Law can reasonably be defined to include all doctrines that affect individual decisions or the settlement of disputes and that derive from sources perceived to bear authority. In this sense, law is not just statutes and the way judges advise juries; it is also administrative decisions and the way lawyers advise clients. Even business customs that lack formal sanctions can serve as a means of making decisions and settling disputes that is as effective and as regularly applied as judicial action. Some authors even regard the language and concepts used to define disputes as a form of law, because they shape the settlement of the disputes.[1] Thus there can be a kind of law that bears little resemblance to formally enacted statutes supported by formal sanction.[2]

International law is almost completely within this wider definition of law. Like domestic law, it is not always enforced, let alone obeyed. It includes specific principles and doctrines, and affects the international behavior of governments and government decision makers. But the mechanisms by which international law is created and applied differ drastically from those of domestic law, which is usually enacted by a clearly defined process and enforced by means of state-authorized sanctions.

There are at least three mechanisms that give international law its effective binding force. The first mechanism rests on the statesman's personal sense of duty to obe   in norms in directing his nation's diplomacy. This r   flects a concept of natural law that places the   n restrictions; for example, the state shoulc   ns' territorial sovereignty and refrain fro. mechanism is weak, as often happens wit cause its principles are abstract and subject in application. Moreover, the concept is undei   ck by those who argue that international relations   nd indeed should be, amoral. Yet this mechanism is both the historical source of most international law and a major force for the reform of that law. For example, there are fundamental notions of justice underlying both the demands of the developing world for self-determination and the opposition of the developed world to havens for terrorists.

The power of this ethical mechanism can also be seen in the decision maker's strong compulsion to explain his actions; a declaration of war, for example, usually contains an explanation cast in terms of law or justice. The apologias of national leaders are often mere rationalizations or cynical efforts to gain public or international support. Nevertheless, they continue to be issued, as much for the sake of their author as for the sake of the author's relations with his audience. The need to justify a forcible action by appeal to universal principles is a deeply human one, reflecting ethical concerns and perhaps biological impulses. The psychological need to give a persuasive explanation undoubtedly has some influence on what action a leader chooses to take.

National self-interest is the second mechanism. The creation and observance of some rules serve the interest of all nations. For example, all nations benefit by obeying a rule against mistreating one another's diplomats. Similarly, nations are able to gain the benefits of making agreements only if they generally honor their agreements. To be effective, these rules require a particular balance of interests; and as long as that balance is present, the mechanism can operate effectively, despite the theory that international relations are amoral. It is norms based on self-interest that are the most effective rules of international law today. Some of the rules are left relatively unarticulated, as in the understandings between the great powers to respect each other's zones of special influence and to permit certain intelligence activities. Other rules are defined in elaborate treaties or laid down by international organizations such as the International Monetary Fund and the European Economic Community.

The third mechanism consists of restraints that the citizens of a nation place on their own government's conduct of foreign relations. Two examples of this kind of restraint are the provision of the U.S. Constitution giving Congress the exclusive power to declare war and the much less formal Swedish tradition of neutrality. In some situations, the strength of this mechanism may come from little more than the government's need to weigh the potential costs of domestic discontent when it formulates a particular foreign policy. In other situations, this mechanism will have the nearly absolute force of constitutional law. The growing interest of citizens in international issues suggests that this mechanism may grow in importance.

THE HISTORICAL DEVELOPMENT OF INTERNATIONAL LAW

The roots of contemporary international law lie in a traditional law that was undifferentiated from morality. The traditional law was believed to come directly from God and to govern both the civil authority and the citizens. In the Christian West during the Middle Ages, the civil ruler was charged with little more than filling in the details and applying the God-given natural law. The Imperial Chinese leader ruled by the mandate of heaven. The Muslim sharia was also viewed as coming from God; the civil ruler's duty was to enforce it, not to change it.[3] Such legal systems drew no distinction between religious duty, positive law, and restraints on civil rulers, all of which bore the same ultimate authority and in many ways had the same content.

Strictly speaking, international law was impossible in such systems, for there were no nations. Most of these traditions did, however, allow for treaties and trade with foreign peoples; and some traditions, particularly the Muslim, developed elaborate principles for dealing with them. The civil rulers were also bound by certain legal restraints in their relations with other civil rulers of the same religion. Sometimes these restraints were feeble and widely ignored, as in medieval Europe. In a few cases, such as that of Persian absolutism, restraint was philosophically rejected. Nevertheless, there were usually some restraints that had strong legitimacy, because each leader was faced with morally binding obligations deriving from a nearly universal ethic. Purely local interests were legally subordinated to broader ones, even if only in theory.

In Western Europe this system broke down with the Reformation, when it became clear that a European order based on religion would no longer be possible. The result of the religious wars, embodied in the Treaty of Westphalia (1648), was an agreement to disagree, a separation of morality and politics.[4] Political authority would be severed from religious authority. The reverse side of the coin was that no moral test was available to apply to politics. Political authority now rested on a theory of absolutism, developed by such philosophers as Jean Bodin, Thomas Hobbes, and Emerich de Vattel.[5] An indivisible sovereignty and the nation-state system became philosophically conceivable. International law was now needed, but its only possible intellectual foundation was the positive consent of sovereign states. The content of international law was therefore limited to those doctrines that were in the interest of the all-powerful sovereigns, or that carried so little content that they could be enforced by the vague moral consensus that remained.

It was in this cultural context that the Western world developed an international law of war. The wars that followed on the religious wars were comparatively small and required relatively little citizen participation. Facing the weakness of international law and the relatively low cost of war, theorists of international law such as Hugo Grotius sought not to prohibit war itself, but instead to control the conduct of war. These theorists may also have feared that the traditional rules distinguishing between just and unjust wars would invidiously tend to become rules justifying war, as had happened during the Crusades and the religious wars. They thus developed a law of war, as opposed to a law against war. The law that emerged included elaborate doctrines of neutrality and rules designed to protect noncombatants. Later, in the nineteenth and twentieth centuries, new rules were added by treaty to govern the treatment of prisoners of war and to prohibit certain weapons.

When war had again grown costly, following the Napoleonic era, the tacit acceptance of war eventually came into question. The nineteenth-century Concert of Europe sought to improve the diplomatic mechanisms for preventing war; and at the same time, reflecting the dominant political orientation of Europe, it sought to protect monarchy from democracy. By the twentieth century, governments desperately tried to mobilize their populations in wartime by promising to change the world order so that war would no longer occur; for war was becoming so horrible that all wanted to put an end to it. Among the results were the Kellogg-Briand Pact of 1928 and the prohibition of aggressive war by the United Nations. These efforts to outlaw war rested on the thin foundation of a consensus of nation-states. The general failure of such laws is apparent. Yet no firmer basis for international law was available until new forms of international organization and the concept of arms control—first seriously considered in the 1920's—emerged, apparently offering a greater potential.

Among the elites of the developing world, the Western approach to international law has replaced traditional doctrines. The Western view, that international law is based solely on the consent of sovereign states, has therefore become the dominant view in many societies that once had their own distinctive law. Because of the West's unwillingness to recognize any philosophical basis for its own international law, and because of the difficulty of relating the Western doctrines to traditional local culture, the developing world's concept of international law often tends toward a cynicism based purely on national self-interest. The support that Western doctrines of international law have often given to imperialist interests in opposition to the interests of the developing world heightens this cynicism about Western law. In defending its interests, the developing world has sought to define a new international law in order to pursue such goals as self-determination, racial and economic equality, freedom from colonial domination, and the proposed New International Economic Order. Though these demands often seek only to change legal doctrines, they can lead to theories that support war.

It is in Marxist doctrine that cynicism about international law reaches its extreme. According to the Marxist view, law is purely a tool. It can be manipulated by capitalist governments to subordinate the working class; and it is available to Marxist governments to support the dictatorship of the proletariat. International law, in the Marxist view, is correspondingly a tool of conflict between the socialist regimes and the imperialist ones; thus a war of liberation is considered fundamentally different from an imperialist war. The historical dialectic of Marxism provides a test by which the international behavior of governments can be measured; nevertheless, the concept of law as a restraint on government is fundamentally even weaker in Marxism than in non-Marxist Western thought.[6]

The general world concern with preventing nuclear war is not enough to create a new ethical basis for international law. In the short run, therefore, the strongest mechanism available for restraining governments remains national self-interest. Even the explosive growth of special-purpose international organizations, because it is mainly centered on technical issues, is unlikely to offer a more solid foundation for international law. In the long run, national cultures might evolve toward a greater international unity, and domestic efforts to limit governmental power might create more effective international restraints. But the immediate status of law and therefore arms control is one in which national self-interest determines both the existence and the effectiveness of agreements; cultural factors contribute little more than an additional motivation that may reinforce self-interest.

LAW BASED ON NATIONAL SELF-INTEREST

National self-interest can support a substantial and significant body of law. This mechanism and its limitations are readily seen in tracing the rise and decline of the law of maritime neutrality. The very concept of neutrality represented an enormous intellectual break with the legal traditions of the Middle Ages. These traditions had implied a duty to fight; one could not be neutral in a conflict between God and the foes of God. The Crusades were a particularly striking example of such a conflict, but the fundamental problem is posed by any doctrine of just war: if a particular war is just for one belligerent and unjust for the other, can a third state remain a neutral?[7]

This general view of war changed as the Renaissance brought an end to medieval universalism and as nations began to consider how they might rearrange trade relationships for mutual benefit in time of war. Thus, as early as 1303, England and France entered into an agreement under which each promised not to trade with the other's enemies.[8] The next step was for nations to protect themselves from the spread of war, a goal that coalesced with the broader legal tendency to restrain war. In the late fifteenth century, for example, Liège entered into agreements with both parties to an anticipated war, promising its neutrality to each.[9] The potential belligerents gained a promise of nonsupport for the enemy; though perhaps not as good as an alliance, this was still desirable. At the same time, Liège protected itself from both belligerents.

After agreements such as these had shown that neutrality could benefit all sides, the concept was picked up by admiralty courts, the national courts that already existed to approve or disapprove maritime seizures.[10] In developing the law governing seizures, these courts, although representing particular nations, were facing well-balanced interests. For a nation entering into a neutrality treaty, the benefits of the other party's neutrality in future wars had to outweigh the costs to its own commerce of being neutral and restraining its own trade during the other's wars. These two interests always figure in a neutrality problem; they were both present in the admiralty courts, which in effect had to balance military interests against commercial ones. The admiralty courts of the various European nations were thus able to articulate widely accepted principles governing such issues as the definition of contraband and the right of search and seizure. Trading nations that fought few wars tried to define contraband much more narrowly than nations that traded less and fought more.[11] Nevertheless, two-fifths of the decisions of Lord Stowell, a British prize judge of the late eighteenth and early nineteenth centuries, were in favor of neutral claimants against the crown.[12] England and France had enough confidence to negotiate admiralty procedures as early as 1497.[13]

Even though the relative independence and fairness of the

admiralty courts were important factors in the development of the law of neutrality, the courts would not have been allowed to develop this law had neutrality not served the interests of the national governments. For the balance between the military and commercial interests to favor the doctrine of neutrality, two conditions had to be met. The first was that the neutrality doctrines would have a relatively mild and generally symmetrical effect on the ability of countries to prosecute war. The second was that the gain one belligerent might achieve by breaking the law could quickly be counterbalanced by retaliation from the other.

So long as these conditions were met, the law of neutrality was fairly stable and effective. The law was able to deal with the shipping of contraband, for example, by using doctrines that permitted the searching of neutral vessels[14] and that defined situations in which a party's violation of its neutrality could be presumed.[15] The neutrals eventually responded, however, with "armed neutralities," which amounted to convoys.[16] Neutrals could thus more easily violate the rules; and as economies changed, this violation became extremely profitable. It eventually became impossible for belligerents to be sure that neutrals were carrying on no contraband trade with their opponents. All this weakened the law of neutrality; it finally became nearly a dead letter when trade became the difference between victory and defeat, and when submarine warfare took from belligerents the opportunity to inspect a vessel's cargo before sinking the vessel.

By generalizing from the example of neutrality, it is possible to define the balance of interests necessary for national self-interest to support effective international law.[17] First, if both nations obey the law, each must be better off than if both disobey it, and neither must lose anything it considers vital as a direct result of its own obedience. And second, if one nation violates the law, any advantage it gains must be minimal or short-lived, and the innocent nation must readily be able to compensate for such an advantage by retaliation. Thus, in the case of neutrality, the first condition was that the economic value of unrestricted trade should outweigh the military value of interfering with the opponent's trade, and that the opponent's commerce would not be decisive in the war. The second condition was that the threat of retaliation could be used to deter the violation of neutrality.

A similar balance of interests essentially underlies nearly all the doctrines of the international law of war. For instance, the international rules protecting civilians in wartime support a large interest, the survival of civilians, at the expense of a smaller interest, the limited military benefit of killing civilians. These rules are therefore least likely to be obeyed when the killing of civilians appears militarily helpful, as in the bombing of cities during the Second World War, or when the chance of retaliation is small, as in terrorism by underground groups. Because this kind of law relies on the possibility of retaliation, it is much more likely to be effective among nations of nearly equal power than among nations differing radically in power or in tactics. This is one reason why the laws of war are so poorly observed in colonial wars.

Though supported by self-interest, most laws restraining warfare have an ethical basis, such as the desire to protect civilians, that may ultimately derive from the cultural norms that were once the source of international law. The first criterion of self-interest discussed above, that obeying a law must bring a greater benefit than disobeying it, is in fact similar to a criterion often used in casuistry to evaluate an action with mixed effects: for the action to be approved, its good effects must outweigh its bad ones. But any ethical basis for international law has been losing importance; when rules of war are not backed by an appropriate balance of interests, they typically disappear. Thus the law of the declaration of war, although codified as recently as 1907,[18] is now meaningless and ignored, presumably because the necessary balance of national interests no longer exists.[19]

A balance of interests may not always be enough to sustain

international law, because of the chance of a breakdown after small or unclear violations. In the face of such a violation, the innocent party must make the difficult decision whether to retaliate or to ignore the violation. Retaliation may be hard to justify publicly and may risk further counter-action by the original violator. But the failure to retaliate may undermine the credibility of the nation's commitment to maintain the rule, and may erode the rule itself. One pattern of this erosion can be seen in the decline of the doctrine of neutrality. The sequence of events was: violation of neutrality, development of counter-doctrines by the belligerents, armed neutralities, and ultimately the breakdown of neutrality altogether.

Such a breakdown may be avoidable if both sides believe the other is acting in good faith. Thus, in the case of the Limited Test Ban Treaty between the United States and the USSR, when the underground nuclear tests of either side have technically violated the treaty by breaking the earth's surface, both sides have had a strong incentive to regard the violation as accidental. If either side had seriously suspected the other of cheating, the entire structure of the treaty would have been in doubt.

A neutral party can also help the law survive by defining it precisely and applying it with flexibility to new situations.[20] The admiralty courts, for example, could adjust the legal doctrine in response to changes in warfare and economics. And in particular judgments they could save governments from having to decide whether or not to retaliate. Moral and cultural attitudes sometimes suggest specific distinctions that help preserve the law. For instance, the difference between the rules for prisoners of war, for civilians, and for combatants rests on widely shared attitudes reinforced by the use of uniforms to show who is entitled to what protection. A treaty can be negotiated to stabilize rules, but the credibility and rationality of the distinctions embodied in the treaty are crucial to its success.

The technical legal norms just described rely on the same

process of balancing interests as the tacit norms governing intelligence activities and defining spheres of influence in the Cold War. The balance of interests is exactly parallel in the two cases; only the verbalization of it is different. Indeed, these examples from the Cold War show the ubiquity of the self-interest form of law; whenever there is the necessary reciprocity of interests, such law will almost automatically arise, even if it is expressed only in internal government calculations.

A reliance on the more formal structure of treaties is more likely when the underlying norm has broad popular appeal, when diplomats fear that the norm may otherwise erode, or when diplomats make a deliberate political decision to pursue one of a number of possible patterns of self-interest. As an example of this last process, one issue at the Conference on Security and Cooperation in Europe in 1973–75 was whether it would be wiser to have a tacit understanding to maintain a nearly impermeable line between Eastern and Western Europe, or an explicit set of rules designed to break down this line in a controlled way. In creating this kind of law, the diplomat works at the margin of the problem, seeking less to find new interests to assemble in international agreements than to decide which interests to emphasize and convert from tacit to explicit form.[21] The pursuit of self-interest may continue in efforts to shape the details of explicit agreements and to make the balance of certain interests more formal or stable and others less so. Although the law resulting from treaty negotiations is important, it is unlikely to be surprising or revolutionary. It is least likely to place strong direct limits on war.

THE POTENTIAL OF THE OTHER MECHANISMS OF LAW

The balancing of self-interest just discussed is characteristic of the activity of a government arms control staff. Hence arms control, as a special kind of international law, is correspondingly limited. But much of the political support for arms control derives from a much broader base than self-interest: from ethical attitudes and from the efforts of citizens to control their national governments. Thus arms control can tap the other mechanisms that support international law. Even though these mechanisms are currently quite weak, it is important to examine their potential.

Among the many factors that weaken the ethical roots of international law are the diversity of legal doctrines and the widespread assumption that ethics is irrelevant to international behavior. Furthermore, law is commonly viewed as highly technical; in both domestic and international affairs, law has lost much of its connection with the sense of justice that usually motivates and affects people as individuals. Among major contemporary societies, China is the only one that may have avoided this separation; and if China has indeed avoided it, this has happened only as a result of a particular Confucian tradition, and possibly at a substantial cost to freedom. The separation between law and justice has many possible explanations—the complexity and cultural pluralism of present-day society and the rise of bureaucracies, for example—and almost certainly has historical and sociological causes. This separation is especially wide in the often esoteric field of international law.

In the face of such a technical view of law, it is hard to bring ethical pressure to bear on national leaders. There are international movements seeking to impose ethical standards in such areas as environmental protection and international economic redistribution. So far these movements have tended only to create new, equally technical international laws and organizations; and the new creations have tended to lose sight of their ethical origins and their appeal to public constituencies. The most interesting exception is the human rights movement, which could fundamentally change international politics. But so far, though this movement is genuinely international, its constituency is rather restricted.

Moreover, the diversity of cultural traditions and philosophies creates a specific barrier to the evolution of a universal, ethically based international law. In Europe and some other areas, international law is indeed growing stronger, but this is a regional phenomenon only. At the global level the idea of justice varies greatly as a result of maldistribution of wealth, racial discrimination, and above all, the tension between justice and peace, the problem of whether war is a proper way to right a wrong. The differing concepts of justice make a worldwide international law based on ethics unlikely.

Some ethical norms might conceivably emerge among the elites that actually conduct foreign policy. The members of a profession often follow an altruistic code; the judiciary and the professional military are examples that show the force of such a code, even in professions closely involved in the use and control of violence. One could visualize a parallel code emerging in the area of foreign policy. The internationalism of the diplomatic corps probably helps account for the European peace that reigned almost unbroken between the Napoleonic Wars and the First World War. Today many leaders of different countries share a common educational background and many common values. On the other hand, current ethical principles urge putting the national interest ahead of both one's own interest and the interest of any other nation or person: *raison d'état* and nationalism both tend to prohibit generosity to a foreign nation at the expense of one's own nation. And in nations whose leaders are self-selected by raw power and manipulation, the leaders are unlikely to be highly responsive to ethical concerns. Thus any development of an international ethics of foreign policy may depend on greater communication among the elites of different cultures and on philosophical shifts in both the developed and the developing worlds.

Bureaucracies too can often provide support for international law. The bureaucratic process brings in many actors, and some of them may obey a legal or ethical norm to oppose an illegal action. For example, the U.S. government would find it very difficult to plan a concealed nuclear test in violation of current treaties. Around 1960, when particularly sensitive nuclear tests were actually carried out in Project Argus, information about them was leaked to the *New York Times* (which chose not to publish a report), even though the tests were not illegal at the time. Because of such bureaucratic opposition, those who want to test nuclear weapons will tend to propose legal methods. Bureaucratic pressure will most strongly favor obedience to international law when the law coincides with the parochial goals of a substantial part of the bureaucracy. That part of the bureaucracy can then use international law as an argument in the internal political debate preceding the government's decision;[22] and such an argument is naturally strongest if the law is codified in a treaty. Thus a bureaucracy can strengthen a law deriving from self-interest, but it is not likely to be innovative; indeed, bureaucratic conservatism may even obstruct the development of new norms.

Sometimes bureaucracies can even weaken the application of existing legal norms. The essence of bureaucracy is the diffusion of the power to make decisions, so that the participation of any one bureaucrat in shaping a policy is so small as to eliminate any moral or legal scruples he may have. The final bureaucratic action is thus essentially amoral; and some bureaucracies, such as those dealing with intelligence, may even institutionalize the violation of law. In any event, bureaucratic pressure is likely to be nearly meaningless when a government is overtaken by revolution or by strong individual leadership.

Domestic legal and constitutional provisions have been only partially successful in restraining the international behavior of governments, because judges hesitate to enforce such provisions. Even though the U.S. judicial system, for example, has frequently struck down executive or legislative actions in the domestic area since the early nineteenth century, it has rarely done so in foreign affairs, even when constitutional language could be found to support such action. In one case, the Supreme Court went so far as to state an elabo-

rate theory that the foreign policy power of the federal government derives directly from the government's "external
sovereignty," and does "not depend upon the affirmative
grants of the Constitution."²³ The constitutional result is a
broad executive discretion in the area of foreign policy, effectively unrestrained by the courts even in the case of action
traditionally prohibited under ordinary domestic constitutional law.²⁴ Japanese courts have shown a similar timidity in
interpreting Japan's pacifist constitution.

The fear that the executive would ignore a court's decision
and thus hold the court up to ridicule sometimes explains this
judicial position. And there are other pragmatic concerns.
Courts doubt that the judicial process is rapid enough or that
it is able to obtain the sort of evidence needed to review the
conduct of foreign policy. Further, courts may fear that international law is too vague and undeveloped to offer the variety
of doctrines and distinctions necessary for applying it wisely.
But the courts have often sidestepped foreign policy issues
even when these pragmatic concerns are absent. In a particularly disturbing series of cases, for example, the U.S. Supreme Court appeared to change its constitutional standards
for wartime powers depending on whether or not the war
was over.²⁵

The courts appear to be responding to a fundamental sense
that foreign policy knows no norm, that legal bars should not
be placed in the way of national defense, and that international law is a matter for the discretion of the executive, not
the rulings of the judiciary. No judicial system is likely to impose severe restraints on the execution of foreign policy unless given a very clear mandate to do so. The Court of Justice
of the European Economic Community, one of the few courts
that intervenes sharply in foreign policy areas, is clearly
created and mandated to apply specific international rules to
economic questions. In general, given their timidity and conservatism, courts are unlikely to develop any novel principles
of international law, and will enforce only those principles

they are specifically directed to enforce. An international court such as the International Court of Justice usually has a still weaker political position, and tends to be even more ingenious in avoiding decisions that call for a change in the status quo.[26]

The more innovative pressures are likely to come from the public. Public opinion can sometimes be ignored, and it is frequently a force for war rather than for peace. Nevertheless, in some situations public opinion does place restraints on the international activity of governments. These restraints may be codified as laws or constitutional provisions; or they may work less formally in such ways as influencing a budgetary process and forcing leaders to justify their actions publicly.

This process of justification is particularly important because public opinion usually requires leaders to justify any use of coercion. The doctrines used to justify a coercive action have become a form of law whose effectiveness depends on several factors: the action itself, the leader's need to justify the action to himself, the attitudes of the leader's constituents, and the extent to which the leader believes he has to be logical with his constituents.[27] The need for justification is naturally more important when the leader has to satisfy a thoughtful public and when the action to be justified is relatively violent.

In some cases, this need for a public justification can produce new institutions. Thus the Allies' public statements during the Second World War contributed to the creation of the United Nations and the Nuremberg tribunals. Though the Nuremberg prosecution was in part a response to those who wished to shoot all the Nazi leaders without trial, it provided a legal framework for trying them. The framework was in some respects a parody, for the victors did not prosecute their own war criminals. But the trials were conducted fairly, and logical principles were developed.[28] For example, the court formally announced the principle that a soldier must sometimes disobey his government. This and other Nuremberg principles have since been turned against their makers.[29]

The need to persuade the public of the rightness of a coercive action does have drawbacks as an ingredient in the creation of law. The use of persuasion in support of force can create a law that justifies war, and a justification sometimes becomes an encouragement. Moreover, a law deriving from such persuasion will often be vague. This happens because there are usually arguments to be made for each side of the conflict in any situation relating to war. For example, a norm opposing aggression may be pitted against a norm opposing tyranny. A decision maker, in order to protect his options, is likely to choose as ambiguous a justification for action as possible. Finally, it is only by accident, so to speak, that a government will use a justification that is likely to restrict its freedom of action later. The Nuremberg trials show one such accident, and others might occur as nations seek revolutionary change. But generally, even in justifying a war, nations will attempt to avoid committing themselves.

Nevertheless, this need to persuade the public can become a way for effective, fundamentally new principles to enter international law. To be sure, any law that is created in this fashion may be colored by national self-interest and imperfectly enforced. But the process of public justification of policies is the closest analogue of domestic political representation that is currently found in international affairs. The principles brought out in the process have some force among diplomats, as well as with public opinion.

In the near future, none of the existing mechanisms of international law seem likely to put very severe restraints on national foreign policies; and least of all will they restrain war. Patterns of mutual self-interest are still the most important source of international law. For the other mechanisms to work, the necessary consensus is too weak, the pressure for justice too sharply opposed to that for peace, and the appeal of nationalism too strong. There is little chance that a deep-cutting world rule of law will come soon. At best, one can hope for a contemporary Westphalia, such as a U.S.-Soviet détente, leaving room for the wide application of law based on self-interest.

In the long run, however, the mechanism of justification offers the hope of introducing substantially new doctrines into international law that do not derive from self-interest alone. Governments will not develop self-denying doctrines of their own accord, though they can be restrained somewhat by fear of each other. Any further restraint can come only from the citizens. This is why the international arms control and human rights movements are so important; for these movements, unlike many other current international movements, seek to restrain governments, rather than just to coordinate governmental power to solve international problems. The development of a thoughtful public opinion (at least among the interested elites) is the key step toward a more effective international law and toward overcoming the division between legal technicalities and the broader political culture. A body of thoughtful judgment and criticism outside government is needed in order to define widely accepted principles for contemporary international law. These principles can be most useful if they derive from a confrontation between the different national, legal, and foreign policy cultures, and if they are developed within a persuasive philosophical structure.

ARMS CONTROL AS A FORM OF INTERNATIONAL LAW

Like any other international legal restraint, the restraint of war is still predominantly based on mutual self-interest. Mutual self-interest is usually ineffective as a direct way to prohibit either war or the use of all but a few particular weapons. The nature of total war and the fervor of national demands for justice make victory so important that nations will seldom refrain from using any available weapons. Some of the new weapons, moreover, are likely to be so decisive that the potential user may not be deterred by the possibility of retaliation. Therefore, one or another of the two conditions required for self-interest to work in law often fails.

A possible exception is the emerging restriction against the use of nuclear weapons, and perhaps also against other particularly horrifying weapons of mass destruction such as biological and environmental weapons. There are widespread cultural pressures against these weapons, and they have indeed been little used. Nuclear weapons have not been used since 1945; conflicts have been kept at the conventional level by strategic deterrence, for when both sides possess invulnerable nuclear weapons, the self-interest of both dictates restraint. Yet the principle of not using nuclear weapons has received little formal recognition, and can hardly be counted on to prevent a nation from using nuclear weapons in extremis. Nor does the principle bar the acquisition of nuclear weapons. Nevertheless, the inhibitions against the use of these weapons are growing stronger each year.

With this exception, law has tended to become ineffective in restraining the use of existing weapons. This outcome is explicit in the concept of total war, which emerged in the nineteenth century. The twentieth century brought the opportunity for a new approach to restraining warfare, since its weapons—battleships, aircraft, tanks, and later nuclear explosives—all need extensive prewar research and procurement. The construction of these weapons requires nations to maintain standing forces and to commit enormous resources to military procurement. Further, it is at least plausible that these procurement efforts, and particularly arms races, have been a source of war. These preparations for war, therefore, have become a focus for control, and the law has shifted its attention toward restraining not the use of weapons, but the possession of them.

Besides stimulating efforts to control arms races, there are other ways that national self-interest could contribute to restrictions on the possession of weapons and help prevent war. An arms balance in which each side would have to build new weapons before it could attack, and in which each side would have the information necessary to know whether the other side was building them, could be much more stable than a balance in which the weapons were already available but in which there was an agreement to exercise restraint during a crisis. As pointed out in the preceding chapter, limits on the existence of weapons could help lower the frequency of diplomatic crises and also the risk associated with them. Thus arms control emerges as a way nations can obtain mutual benefits from not having certain weapons.

As will be seen in the next chapter, self-interest is the touchstone of national approval of arms control agreements. Sometimes, however, the agreements reflect the other mechanisms of international law as well. In the Strategic Arms Limitation Talks (SALT), for example, the emphasis is on the mutual benefit to two powers that threaten each other and wish to come to terms with this threat. But as in any agreement to restrict nuclear weapons, SALT also has a more altruistic basis: the shared abhorrence of the weaponry. Arms control is a potentially fertile field for cultivating international agreement because the ability to communicate in order to define self-interest is better in this relatively technical area than in the more traditional areas of politics. Arms control may not be an intellectually satisfying form of international law. It is not foolproof; nor is it very clearly a step toward a more humane world community. Yet it is available.

Arms control is achievable, however, only under certain conditions. The political support needed for defining the permissible balance of forces is most readily achieved when the parties to the agreement have roughly equal arms levels; as will be seen, asymmetrical situations present grave difficulties for arms control. The implicit opposition of arms control to war further implies the acceptance of the status quo. Thus arms control, with the possible exception of that specifically designed to prevent nuclear war, is unlikely to appeal to nations that find the status quo unacceptable. Since arms control negotiations necessarily focus on the level of arms, they must suffer from the domestic political pressures of armaments lobbies pointing out the undeniable virtues of preparedness. This concentration on relative arms levels can also heighten strategic concerns and lead to even higher arms levels. It is understandable, therefore, that diplomats will not be able to negotiate successfully all the agreements likely to be useful. And because the likelihood of war does not depend entirely on arms levels, all war cannot be prevented by arms control agreements, even if the agreements are fully observed. Yet even allowing for all these limitations, the analysis of war in Chapter Two suggests that arms control can make a significant difference.

For the near term, it is necessary to assume that mutual self-interest is the only effective mechanism of arms control. For the longer term, this assumption cannot be accepted, because an arms control anchored in self-interest alone will probably be inadequate to prevent a nuclear catastrophe. The greatest danger is not a U.S.-Soviet war, but rather a nuclear war in the developing world. The problems of asymmetry make an effective arms control difficult in the developing world, where the growth of technology is likely to make nuclear weapons more readily available; and the risks of conflict are great. Therefore, it is necessary to examine possible ways of broadening arms control in order to overcome its present limitations. The principle of self-interest in arms control may be extended so as to reduce the economic or political incentives to procure weapons.[30] In addition, stronger international organizations may be required to help deal with the sense of injustice that makes nations hesitant to renounce war. And more effective arrangements for enforcement will be essential if arms control among unequals is to be politically and militarily feasible.

The chance of creating such arrangements may grow as citizens realize that their governments can no longer protect them in traditional ways when nuclear weapons are freely available. It is also possible, however, that governments will become immune to popular restraint because their ability to use nuclear weapons will not depend on the ability to raise a citizen army or even to raise large tax sums. In evaluating the possible benefits and shortcomings of arms control, I will first analyze the short-run potential of arms control agreements based on self-interest, and then the nearly unexplored longer run of arms control that builds on international organizations and on changes in the nation-state system.

4. Entry into Arms Control Agreements

As is evident from any review of the history of arms control,[1] explicit arms control agreements are much less common than situations in which arms restraint would be mutually beneficial. This is because of important additional political conditions, which derive from three main sources: the general political context, the need to assemble existing political and bureaucratic constituencies into domestic support for an agreement, and the structure of the international negotiation itself.

THE GENERAL POLITICAL CONTEXT

An arms control agreement has deep connotations that transcend the direct military effects that may be expected. There is a human sense that an agreement—almost any agreement—will bring peace, but also a fear that it will compromise the national sovereignty. Negotiation with another nation may carry the positive connotation of overcoming conflict or the negative connotation of betraying loyalties. These connotations can vary radically. In the 1920's they were so favorable that nations negotiated highly idealistic agreements like the Kellogg-Briand Pact; in the 1950's they were so unfavorable that any arms control negotiation was futile. The United States opposed arms control in the 1950's and supported it in the 1960's; the developing world that favored it in the early 1960's had turned against it by the end of the decade. The political factors that shape these attitudes toward arms control are subtle. They are apparently not the same as those that shape mass aggression or the willingness to support large military budgets; for there seems to be little correlation between the historical cycle of arms control and the cycles of national aggression and military budgets.

Only a few of the political phenomena underlying arms control are clear. It is clear that the experience of war produces a direct human reaction that sometimes favors arms control. The classic example of this reaction came in the period after the First World War, which had been a bloody stalemate whose stakes did not seem worth its costs. Even the victors, particularly the United States and England, tended to be interested in disarmament. This tendency, reinforced by the idealistic propaganda used to encourage public sacrifice during the war, created popular support for a far-reaching postwar settlement. Similarly, it was in the wake of the War of 1812 that the United States and England accepted the Rush-Bagot agreement demilitarizing the Great Lakes. And it was after a civil war that Costa Rica amended its constitution to abolish the military.

The reaction to losing a war can be especially favorable to arms control. It can discredit a government that controlled military policies, bring in new leaders who are usually antimilitary, and reduce the popular interest in arms expenditures and military activities. Thus, after the Second World War, Japan accepted a constitutional limitation on armaments. And after the Vietnam War the domestic reaction in the United States undoubtedly helped make SALT I politically acceptable to the American public.

On occasion, the opposite attitude occurs after a war, but there are often special circumstances. An easy success in war may encourage further war and work against arms control. German revanchism after the First World War is partly explained by the harsh terms of Versailles. Moreover, it was the new German government, not the one in power during the war, that was discredited by the peace arrangements. After the Second World War, the image of Munich, which symbolized the need to be prepared, left the West disinclined to enter into broad arms control agreements. After the Korean War, much of the American public turned against the government in the belief that the United States forces could have done better if they had not been restrained by politics. By the time of the Vietnam War, in contrast, the American public better understood the limitations on conflict in the nuclear era. Finding the war itself morally unattractive, the public doubted both the military and the political leadership; it thus became much more receptive to arms control.

Although the reaction to a past war normally favors arms control, the desire to avoid a future war seems generally to work against arms control. The historical evidence for this point is quite persuasive. England and Germany were unable to control their naval competition before the First World War even though the competition was clearly a source of tension. The European countries were similarly unable to negotiate arms control in the early 1930's, again in a time of growing tension. Arms controllers, like generals, may invoke the specter of a future war; but in fact they tend to think in terms of the last war.[2]

It is understandable that a dynamic nation seeking to improve its status is likely to support an arms buildup, giving its military a large role in government and rejecting arms control as idealistic nonsense. Nations like Germany in the late nineteenth century and Japan in the 1920's and 1930's tend to be somewhat mystical about armaments, their leaders vague about the specific conflict in which the arms are to be used. Although one cannot be certain about the future of specific nations, Brazil, China, and India currently present the possibility of such a dynamism; and all tend to oppose arms control. The leaders of such nations might argue that their increase in arms will encourage diplomatic bargaining; or they might justify the procurement of arms by pointing to an inconsistency between what they regard as the nation's proper international role and its present military power.

Even in nations not subject to this sort of dynamism, the

perceived need to be ready in the event of war usually discourages arms control. During the 1950's, for example, the
United States and the Soviet Union found arms control to be
impossible; and Western Europe, equally fearful of war, was
in a similar position. South Africa and the black African countries seem unlikely to reach arms control agreements now or
in the near future. The public in these nations, with war
scenarios in mind, is likely to support arms purchases and to
reject arms control. The domestic discussion of arms control,
indeed, may be viewed as a form of appeasement tantamount
to treating with the enemy.

Perhaps the problem is that the risk of war psychologically
encourages an inclination to rely on strength rather than
negotiation. Moreover, policies based on future expectations
are necessarily subjective. People may have a clear reaction to
the memory of a past war. But their feelings about the risk of a
future war or the possible consequences of arming and dis-
arming are usually uncertain; hence their judgments are
likely to reflect subjective factors. It is difficult to combine an
attempt to negotiate arms control with a prudent mistrust of
the possible opponent.

If this sort of mistrust endures for a long time without war,
a reaction may set in that favors the normalization of relations. Arms control agreements then become possible as
symbols of the normalization. This phenomenon was a major
political component of the U.S.-Soviet arms control of the
1960's and 1970's; the two nations can probably reach arms
control agreements only during such periods of détente.[3] A
long period of enmity without war perhaps produces a
psychological effect similar to that of a stalemated war. People
become willing to accept the status quo and to turn their back
on the enmity. But in addition, a generational change may be
needed for this process to work.

Although war and prolonged conflict probably do the most
to shape public attitudes toward arms control, other motivations can sometimes play an important role. For instance, a

particular foreign policy can become deeply embedded in the public consciousness and thus be very difficult to change. Britain's tradition of naval preeminence would have been an obstacle to a naval agreement with Germany before the First World War even if Germany had been willing. The eagerness of Mexico and Canada to help negotiate arms control may in part come from a traditional feeling that these nations have a mission to look after the nonmilitary interests that their powerful neighbor sometimes neglects. Sweden's traditional neutrality, though it may rest on the solid ground of realpolitik, perhaps makes the nation particularly inclined to support arms control.

Economic factors also shape these attitudes. Nations that believe their economy is dependent on the production of weapons are unlikely to be interested in arms control. The widespread dependence of developed nations on the exportation of conventional arms is part of the reason it is so difficult to control these arms. Developing nations that view military technology as the leading edge of technological progress are also unlikely to favor arms control, whereas those that see a conflict between expenditures for arms and economic development will tend to support arms control. And although the citizen's interest as a taxpayer is usually submerged under many other pressures, nearly every taxpayer has a strong economic interest in reducing expenditures on arms.

The historical record suggests then that arms control agreements may be most likely to occur in the aftermath of a war or a long conflict, and least likely in the face of an impending war. But when the political content of the agreements is considered, history suggests more—that there are specific patterns into which the majority of arms control agreements seem to fall. Three patterns are identified in this book: the settlement pattern, the legislative pattern, and the transitional pattern.

In the settlement pattern, probably the dominant one today, the arms control arrangement is part of the political process of settling a conflict. As in the case of SALT, the nations involved are effectively accepting the status quo defined by the political settlement that accompanies the arms control agreement, and confirming that status quo by the arms control agreement itself. Naturally, the parties to the agreement are most likely to find the status quo acceptable if their military strength is roughly equal. This pattern is probably the one most influenced by the experience or expectation of war. Nations commonly enter into settlement agreements as part of a de-escalation of cultural or diplomatic tensions associated with a past war. In contrast, they are quite unlikely to enter into this kind of agreement as a way to defuse an enmity that threatens war in the future.

The legislative pattern has a somewhat different motivation than the settlement pattern. Lawlike, the legislative pattern is more idealistic, resting on a widespread belief that the world would benefit if all nations refrained from a particular dangerous activity, and that lawbreaking should be penalized or at least condemned. This pattern is exemplified by the Limited Test Ban Treaty (1963) and the prohibition of biological warfare agents. Because such agreements symbolize deep human revulsions, they can gain political support from nonmilitary considerations as well as military. The test ban treaty, for example, built on an environmental constituency, and the Antarctic treaty on a scientific constituency.

The political support for agreements of this type depends to an especially great degree on attitudes toward technology. The anti-technology romanticism that has become important in the developed world generally favors arms control; the pro-technology romanticism so common in the developing world makes arms control more difficult. There are also special attitudes toward particular weapons; the nuclear weapon, for example, evokes deep reactions. Sometimes these reactions are favorable; the Indian and French governments had broad popular support in their pursuit of nuclear devices as a symbol of technology and prestige. But most people, including many in the nonnuclear nations, especially fear nuclear weapons. Even in the United States and the Soviet Union political decision makers have found their ability to launch nuclear war terrifying. Thus nuclear arms control has a uniquely wide constituency. This special attitude toward nuclear weapons resulted in the early support for the Baruch Plan in the United States in the 1940's; it has been at the heart of much of the arms control movement seen since the Second World War.

Whatever the particular weapon being controlled, this legislative pattern of arms control must show equality in the restrictions it imposes, precisely because it is a pattern based on a sense of law and rationality. For example, it seeks for all nations, without exception, to refrain from atmospheric nuclear testing because its goal is more to stamp out the evils of testing than to ensure any strategic balance.

Finally, the transitional pattern describes a small category of arms control agreements exemplified by the interwar naval treaties and the Non-Proliferation Treaty. These were neither balanced settlements nor balanced prohibitions, probably because they were viewed as transitional arrangements, to be supplemented later by broader agreements embodying either a settlement or a new form of law. Thus many in the developing world viewed the Non-Proliferation Treaty as a holding action that would be followed by superpower arms control and by the peaceful transfer of technology in order to effect a broad settlement between the industrialized countries and the less developed ones. Because transitional agreements create these expectations, they are likely to be unstable. The transitional pattern permits asymmetry in both form and effect; but the nations accepting inferiority are likely to become embittered unless the implicit promises to rectify the asymmetry are honored. Honoring the promises usually proves quite difficult.

DEVELOPING A DOMESTIC NEGOTIATING POSITION

The broad attitudes just described affect the political leader's ability to obtain public support for arms control, and perhaps also the leader's ideas about whether or not a particular type of arms control is realistic. In working out the details of an agreement, however, the leader will turn to specialized constituencies and to the government's own staffs. These constituencies and staffs thus have a great influence both on the shape of the government's negotiating position and on the final structure of the agreements themselves.

The relevant constituencies. In most countries there is a wide spectrum of views on arms control. Beginning with those who strongly favor arms control, there is usually a small core whose position rests on pacifist, religious, or anti-technology grounds. Though seldom having direct political power or even direct access to government decision makers, this core frequently projects its influence through the communications media, public opinion, and elite culture. Its ideals have sometimes become the goals of centrist decision makers of a later generation.

Another core group, composed of scientists, has probably been the most effective constituency favoring arms control since the Second World War. This scientific core group provided much of the early thinking about possible U.S.-Soviet arms control agreements. Their motivation may derive from the internationalism of science, from a special awareness of the awesomeness of modern weaponry, or from a sense of responsibility for having helped develop such weapons, particularly nuclear weapons. These scientists often have better access to decision makers than pacifists do. They are also likely to have the information, the skill in presenting their views, and the professional authority to make their points effectively in both private and public discussions. This special role of scientists has probably been strongest in the United States, but it may not survive the emergence of popular doubts about science.

The swing constituency, in the middle of the spectrum, is a much broader elite that includes national leaders, diplomats, military officials, and people outside the government such as educators and journalists. The members of this group support specific arms control measures they believe will help bring specific benefits, and oppose others they believe will not be beneficial. The positions these elites take undoubtedly depend on the psychological factors discussed earlier in this chapter; but other factors, which need not even bear directly on arms control, can be important. Some Soviet leaders, for example, probably saw the Non-Proliferation Treaty essentially as a way to strengthen West Germany's political commitment against nuclear armament; and some Americans evaluated the Limited Test Ban according to their estimate of its effect on fallout. It is clear that this elite will normally be divided, often in ways that cut across traditional distinctions such as those between civilian and military, foreign ministry and defense ministry, and liberal and conservative.

The opposition to arms control only rarely rests on philosophical grounds in the same way that support for arms control can rest on pacifism. A philosophical opposition can spring from the view that international politics is too cynical and power-oriented to make arms control worth considering. To a few, the idea of arms control is an absurd infringement on national sovereignty; those adhering to a particular theory of history may reject arms control as inconsistent with the theory. For most ideological opponents of arms control, however, the crux of their position is a strong doubt concerning the efficacy of arms control. It is sometimes possible to overcome this doubt if a particular agreement can be persuasively shown to benefit the nation. In the absence of demonstrable benefit, these opponents tend to prefer a reliance on strength, fearing that arms control only amounts to appeasement or wishful thinking.

The opposition to arms control by military and economic bureaucracies can be very strong, far overbalancing any support from the same sources. The military and its allied civilian and industrial bureaucracies are usually professionally committed to the procurement of arms. To the extent that this commitment derives from a fascination with arms or from an economic or bureaucratic desire for large budgets and contracts, the commitment may imply an opposition to all arms control. Such an attitude is likely to be held by some military officers everywhere and by many defense contractors. A foreign office, because of its concern with the ability to use power in diplomatic negotiations, may be even more opposed to arms control than a military-industrial bureaucracy.

The military, however, sometimes can affect the bureaucratic balance in a way favorable to arms control. A common military view is that certain specific arms, rather than arms in general, are necessary to defend the nation. Thus the military may be persuaded, perhaps more readily than defense contractors, to support specific arms limitations on the ground that the specific arms are unnecessary or that mutual arms control is preferable to competition in procurement. The military, after all, is more familiar than most with the effects of war. Moreover, the military is itself made up of small constituencies for specific weapons. Some officers may want to buy aircraft carriers; others prefer different expenditures. The result is a competition that has the potential to work either for or against arms control.

The competition between the three services in the United States has probably obstructed arms control because of a tendency to resolve the competition by balancing expenditures among the services. But the competition between the outlays for personnel and for weapons has probably favored arms control. The officers or defense officials who must allocate budgets among the different military constituencies are likely to be particularly receptive to arms control because of their grasp of the budgetary implications of different military alternatives. Thus Secretary of Defense Robert McNamara often favored restraint in the procurement of arms. Similarly, experience in counterinsurgency warfare taught some of the radicalized militaries from the developing world, such as that of Peru in the early 1970's, to emphasize economic development rather than arms expenditures.

In general, however, the attitude of the military is still likely to be somewhat biased against arms control, since the military would normally prefer the risks of too many weapons to the risks of too few. The conservatism of the military, moreover, will often slow its reaction to new technology and new political situations. For example, the British Admiralty applied nineteenth-century line-of-battle doctrines to measure parity with the United States during the naval negotiations of the 1920's, and thus delayed the conclusion of the naval agreements. Interestingly, when the agreements were collapsing in the 1930's, the British Navy then wanted their extension.

The effective power of the military constituency depends on the entire structure of the society. In evaluating an arms control agreement, almost all societies will show some respect for the military's technical expertise. In some societies, however, the power of the military is stronger, even amounting to a veto. In the United States during the 1960's and early 1970's, there was unquestionably a military-industrial-congressional complex. Its power was directly based on the willingness of congressional committees to defer to the military's judgment, and on the economic benefits that defense expenditures could give to congressmen seeking reelection. Ultimately, however, this power depended on the public's being more willing to pay for military spending than for peaceful spending; otherwise the congressmen could just as well have run on a platform of bringing other, nonmilitary federal spending to the district. In contrast to the American pattern, the military's position is more tenuous in some parliamentary systems. In Britain, for example, the military is unable to build such an effective legislative constituency. It must rely instead on its success in appealing privately to cabinet ministers or, on rare occasions, going to the public.[4] In the USSR the military's veto is probably much stronger than in the United States, although this is hard to evaluate with confidence.

Staff work and arms control negotiations. Even when the general political climate favors arms control, an agreement is unlikely unless someone assumes the responsibility for putting detailed proposals before the political leaders and for working out plans to gain the support of the important constituencies. For this a staff is essential; the arms control negotiations since the Second World War show long gaps most readily attributable to the absence of a staff or to the desire of a new leader to have new staff work carried out.

The task of the arms control staff is to define the effects of a proposal as carefully as possible, to fashion the proposal so that those effects are as favorable as possible, and to gain the various swing constituencies' support for the proposal. This task is very difficult, and its uncertainties have a great effect on the shape of possible agreements.

The core of the staff analysis is an estimate of the potential strategic effect of a specific proposal. This must begin with an estimate of the arms level of each of the nations involved. Since these estimates are often derived from intelligence, they are subject to uncertainty. It is also important to know the capability of those arms. This is not only an intelligence problem; it is also a technical problem, because the nature of the weapons must be deduced from the limited information available. Bureaucratic channels are often so opaque (sometimes deliberately so) that information about the capability of one's own weapons may be as limited or as confusing as that about another nation's weapons. The information on the capability of weapons must then be converted into strategic and political capability, based on an understanding of the military roles of weapons, the strategic doctrines guiding their use, the probability of different forms of conflict, and the importance of the national goals that might give rise to conflict. Finally, the entire analysis must be projected into the future. This requires additional intelligence data and estimates of the production capability, the likely procurement decisions, and the likely political evolution of all nations involved.

Ideally, the entire analysis is made both on the assumption that there is no agreement and on the assumption that there is an agreement, so that the net costs and benefits of the agreement can be estimated. Any possible variations of a proposed agreement would also be considered. An analysis based on the assumption that there is an agreement poses new uncertainties besides those already discussed. The obvious new uncertainty is the possibility that the other parties to the agreement will evade it. This makes it necessary to consider the possible technological and strategic effects of such an evasion, as well as the ways in which it might be verified that the agreement is being obeyed.

There are other new uncertainties that might arise. Other parties to the agreement might alter their procurement of weapons in a way that is consistent with the treaty but still brings new military benefits. Between the world wars, for example, Germany designed cruisers that technically complied with the Versailles restrictions, but effectively gave Germany the battleship capability that Versailles had sought to prohibit. The risk that this sort of violation will occur is very difficult to evaluate: novel weapons will be designed because the treaty is likely to prohibit the designs that earlier appeared most rational. A still more important new uncertainty comes from the influence of the treaty on national political goals. Thus the 1963 Limited Test Ban Treaty confirmed the split between China and the Soviet Union, affecting military planning much more dramatically than had been expected. This sort of effect is probably the most important one, and also the hardest to predict.

In reality, the work of the arms control staff is seldom as elaborate or as rational as the process just outlined. Normally only some of the steps in the staff analysis give rise to controversy and demand careful study. For example, the issue of verification dominated the discussions concerning a comprehensive nuclear test ban in the late 1950's and early 1960's; the possible effects of a treaty on future weaponry dominated the discussions of a similar agreement in the 1970's. Sometimes the analytic assumptions prove wrong, as may be seen in the lack of any understanding of the aircraft carrier during the naval negotiations of the 1920's and in the previously noted effort to maintain a balance between the United States and Britain in the same negotiations.

More fundamentally, the evaluation of the consequences of arms control poses severe intellectual problems, for most of the projected risks and benefits with an arms control agreement and without one are not directly comparable. It is difficult, for example, to compare the risk of a continued arms race with the risk of a possible evasion of the treaty, especially since opponents and proponents of the treaty are likely to emphasize different national goals and to reflect different psychological concerns. Thus the role of expertise in arms control proposals is in fact limited, whereas the judgment and initiative of individuals are likely to have a great influence. The actual staff work, therefore, often amounts to no more than a bureaucratic or political advocacy for or against a proposed agreement.

Generally, any bias introduced during the staff work is against arms control. Some of this bias derives from the influence that organizations for gathering intelligence and procuring weapons have in most nations. These organizations, which have substantial expertise in evaluating military capability and which long predate the arms control staff, will either carry out the government's arms control analysis themselves or will have the political power to ensure that their views are heard during the course of the staff work. Sometimes these organizations have a special interest in building certain weapons that may bias their judgments. Always, because these organizations are responsible for maintaining the national security by traditional means, they have a duty to be conservative in evaluating the risks of proposed policies. This conservatism, when applied to arms control, may lead to an overestimation of the opponent's capability and an underestimation of the nation's own capability, and a consequent bias against arms control.

On occasion, this bias counterbalances other biases, particularly those regarding proposed new weapons. It is hard for the advocates of a new weapon to avoid consciously or unconsciously overselling their proposal. Thus, during the budget-making process, the capabilities of any proposed weapon are likely to be overstated (and those of existing weapons understated). Before the new weapon has received careful scrutiny, it is likely to appear too valuable to give up as a part of arms control. When the weapon is considered carefully during the arms control staff work, however, the conservative bias may cancel out any exaggeration. Thus the capability of the American antiballistic missile system was consistently overestimated during the repeated discussions about procurement in the 1960's; but in the different bureaucratic context of the staff work for SALT, the weapon's limitations were recognized and it was effectively rejected. In a similar way, in the early 1970's the process of developing a position for European force reduction talks may have encouraged NATO leaders to rethink their deployment patterns in Western Europe. This process sometimes fails, however, as happened most dramatically in connection with the multiple independent retargetable reentry vehicle (MIRV) program during SALT I. Those who doubted the strategic desirability of the MIRV's thought their ability to move the bureaucracy would be stronger if they waited to raise the issue until the USSR had shown an interest in placing limitations on MIRV's; but though the USSR hinted in this direction, it never did so clearly enough.[5]

Another bias, which is generally unfavorable to arms control, arises because of the contrast between technical military calculations and intuitive political estimates. The military calculations are relatively quantifiable, and consequently tend to be persuasive. It is impossible to make an equally precise calculation of the risk of war or of the projected political course of events with an agreement and without one. This contrast in precision was evident in the 1963 congressional hearings on the Limited Test Ban. Almost every witness gave only a short statement on the political issues of whether the treaty would favor détente and help control the arms race; but each then went on to comment at great length on the military and technological questions of the verification of compliance with the treaty and of the effect of the treaty on the relative nuclear strength of the United States. This bias in favor of military calculations can do more than affect the persuasiveness of the arguments for and against an arms control agreement; it can also distort judgments of ways to prevent war. The calculations of military risk claim no more than to help predict the outcome of a war that is initiated with given force levels. The analyst, however, finds it difficult to avoid turning this military calculation into a tool for preventing war by making the implicit assumption that the primary way to prevent war is to ensure that the military balance is favorable. The more subtle but no less important political factors tend to be forgotten. This problem is inherent in arms control itself, which almost by definition overemphasizes the relative force levels and encourages a reliance on the balance of power.

Finally, a type of bias derives from the influence of military theories and doctrines such as the theory of strategic nuclear deterrence. These theories can aid in the procurement of weapons and in the designing of tactics to be used with the weapons. It is not clear, however, whether the theories play a great role in actual decision making; they may sometimes be only a language of debate. Each theory is, after all, the raison d'être of a particular branch of the military; and it is sometimes only the political strength of these branches that determines which theories dominate in a particular decision. To the extent that any theory is applied, the resulting bias is probably a conservative one, tending to reflect the beliefs of the politically dominant elements of the military. The agreements that result will be aimed at maintaining the status quo approach to military balance. Theories also tend to go through styles. Thus, since there was little fear of nuclear terrorism until the 1970's, the problem of terrorism was ignored in earlier arrangements for nuclear materials; later, however, it became an important concern. Moreover, the possibility that different parties to an agreement and different factions on each side adhere to different theories can complicate the process of making an arms control agreement. Many Americans, for instance, analyze SALT on the basis of a theory of strategic deterrence. Other American analysts, however, doubt certain aspects of this theory and believe the Soviet Union has the same doubts. In the light of this, it may be very difficult to formulate an agreement acceptable to both American schools of thought and to the Soviet Union as well.

Fundamentally, the burden of proof seems to be on those who favor arms control. Because those who make decisions in connection with arms control are dealing with national security, they are understandably cautious. If they accept an arms control treaty, their decision is much harder to reverse should it prove wrong than a unilateral decision against building a specific weapon. The parties know they are negotiating with possible opponents, and are naturally concerned that the opponent's proposal may be a trap; they cannot count on the other party's understanding in the interpreting or renegotiating of the agreement. Because of these difficulties, many arms control advocates urge tacit agreements and almost all actual agreements have very generous withdrawal clauses. Arms control agreements are still novel, and must bear a special political burden. In the more familiar patterns of agreement, this burden is absent. Armistice agreements, for example, are in content very complex arms control agreements designed to achieve a theater balance of power. Yet their military aspects are often quickly negotiated and approved, probably because they provide for a return to the "normal" situation of peace and because the costs of a continuing war are so clear. Arms control, in contrast, is widely perceived as creating an abnormal situation; it must therefore be justified more carefully.

The building of a consensus. In a few nations, a key individual and a staff have the ability to develop a national position on arms control. During the late 1960's and early 1970's, Alfonso García Robles of Mexico and Alva Myrdal of Sweden were each able to participate in arms control negotiations from a nearly independent power base. In most nations, however, only the chief executive is able to command the consensus needed for a major arms control agreement. In the United States, for example, though a treaty formally requires only the assent of the president and the Senate, many components of the bureaucracy have independent constituencies in Congress. Only the president normally has the capacity to overcome these political pressure groups or to work out binding compromises among them. Even authoritarian governments may need the acquiescence of the military, the bureaucracy, or the dominant political party. To gain a consensus, the chief executive may have to be in a relatively strong position. President Nixon was unable to resolve a disagreement over nuclear strategy between his secretaries of state and defense in May 1974, and was therefore unable to conclude an effective agreement; similarly, President Carter could not conclude a SALT agreement in 1979 for lack of congressional support.

Even when the chief executive is strong, the process of gathering a domestic consensus can profoundly change a possible arms control agreement. To persuade the various constituencies to accept the proposed agreement often requires arguments contrary to those made in the international negotiations. At home, the government must declare that the agreement would strengthen the nation, and that any concessions it made were small compared to those made by the other parties. These arguments, though they may already have been made privately, have to be made publicly when the treaty is ratified; this may embarrass the other parties to the treaty. The public statements may also make the other parties less willing to enter into future agreements; this can weaken any momentum that the negotiations might have generated. At the same time, the rhetoric of domestic opponents of the treaty may appear threatening to other nations.

To obtain the support of the military for an agreement, governments have also typically promised to support the development of new weapons and generally to interpret the treaty in ways that hinder military preparedness as little as possible. Thus, when the Limited Test Ban was up for ratification, President Kennedy promised to maintain programs to detect Soviet nuclear tests, to advance the capabilities of nuclear weapons by underground testing, and to be prepared to resume atmospheric testing. Similarly, President Nixon, when SALT I was ratified, promised to support new weapons systems. These commitments can be viewed as payments for bureaucratic or congressional favors. They can also be viewed as the logical assurance that, for example, a prudent military officer requires in order to feel justified in telling the Senate that a treaty will not harm the national security. Such commitments are probably made in other nations as well; both the United States and the USSR increased their underground testing after the Limited Test Ban. The clearest counterexample in American history was a very special case—the Geneva Protocol of 1925, which was finally approved by the Senate in 1974. In the wake of the Vietnam War, the Senate almost unanimously opposed the intention of the executive to interpret ambiguous language in the treaty so as to permit the use of herbicides and tear gas. It finally forced President Ford to agree not to use these chemicals in war.

It is almost impossible to achieve a consensus in favor of an agreement that leaves the nation in a position regarded as inferior in any way. Many people would consider such an agreement a symbol of defeat that should be rejected, regardless of any counterbalancing benefits that it might bring. Thus Senator Henry Jackson felt that the American negotiators had erred in SALT I by accepting certain numerical inferiorities in strategic missiles (although many other strategic analysts considered these inferiorities irrelevant). Senator Jackson gained enough support that Congress prohibited the government from taking such a negotiating position in the future. He probably also forced the administration to purge lower level officials who had been associated with SALT I. In SALT II the critics were even more demanding, some senators wanting a return to U.S. missile superiority. Since similar processes are probably at work in all nations, agreements dealing with force levels must usually provide for symmetry in respect to both the levels of arms permitted and the particular arms forgone.

The pattern of relations involving the military, the citizens, the executive, and the legislature can vary radically with time and place. Nevertheless, the effects just suggested—the opposition between internal and external arguments, the trading of new weapons programs for military support, the political need to avoid inferiority—probably occur in most countries. It is also possible to generalize about the forms of agreement that are most likely to gain a consensus. Comprehensive schemes, for example, are likely to provoke broad military opposition; narrow agreements, on the other hand, provoke less opposition and usually can obtain support thanks to the fear of a particular technology or the desire to make peace with a particular opponent. Consequently, narrow treaty packages have a better chance of acceptance than broad ones. In general, proposals with an uncertain impact, such as the limitation of research and development, tend to rally the forces opposed to arms control more effectively than those in favor of it.

Bureaucratic limitations probably also make it difficult to negotiate the exchange of different kinds of arms. There was some talk in the early 1960's, for example, about an agreement by which the United States would give up its numerical superiority in strategic missiles in return for the Soviet Union's giving up its numerical superiority in tactical ground forces. The problem with this plan was that its benefits in the eyes of the American tactical force constituency and the Soviet missile constituency could not compensate for the outrage felt by the American missile constituency and the Soviet tactical constituency.

THE INTERNATIONAL NEGOTIATION ITSELF

No nation will voluntarily accept a treaty unless its leaders expect the treaty to benefit the nation. Arms control staffs are set up to assure this benefit. Each party to a treaty, making its own evaluation of the potential costs of maintaining arms and of fighting a war, must conclude that it is better off with the treaty than without it.

The stated benefit of arms control agreement—to reduce the risk and the human cost of war—is therefore not necessarily the immediate goal of the negotiators.[6] Each negotiator seeks to obtain advantages for his own nation. As Salvador de Madariaga wrote in 1929, "in effect every delegation goes to the conference determined to secure an increase in the *relative* armaments of its own nation, even though the conference may lead to an all-round reduction of *absolute* armaments."[7]

The advantages sought may not even be those of the agreement itself. For example, the USSR long used arms control negotiations as a forum in which to condemn American foreign bases. Presumably, it had no expectation of obtaining an agreement and instead hoped to turn world public opinion against the United States. During the late 1950's and early 1960's, the United States and the USSR discussed general and complete disarmament; each side's proposals were probably unacceptable even to the proponent, but both thought they could make gains in public opinion. Just as disingenuously, Nixon and Brezhnev negotiated minor agreements in May 1974 that were probably expected to demonstrate achievement to the public but not to change arms levels greatly.

In spite of the pursuit of propaganda victories and unrealistic arms balances, and in spite of the need for an agreement to benefit all parties, arms negotiations can achieve significant agreements. Such agreements, as a form of self-interest international law, require a situation in which cooperation enables the parties to gain a benefit not otherwise available to them.[8] There are many such situations. For example, in the negotiations over naval forces in the 1920's, the United States and Britain each placed a high value on naval parity with the other and a high cost on further naval construction. By agreeing on force levels, both nations were able to gain the benefits of parity and to avoid the cost of construction. In the 1960's, many in both the United States and USSR believed the construction of antiballistic missile (ABM) systems would make nuclear war more likely, or at least make the strategic arms competition more costly, without benefiting either side. The two therefore agreed on a treaty to limit the number of ABM's. In such negotiations an element of antagonism is usually intermingled with the cooperation, for there is usually a range of possible force levels, each of which can provide benefits but some of which favor one side more than the other.

Any arms control treaty thus amounts to a way that nations collectively renounce activities they would already prefer to renounce individually. This may not have been apparent during the 1950's, when negotiations were marked by propaganda as well as idealism; it is clearly revealed by the limited character of the agreements actually reached during the 1960's and 1970's. In evaluating SALT proposals, for example, each government uses essentially the same procurement doctrines, the same weapons capability estimates, and the same intelligence data (since SALT is verified by "unilateral technical means") that it would use in deciding whether to procure additional weapons. Thus SALT can end the strategic arms competition only when neither side wishes to arm further. Since nations are much more likely to renounce future weapons than current ones, it follows that treaties are more likely to freeze current force levels than to roll them back.

It further follows that arms control is a weak tool for dealing with a nation, like Germany before the Second World War, that seeks to increase its military strength relative to others. The nation will not accept an agreement that does not provide for such an increase, and its neighbors are unlikely to accept an agreement that does provide for it. Moreover, an arms control agreement that changes the balance of power affects the ability of the relevant parties to exert diplomatic pressure, and thus shapes the resolution of future international disputes; and nations will not voluntarily weaken their position in future negotiations. It is probably this problem that ultimately defeated the Baruch Plan: regardless of the good or bad faith of either side, the USSR could not accept inferiority in a world so far from its ideal, nor could the United States give up its superiority. Arms control is not a means of directly changing the balance of power; at best it can protect an existing balance against upset. Ideally, as technology and the perceptions of national interest change, new agreements may then help build a broader mesh of restraints.

Settlement agreements and the problem of balance. An agreement setting the force levels for two countries or blocs tends to come about only when the levels prior to the treaty are approximately equal. The treaty can then require equal adjustments in force levels, and permit equal changes after the treaty is in effect. The tendency toward symmetry is so strong that any asymmetry accepted by the treaty is likely to be concealed by a formal symmetry. The SALT I agreement on offensive forces allowed unequal post-treaty force levels, but disguised the inequality by its definition of a freeze at existing levels. In the SALT II draft, a similar technique was used to resolve an imbalance in the category of large land-based missiles. This need for symmetry rests in part on the fact that neither party is willing to accept an unfavorable modification of its military position. It is very difficult for nations starting at unequal strength to define force reductions that—in both nations' eyes—fairly reflect the disparities that existed before the treaty.

But the tendency to negotiate only when in balance also reflects less visible factors that are rooted in the character of the political support available to arms control. The normal political motivation for two sides to negotiate arms control is the desire to settle a dispute that has divided them. This desire is likely to arise only from a stalemate and a sense that the balance of forces is likely to continue indefinitely.[9] Indeed the 1972 Jackson Amendment controversy in the United States shows that it is politically difficult to accept even a minor imbalance if substantial constituencies believe the other party is not really interested in a broader settlement. The 1979 Senate attitude toward SALT II went even further, demanding Soviet compliance with détente as a prerequisite for any formal bilateral arms control.[10]

The negotiation process, by focusing on asymmetries, exposes the political decision maker more fully than a simple decision not to acquire a particular weapon. In the face of an asymmetry, then, a tacit agreement may be more feasible than a formal one. In a tacit agreement, each side restricts its own arming and hopes that the other will accept the implicit offer by restricting itself. The requirements are again comparable to those for the self-interest pattern of law: a reasonable, shared confidence that both parties want the restriction, adequate time to deploy countermeasures should one party violate the understanding, and a common view of the scope of the tacit agreement. The last of these requirements is often the most ticklish; when technology is changing or force levels are constantly varying, a more formal understanding may be necessary to define what is permitted and what is not. Nevertheless, there are a number of examples of successful tacit agreements. One of them has helped limit the role of nuclear weapons in the Middle East conflict, because either side could expect its open acquisition of nuclear weapons to be quickly matched on the other side and at the same time to weaken its political support from the great powers.[11]

When politically possible, a formal agreement can add substantially to the force of a tacit understanding. Although the process of ratifying a treaty can bring problems, it can also strengthen the political commitment to the agreement and make the violation of it much less likely. A formal agreement is much more likely than a tacit one to be respected should a new government come to power, and is more capable of with-standing the pressure of changes in politics and technology.

Typically, nations have had either of two specific goals in making a formal settlement agreement: to stabilize an arms balance against change or to reshape an arms balance so as to decrease the risk of war. The first of these goals is to ensure that an existing balance will continue in the future at as low a cost as possible. The two parties seek to avoid the cost of mutually canceling improvements in their forces and to de-crease the risk of an asymmetrical technological breakthrough that might create an imbalance and encourage war. Assuming no one can predict which side is likely to make such a break-through, both sides may prefer to maintain the balance by mutual consent. Although this goal might sometimes be at-tained by tacit agreement, a formal agreement can add politi-cal stability. Formal terms may also help if the two sides are engaged in an arms competition of the interactive, or action-reaction, type, in which each side builds arms to balance those it fears the other is building.[12] The lag time in research and deployment combines with the uncertainties of intelli-gence to force each side to expect the worst and to arm itself accordingly. In such a context, an improved flow of informa-tion and an increased confidence about each other's plans could help slow the competition.

SALT reflects such thinking. Both sides recognized the stabilizing value of information derived from satellite surveil-lance, and therefore agreed not to interfere with each other's "national technical means of verification." Both sides effec-tively rejected antiballistic missile systems partly because these systems pose enormous technological uncertainties that could easily lead to an action-reaction arms competition. And both sides supported the general arms ceilings of Vladivostok and SALT II, albeit not very persuasively, as a way to permit more restrained planning on each side.

In practice, however, it has proved very difficult for arms control to halt an arms competition. SALT has been only partially successful, and the Anglo-German efforts before the First World War failed completely. Some of the reasons for this are already familiar. Only rarely is there a parity of arms combined with a political willingness to settle. An agreement usually has to define a balance between different military systems, and this balance must be able to survive any technological change. The underlying technical evaluations are difficult, especially when technological innovation is at issue, for the innovations will be only partly understood and will make verification especially difficult. An agreement is also likely to draw the opposition of formidable armaments lobbies, which can point out the need for continuing sales and research in order to maintain a standby capability in case the adversary violates or abrogates the agreement.

There are also less familiar difficulties. First, the need to reach an agreement usually does not seem urgent. Arms negotiations are not like labor negotiations in which a strike imposes great pressure to resolve the dispute immediately.[13] A delay in arms control only rarely appears particularly serious, as when a destabilizing technology like the ABM in the 1960's lurks just over the horizon. But by the time the new development becomes visible, it may already have a strong constituency. Second, there are often no obvious outcomes to aim for in the negotiations, such as a fifty-fifty compromise.[14] If the two sides are symmetrical, a future arms equality can provide a focal point for negotiation, but it is still necessary to define the level at which the equality will be fixed. If the sides are not symmetrical, a focus becomes even more difficult to define because of the problem of comparing different systems. Third, each side seeks to enter the negotiations with as high a level of forces as possible. Even during the negotiations a nation may work on new weapons that can become part of a new status quo or be bargained away in return for concessions by the opponent. During SALT I, for example, the USSR substantially increased its offensive missile force and the United States worked on an ABM system. The history of the negotiations suggests that these two programs were influential in shaping the final agreement.

The effectiveness of "bargaining chip" programs, those designed with the specific purpose of affecting the negotiations, is less clear. For example, a threat to build weapons across the board in order to demonstrate to an opponent that it has no choice but to accept an inferior force position probably makes an arms control agreement extremely unlikely. At best, it might produce a tacit agreement; at worst, an embittered enmity. But the experience of SALT shows that a threat to outbuild the opponent in some capabilities, balanced by the opponent's threat to outbuild in other capabilities, may produce concessions that balance each other. It is doubtful, therefore, that bargaining chips can be effectively used by only one party; and it is clear that the use of them by both parties raises the level of forces that the agreement will allow.

The SALT I agreements show the effect of these factors. The agreements greatly increased strategic stability; but they did not substantially slow the arms competition, and perhaps even helped accelerate it. [15] The agreements stopped only one deployment that was actually in progress, one of the American ABM systems. The basic concept of the agreement was to freeze the existing force levels, but the agreement dealt with asymmetries by "upward arms control," allowing each side to do what the other had already done. The agreement thus allowed each side to build an additional ABM system to balance the other side's ABM's, and also permitted the USSR to deploy new submarine-launched missile systems. (The freedom to deploy additional ABM's was eliminated in 1974, after it became clear that neither side wanted to exercise its option.) The U.S. administration apparently promised to support new American weapons programs in order to obtain favorable military testimony before Congress. And the need to have bargaining chips for SALT II was used as an argument to obtain congressional approval of the new weapons systems.

History not only gives grounds for a general pessimism

about the ability of arms control to halt an arms competition. It also gives grounds for a special pessimism about the logic often used to argue in favor of narrow arms control agreements—that one agreement can build on another step by step. There are two historical examples of such a sequence of agreements. In one, the 1922 naval treaty was reached with relative ease; it was expanded in 1930 only after several failures and at the cost of enlarged escape clauses; and the next stage, in 1935, was a nearly empty agreement. In the second example, it is clear that SALT II did not flow readily from SALT I, even though the future of the SALT I agreements was made contingent on the conclusion of a SALT II agreement by a stated deadline. The SALT II draft contained a similar protocol posing certain arms restrictions for a limited period pending new agreements; the U.S. Senate was not unreasonable in its concern about the status of the protocol restrictions should the new negotiations have failed.

The general problem of the step-by-step approach seems to be that the easy issues are settled in the first agreement, leaving only difficult ones for the second. Moreover, the political circumstances are likely to be less favorable at the time of the second negotiations: the need for a symbolic settlement is less urgent, and the debate over the ratification of the first agreement may even have created new barriers to a second one. A step-by-step concept is valid only when each step creates new political conditions conducive to future steps. These conditions may be met with legislative arms control, or with settlement agreements when political steps are successfully intermingled; but the conditions are difficult to meet when the more technical aspects of an arms competition have to be handled in sequence.

The curtailing of an arms competition is so difficult that arms control talks almost seem to be directed toward the joint management of a continued arms competition rather than the termination of it. A joint management may help maintain a balance in the face of technological change; it may also become a way for the leaders of the two sides to cooperate in persuading their more reluctant constituencies to support arms increases. Therefore, some critics have sought to change the structure of arms control negotiations, arguing that it is the idea of negotiating toward fixed numerical limits that creates the problems just discussed. These critics suggest, for example, a negotiated limitation on military budgets, which might control arms competition more effectively by separating the bureaucratic politics of budget allocation from the politics of negotiating specific relative force levels. It is doubtful that a bureaucracy could be deceived this easily; so far, this approach has met strong opposition without offering an appealing focus to attract support. Another proposal would emphasize limitations on testing as an indirect way to slow arms development.[16] So far, this proposal has also failed, for testing has as broad a constituency as development. Moreover, this approach poses technical problems stemming from the differences between American and Soviet ideas about testing and from the need for tests to confirm the reliability of existing weapons. Perhaps the underlying problem is simply that the domestic political context in one or both nations is so unfavorable to any arms limitation as to make the national leaders unable or unwilling to work for significant restrictions.

The second general goal of the settlement pattern of arms control is to shape a strategic balance that will decrease the chance of war. The mutual benefit is similar to that of the buffer zone of traditional diplomacy. A buffer between two major powers would increase the warning time of an invasion and decrease the frequency of incidents that might provoke a war. Present-day analogues, such as the American-supervised demilitarized zones in the Middle East and the various proposed arrangements for separating Eastern and Western forces in Europe, form an extremely important pattern of arms control. Though these arrangements tend to restrict only the deployment of forces, rather than their level, they undoubtedly lower the probability of war. Where the risk of war is evident, such agreements are negotiated with relative ease. The military positions defined by the agreement naturally have to be well balanced and may have to be verified. These agreements are close enough to settlements that they must meet the corresponding political requirements, albeit in weakened form, for the benefits of an agreement are very clear if an unwanted war is actually likely.

In Europe, for example, the risk of war has been so small, and the tendency toward a political settlement so weak, that historically there has been little pressure to make an agreement that would either accept or change the East's numerical military superiority. But in the Middle East, even though territorial issues are central to the political disputes, buffer zones have been created, complete with local force limitations. The settlement pattern is obvious in the case of Israel and Egypt; but there are also buffer zones between Syria and Israel, in spite of the lack of any political settlement. This pattern of disengagement is one likely to be seriously considered almost any time it might be useful, and the political barriers to its use are much lower than those for many other forms of arms control.

With modern weapons, a kind of strategic stability similar in its effects to the use of a buffer can sometimes be achieved by limitations on weapons. Nations share a strong interest in avoiding military postures that could increase the risk of war, particularly nuclear war. This goal of strategic stability was at the heart of SALT I, at least for the United States. The idea was to decrease each side's military incentive to strike first in the hope of gaining a great advantage or out of the fear that the opponent would gain an advantage by striking first. Many Americans believed that the ABM might encourage such a first strike, and that limiting the development of the ABM could therefore add to strategic stability. (The fact that such arguments were not available for SALT II helps explain that treaty's difficulties.) In the Middle East and elsewhere, nations might similarly pursue arms control to prevent the deployment of weapons that might encourage preemptive warfare. Although no such agreements have yet been achieved in the Middle East, there has been a reasonably effective tacit restraint on the use of long-range weaponry against cities and on the open possession of nuclear weapons. Of all the possible goals of an arms control based on mutual self-interest, the one with the greatest political potential is probably that of a strategic stability that forestalls preemptive war. This goal has supported significant tacit agreements; it can probably support some explicit agreements as well, even in the absence of a full settlement.

Multiparty negotiations and the legislative pattern. When there are more than two parties, the pattern of arms control negotiations is radically different. Because of the variety of power balances and coalitions that must be considered, it is nearly impossible to negotiate the level of forces for all parties. Historically, the series of naval agreements that were made between the world wars has been the only successful use of negotiation to set the force levels for more than two parties. In that instance, only a few combinations of forces were relevant, and the likely coalitions and conflicts were fairly easy to predict. The balance of forces in the Atlantic did not depend very strongly on Japanese power in the Pacific; in the Pacific calculation, the balance was supplemented with changes in the Anglo-Japanese alliance and with limitations on the use of bases.

Multilateral arms control is limited even more stringently by political requirements than by technical force balance requirements. If arms control is normally possible only in an atmosphere of détente, an effective multilateral negotiation is likely to require a multilateral détente. But a détente between any two parties is likely to provoke the suspicions of others. In the naval negotiations of 1935, for example, France was troubled by a naval agreement between England and Germany, fearing that it would legitimize Germany's renunciation of the disarmament provisions of the Versailles Treaty. European leaders today have sometimes feared their interests would be ignored in the American SALT diplomacy. It is extremely difficult to visualize the combined détentes necessary for the negotiation of force levels between the United States, the Soviet Union, and the Peoples Republic of China, since any benefit to each pair of parties would give the third party reason for suspicion.

This kind of barrier is nearly insurmountable. Hence multilateral arms control must generally seek a different pattern: a rule that applies uniformly, rather than a set of assigned force levels. All the parties would then benefit if each refrained from certain actions, such as the testing of nuclear weapons in the atmosphere. By prohibiting certain actions, a treaty encourages individual restraint and effectively defines a law. The law might have different strategic effects on different nations; but it will, at least formally, apply uniformly to all. In this way, negotiation becomes feasible.

Multilateral agreements of this type gain political force from their legislative character. The domestic political debate on such agreements may focus on the need to restrain one's own government by means of the treaty, whereas the debate on settlement agreements necessarily focuses on the forces permitted to one's own nation as against those permitted to others. The politics of a legislative agreement emphasizes the joint prevention of a particular evil, such as the fallout from atmospheric nuclear tests or the inhumanity of biological warfare. Such agreements can gain broad multilateral support owing to their persuasive philosophical basis and their appeal to idealism. This happened, for example, with the Latin American Nuclear Free Zone, which was taken as a demonstration of the path toward a more peaceful world.

Although the political support for these agreements may be strong, the staff process will usually reject or reshape any proposal that might seriously restrict a signatory. No nation will give up the right to conduct an activity it views as important. Each will seek protection against the possibility that other nations will refuse to sign or will violate the agreement. Thus the treaty has to satisfy the general conditions for international law based on self-interest. In a multilateral context, these conditions are quite stringent.

The negotiations themselves also pose problems that limit these agreements. Only a few powerful nations are fully able to participate in shaping a treaty so as to maximize its benefits and minimize its costs to themselves. The weaker nations, with little chance of upsetting the balances carefully negotiated by the leading powers, are thus presented with a take-it-or-leave-it choice between adherence and abstention. Sometimes, as in the case of the Seabed Arms Control Treaty (1971), the leading nations are willing to revise a draft agreement in order to obtain a broader participation, but this seldom involves the weakening of any provisions crucial to the great powers. It is impossible for all to participate as equals; but near-great powers are likely to be especially sensitive to their position of inferiority, and therefore unwilling to participate as unequals. France and China, for instance, rejected even the legislative form of arms control in the 1960's; India, Brazil, and others joined in the opposition in the 1970's. The probability that such nations will not participate, the particular problems of multilateral agreements, the relatively severe tests before nations will give their approval—for these reasons legislative treaties have only been able to impose relatively weak restrictions on the behavior of nations.

Some of these agreements have sought to denuclearize or demilitarize a specific geographic area, such as the Antarctic, outer space, or the seabed. By preventing dangerous incidents, damage to the environment, or arms races in these areas, the agreements offer mutual benefits at the relatively minor cost to each nation of forgoing military operations in the specified area. Other agreements of the same general pattern have attempted to direct arms competition away from particular areas of technology. It is difficult for nations to renounce the potential of a technology; the only such agreements so far are conventions to control biological and environmental warfare. These types of warfare create a strong emotional reaction; neither offers any clear military potential in the near future. The control of chemical warfare, which has been only partly successful, shows the limitations of this pattern of agreement: though chemical warfare triggers a strong sense of revulsion, it may have military potential, and the verification of compliance with restrictions would be difficult. Hence recent efforts to strengthen the 1925 convention on chemical warfare have failed. Moreover, the Limited Test Ban of 1963, although sometimes viewed as a way to control the technology of nuclear weapons, was not ratified until its proponents had shown that this technology could be advanced by the underground testing that the agreement left uncontrolled.

Other forms of legislative agreement are designed to prohibit the use of a weapon, rather than the construction of it. Initiating the use of poison gas has been prohibited, and restrictions on the use of nuclear weapons have often been proposed. In a sense, such agreements are unenforceable. The possibility of retaliation provides a kind of enforcement, but this requires that inventories of the weapons be maintained. Nevertheless, these agreements effectively prohibit any explicit threat to use the particular weapon. This point is particularly important in the case of nuclear weapons. Nuclear threats may currently help prevent a conventional conflict in Europe and the Far East. On the other hand, if nations agreed to abstain from making explicit nuclear threats, the prestige value of nuclear weapons might decline and with it the incentive for other nations to obtain these weapons. Except in special cases, proposals like these attract relatively little support from those who oppose the actual construction of weapons, yet at the same time they create opposition within both the defense and the foreign policy communities, which do not like to deprive themselves of capabilities that might someday be useful. Agreements of this sort were regularly rejected by the United States until President Carter's unilateral commitment in 1978 restricting the use of nuclear weapons against nonnuclear nations.

The nuclear free zone is a kind of agreement that combines several mechanisms of control. Among the nations within the zone, a nuclear free zone represents a law designed to decrease the risks of one-sided nuclear arming; this legislative aspect provides part of the underlying political force of the agreement. The concept of a nuclear free zone also usually requires the commitment of outside nuclear nations not to use nuclear weapons against nations within the zone. This gives a measure of protection to the region; but there must already be some sense of harmony within the region, as well as a global balance of interests such that the nuclear nations are willing to make the necessary commitments. So far the Latin American Nuclear Free Zone is the only such proposal that has reached the status of a treaty. Some of the necessary commitments, however, were still being sought in 1980; without them, several important nations are not yet bound by the treaty.

The legislative dynamic in arms control has thus led to agreements only in special situations. Nations have rarely if ever agreed to give up weapons that might be useful to them. This dynamic, however, might become much stronger in the future, since it rests on a broadly based politics that emphasizes the benefits of cooperation. A major nuclear incident, for example, might create a political reaction in favor of legislative agreements. Moreover, because these agreements are based on a public concern about specific, evolving risks of weaponry, they can build on one another more readily than settlement agreements. More than settlement agreements, legislative agreements are amenable to political pressure to extend them and to close loopholes. In the 1970's, for example, the U.S. Congress wanted to extend the earlier prohibition on poison gas, in striking contrast to its behavior regarding SALT.

Transition agreements and asymmetry. A very few arms control agreements lack the symmetry of either the settlement pattern or the legislative. A disarmament imposed at the close of a war, such as that established at Versailles, is one example that is easily understood in light of the unequal bargaining power at the time. Some asymmetrical agreements, however, have been more fairly negotiated. The prime example is the Non-Proliferation Treaty; it formally confirmed the imbalance between nuclear and nonnuclear nations, prohibiting the latter from building nuclear weapons yet placing relatively little restraint on the former. The treaty held some benefits for the nonnuclear nations. It reduced the risk that other nonnuclear nations would build nuclear weapons, though few nonnuclear nations seriously considering the construction of nuclear weapons signed the treaty. But part of the explanation for this agreement, which was unbalanced in both form and effect, lies in its side arrangements. The nuclear powers supported a UN resolution assuring the nonnuclear signatories that the nuclear powers would consider assisting them if they were threatened by another nuclear power. And of greater political significance, it appeared possible that the nuclear powers would end peaceful nuclear assistance to nonnuclear nations that rejected the treaty.

Whatever the benefits of the Non-Proliferation Treaty, however, it is fully intelligible only if viewed as a transitional step. From the standpoint of many nonnuclear nations, the most important side commitment of the nuclear powers was their promise to work for arms control among themselves. With this commitment, the agreement effectively became more symmetrical. As a step toward greater arms control, it could draw strength from both the legislative motivation of controlling nuclear weapons and the settlement motivation of establishing a new balance between the developed and the developing nations. The symmetry would come in the future. Similarly, the interwar naval agreements that gave Japan an inferior role were at one time expected to lead to more important agreements. Asymmetric arms control is probably impossible without such an appeal to the future.

An asymmetrical agreement usually ends up by causing resentment, because the nations given superiority fail to honor their express or implied commitment to take further steps. Germany defended its breach of the Versailles disarmament provisions by pointing to its neighbors' failure to reach disarmament agreements, and there are many indications that the nonnuclear nations may become equally bitter about the Non-Proliferation Treaty. If nations have no faith in the future negotiations, asymmetry is likely to be unacceptable. Thus the Non-Proliferation Treaty would probably no longer have been negotiable in the mid-1970's, just as the asymmetry that Japan accepted in the 1922 naval treaty was no longer tolerable to that nation in the 1930's.

The decision to enter into an arms control agreement relies on balance-of-power calculations even more heavily than a decision to procure weapons or to initiate a war. The precondition of balance is almost certainly the most severe barrier to an arms control agreement—far more severe than the problems of control and verification that are commonly mentioned. Any agreements directly affecting the level of forces are most likely to be negotiated as part of a process of détente, at a time when diplomatic and cultural changes are already working toward a settlement. Even in those circumstances, however, it is difficult to terminate an arms competition.

Since the settlement dynamic is likely to be much stronger for the initial arms control agreement than for follow-up agreements, one should be very dubious about the step-by-step approach in this context. It may be wise to make the initial agreement as strong and as broad as possible, even though bureaucratic constraints tend to favor narrow, specific agreements rather than those that cross different areas of weapons technology.

The greatest potential for arms control in the future probably lies in the legislative pattern of agreement. Though this pattern has so far failed to achieve more than minor arms limitations, these agreements restricting specific weapons technologies can probably build on one another more readily than settlement agreements attempting to set the specific level of forces. Moreover, because legislative agreements gain strength from a global public consensus, they are likely to retain a constituency that is broader than the constituency for settlement agreements.

5. The Impact of Contemporary Arms Control

THE ULTIMATE test of the process of arms control negotiation just described is whether the resulting agreements help prevent war. To evaluate this, it is necessary first to examine when the agreements are likely to be successful in restricting arms, and then to examine how these restrictions can affect the mechanisms that generate war.

THE POLITICS OF COMPLIANCE AND VIOLATION

One is tempted to think of the problem of treaty evasion primarily in terms of verification and sanction: the likelihood that innocent parties to an agreement will detect a violation and react. Undoubtedly, a potential violator carries out this calculation and is influenced by the result. But the pressures that most strongly shape compliance or violation arise well in advance of this calculation.

At the outset, an arms control agreement must appear advantageous to the signers or they will not enter into it. As long as the initial expectation is borne out, compliance is per se in the national interest; violation is not seriously considered. Thus neither the United States nor the Soviet Union has so far been inclined to build ABM systems in violation of their agreements. Nor has any nation seen value in establishing a military presence in the Antarctic contrary to the Antarctic Treaty. This correspondence between national interest and obedience to a treaty is the main reason why nations comply with contemporary arms control agreements.

The pattern of incentives in arms control is the same as that in other international law based on self-interest. The first condition—that mutual compliance be preferable to mutual violation—is automatically met at the time the agreement is reached and will normally continue to be met if the agreement is well conceived. The second condition—that a violation by one nation be sufficiently likely to provoke other nations to take countermeasures—will be met if the arrangements for verification are adequate and if the injured nations are politically willing to respond. A nation's self-interest will tend to make it comply so long as these conditions are met, even if some specific violation might appear desirable. Thus the United States and the Soviet Union both refrain from any serious violation of SALT I precisely because each judges that a major violation would lead to a costly arms race. Arms control agreements recognize this concept of self-interest in their abrogation clauses, which typically permit the termination of the agreement a specified time after a nation gives notice that it believes its supreme interest would otherwise be jeopardized. The threat of abrogation amounts to a kind of enforcement.

This pattern of compliance resting on mutual self-interest can fail in several ways. First, it is conceivable that the pattern will never be established because a violation is planned from the start. A nation might enter into an agreement as a trick to obtain a short-term advantage over an opponent. Germany, for instance, may have had no intention of honoring its naval accords with Britain after the First World War. It is hard to find similar examples of bad faith in the arms control agreements since the Second World War; the agreements have been so limited that the political costs of such cynicism would almost certainly outweigh any military advantage that could be gained by it.

Second, national goals change, most commonly as a result of a change in government. The Weimar government of Germany undoubtedly disliked the arms control provisions of

Versailles, but it generally honored them. The Hitler government saw German interests differently and violated the Versailles agreement, covertly at first and later openly. One can
imagine a party to the Non-Proliferation Treaty similarly deciding to violate or abrogate it, perhaps after a coup d'état or
in response to the acquisition of a nuclear capability by a rival
power. The termination clause of this treaty permits abrogation with as little consequent harm as possible to a nation's
fabric of international commitments, but an ideological opponent of the treaty might not bother with the formal termination procedure. A unilateral rejection is most likely to occur
in the case of an imposed treaty like the 1922 naval forces
agreement. The Japanese government had entered into that
treaty judging it the best arrangement obtainable in the light
of Britain's decision to revise the terms of its alliance with
Japan. But by the 1930's the only feature of the treaty that had
political importance in Japan was its inequality; compliance
no longer appeared to serve the national interest.

   Third, and less dramatically, an agreement may erode because of the strong tendency to push at its edges.[1] To obtain
domestic support for a treaty, for example, leaders often
commit their governments to maintain substantial military
programs in areas at the edge of what is permitted by the
treaty. Often the negotiating process highlights these areas.
Because the treaty brings mutual benefits, other parties to it
are reluctant to respond by threatening to abrogate it; instead,
they will explore similar military areas. Depending on the
clarity of the treaty and the extent of verification, the content
of the treaty may gradually be eroded. One instance of this
sort of erosion is the world's effective toleration of the Soviet
fractional orbital systems even though these systems arguably violated the Outer Space Treaty. Cease-fire agreements
often provide clearer examples; both sides loosen their interpretation of the agreement until ultimately the entire structure collapses.

   The other, weaker mechanisms of international law also influence the character of compliance and violation. The force of moral authority, for example, can occasionally be seen in the phenomenon of a nation complying with an agreement even though it is not formally a party to it. Thus France, which had not signed the Limited Test Ban, chose to terminate its atmospheric nuclear testing in 1974, albeit under the pressure of world public hostility and a pending suit in the International Court of Justice. Moral pressure can present a particularly strong barrier to the violation of legislative agreements that have wide popular support, such as the Limited Test Ban and the Biological Warfare Convention.

Moral pressure can also cause a nation contemplating the violation of a treaty to employ legal rationalization. India argued that its nuclear explosion in 1974 was peaceful and therefore consistent with its commitment to Canada, which had supplied the reactor that produced the nuclear materials. (Though India might have exploded its bomb without this loophole, its decision to do so would have been somewhat more difficult.) Another form of legal rationalization is to attack the underlying agreement. Hitler argued that the Versailles Treaty had been imposed on Germany. Theorists of wars of national liberation might argue that a treaty must be ignored in the name of some higher good. Such justifications are easiest for radical regimes; in the context of revolutionary change, it is especially easy to dismiss previous treaties, even legislative ones, as no longer valid. But even in less radical regimes, public opinion can favor violation; the Indian government obtained broad national approval for its nuclear explosion.

It has been argued, particularly during the SALT I debates, that the nature of bureaucracy favors compliance with treaties.[2] In part, the argument is that a plan to violate a treaty is unattractive to the most capable bureaucrats. These people are eager to build reputations by identifying themselves with important efforts. They will therefore avoid programs that violate a treaty, because in their view such programs are unlikely to be carried out or to attract substantial funds. More-over, bureaucratic planning normally assumes that existing agreements will be obeyed, since it would require a high-level decision to plan a violation. A second prong of this bu-reaucratic argument is that the use of a bureaucracy is likely to make a violation particularly visible. To plan the evasion of a treaty within a nation's basic bureaucracy would require the informing of many people, some of whom could be expected to reveal the plan publicly. Yet the creation of a special bu-reaucracy for this illicit purpose might itself reveal the plan.

Although this argument has some force, it is subject to a number of important limitations. First, experience has shown that bureaucracies are often willing to undertake questionable activities. Second, as Henry Kissinger has pointed out, many of the most important decisions in government are indeed taken outside the bureaucracy;[3] and once high-level officials have suggested that the evasion of a treaty should be consid-ered, the bureaucracy can follow quickly. Third, a bureau-cratic agency may be deliberately designed to maintain the government's option of violation; the agency might function in programs that serve permitted purposes but that could also serve forbidden ones. To the bureaucrat, this might appear to be no more than normal contingency planning. Fourth, a well-disciplined bureaucracy might have little difficulty in supporting the violation of a treaty that the nation has en-tered into in bad faith, for there would then be none of the bureaucratic struggle associated with the transition from compliance to noncompliance. In a talkative bureaucracy like that of the United States, however, such planning may be impossible.[4]

The psychological and political difficulty of undoing a gov-ernmental decision creates an important internal force that works for compliance as long as the regime that made the treaty is in power. For a government to enter into an interna-tional agreement, its leaders must stake their reputations; internal power balances must be tested and found to favor the agreement. To reverse the decision and ignore the agreement is then very difficult, even if the agreement appears to have been a mistake. This weight of past decisions was seen in the American policy toward China, which survived for nearly a generation in spite of constant criticism by experts; the policy was ultimately reversed only by a new generation of leaders. Similarly, an arms control agreement is likely to be reversed by a deliberate decision to violate it only after new leaders have come to power and domestic attitudes toward the agreement have clearly changed.

The evolution of domestic attitudes toward an arms control treaty normally reflects the broad political context and symbolic significance of the treaty. A settlement agreement, for example, builds on a complex of views about the opposing nation. Compliance with the treaty is then shaped by the general relations with that nation, whether or not it technically violates the agreement. The importance of the international context of a treaty is most clearly seen when further agreements are to be negotiated. Bad relations between the United States and the USSR, for example, have made the negotiation of SALT II very difficult. Although it is unlikely, these bad relations could even lead to the abrogation of SALT I.

When an agreement is unequal and accompanied by growing tension, as is typical with transition agreements, compliance is less likely. Thus the Non-Proliferation Treaty, because it is resented in parts of the developing world, may tend to lose its legitimacy over time. The inequalities of the Washington Naval Treaty of 1922 similarly grew onerous to Japan; this may have contributed to the atmosphere in which Japanese militarism emerged.[5] In a few cases, moreover, attitudes outside arms control may affect compliance. The growing doubts in the developed nations about nuclear power, for example, make it difficult for them to give the developing world the technology that was to be the quid pro quo for a commitment not to acquire nuclear weapons.

The political attitudes toward a treaty and a rival nation often fall into patterns. Thus Americans who supported détente with the USSR and saw SALT I as a symbol of the détente generally believed that the United States should interpret the treaty broadly and even refrain from building some strategic weapons permitted by the treaty. These advocates of the treaty also tended to minimize the likelihood that the USSR would violate the agreement. Those Americans, however, who emphasized power rather than détente in dealing with the Soviet Union often argued that SALT gave an advantage to the USSR. Further, these opponents of SALT tended to believe that the USSR was likely to cheat on the treaty; they wanted the United States to interpret the treaty as narrowly as possible, building all useful strategic weapons not clearly inconsistent with the treaty. A transfer of power from the first group to the second or a radical shift in opinion would be nearly an absolute precondition for the United States to abrogate the treaty.

Political pressures of this sort usually lead to strong support for compliance once the treaty is concluded. The balance of attitudes reached at the time of ratification is likely to be highly durable. The extreme example of durability probably occurred in the 1930's when the United States and the United Kingdom negotiated a follow-up to earlier naval arms control treaties due to expire. As late as 1936, in the face of obvious tension in both Europe and the Pacific, these powers were so committed to the maintenance of the arms control system that they negotiated very weak agreements rather than admit a failure to reach agreement.[6] And Japan, even though it had withdrawn from the arms control system, continued to honor its agreements until shortly before the Second World War. An unbalanced or dangerous agreement provides an easy target for disaffected politicians and groups; but an agreement must be extremely unbalanced or dangerous before its violation or abrogation becomes likely. The pressures for violation or abrogation normally arise only a long time after the agreement has been concluded, and they may be ineffectual unless reinforced by political or economic turmoil like that of the 1930's.

In summary, the entry into an agreement with the intent to trick an opponent into weakening its forces is possible only when a nation has strong bureaucratic discipline. In an open society it would be very awkward to conduct a debate over the ratification of such a treaty or to justify its violation later. In general, the possible benefits of entering into a present-day arms control agreement in bad faith are so slight that it is hard to imagine any nation doing so at the risk of losing the credibility of its other treaty commitments. The erosion of an agreement by repeated minor violations and infringements is more likely, especially in the case of ambiguous agreements and, a fortiori, tacit agreements.

The most common violation of an arms control agreement is one consciously decided on some time after the treaty is ratified, when circumstances have changed or a new government has taken power. The historical examples of this show that the violation is often open and unconcealed; an intelligent observer can almost always predict it. The violator may or may not carry out the formalities of denouncing the treaty, but he will usually argue publicly that the treaty is illegitimate and that the violation is therefore legal and desirable. This kind of violation is most likely to be directed by an ideologically oriented revolutionary government against an unequal treaty or one that was barely accepted. Treaties like these are most commonly of the transitional pattern, though they can be of other types as well. By contrast, the treaty least likely to be violated is a reasonably balanced one, perhaps of the settlement pattern, that has been ratified after vigorous debate and that has brought the promised political benefits.

VERIFICATION

The political factors just described are clearly the primary guarantee of compliance with an arms control treaty. However, they are seldom considered adequate. In the face of the secrecy that surrounds many military activities, each party to a treaty usually wants information to verify that the others are complying with it.

The exact purpose and the desirable degree of verification are controversial; three different standards of verification have been seriously proposed. The first, a juristic standard, rests on the assumption that any violation of the agreement is dangerous; ideally, it requires a perfect system of verification. The second, a strategic standard, is based on an analysis of the advantage that an evasion of the treaty might confer. Thus the verification must be able to detect any strategically significant evasion in time for a defense to be deployed. The third, a political standard, looks to the motivation of the possible evader. The verification, when added to all the other motivations affecting compliance with the agreement, must make the chance of being caught in a violation high enough to discourage evasion.

The juristic standard, demanding that every violation be detected, may appear absurd, for the importance of verification would seem to depend on the actual strategic significance of both the agreement and the violation. Nevertheless, the United States has often sought to meet this standard in its negotiations toward a comprehensive nuclear test ban, especially in the early 1960's. It sought, for example, the right to visit the site of every seismic event that might be a nuclear explosion (or at least a substantial sample of such sites) in order to verify that the event was not in fact a nuclear explosion.

This American pursuit of a very high standard in the area of nuclear testing might have been quite rational; depending on the state of technology, a single series of tests or even one test could conceivably provide knowledge of immense value in the future design of weapons. Yet the American argument for perfect verification probably rested on broader grounds than that. The Soviet commitment to compliance was unknown, and the possibility of bad faith could not be readily dismissed.

Americans felt a need to build powerful mechanisms of detection, if not of enforcement. Moreover, the aura surrounding arms control in the 1960's was more legal than strategic; and whereas arms control of the legislative type does not necessarily require juristic verification, a legalistic view of arms control does require it. Even though in domestic law the mechanisms for verifying compliance are rarely airtight, it was generally assumed that airtight mechanisms would be needed in this new international area.

In contemporary agreements the strategic standard is more common; the verification must be sufficient to preclude any serious risk should another nation evade the treaty. At first blush, the calculation of this degree of verification appears quite straightforward. One estimates the time necessary for the evader to develop and deploy a force that substantially affects the balance of military power. The necessary verification must then confidently be able to detect the preparation for such an evasion early enough to enable innocent nations to build a counterforce before there is a significant imbalance. The analysis must consider ways that the evader might seek to avoid early detection; but at the same time it can allow for the fact that any such secrecy is likely to increase the development time for weapons or to result in less effective forces.

The difficulty of the strategic standard is that it may be impossible for both sides ever to be formally satisfied. If one nation has a stronger economic base, it may always be able to outbuild the other, and eventually it may achieve a significant advantage. In such a situation, a resumed arms race can never help the weaker side; no amount of warning is adequate to ensure that stability will be restored.[7] Thus the strategic standard of verification can sometimes be useful only for the stronger nation. This is perhaps one of the less obvious reasons why the United States, which is fundamentally stronger than the USSR, has been more concerned about verification than the USSR. However, when two adversaries have an equal capacity for building arms, or when an adequate counterforce can be smaller and more rapidly built than the illegal force, both sides can be satisfied by the standard of verification. With ground forces, for example, a successful attacking force traditionally had to be substantially larger than the defending force. Similarly, in strategic deterrence a very large numerical advantage is generally required to gain a significant strategic advantage. Hence a new deployment can generally restore the balance in spite of any head start achieved by evading a treaty.

In order to apply the strategic standard, each nation must be able to predict the character of the other's illegal actions and to evaluate their strategic effects. This evaluation is impossible for agreements designed to restrict the development of an unknown technology, since no one can predict the effects of an unknown development or define the necessary countermeasures. If the technology is believed important, nations react to this uncertainty by moving to impose an absolute standard, as the United States did for the comprehensive test ban. If, however, the technology is believed unlikely to affect the balance of power, nations tend to accept a weaker standard. The verification of the Biological Warfare Convention, for example, relies on a political process in which the UN might investigate a suspected violation. When nations judge that they cannot adequately evaluate new technology or new tactics, an agreement may even become impossible. Thus precision-guided munitions probably cannot be controlled by agreement until nations understand the weapons better.

The strategic standard of verification takes into account military costs and benefits but ignores the political factors that frequently make evasion unlikely. It also ignores the fact that both sides usually have an interest in compliance. Many people therefore have urged that a lower, political standard of verification be used. By this standard, nations are presumed unlikely to evade a treaty secretly; the necessary level of verification, then, is one that adequately reduces any remaining temptation to evade. All the factors already discussed are considered, and new ones besides: the mutual interest of the parties in obeying the treaty, the character of likely responses to a violation of it, and the relative attractions of illegal and permitted ways that a party might improve its military capability.

The emphasis of this political standard of verification is on balancing risks and on increasing the incentive to comply with the agreement. Although the innocent nation might prefer to have a very high level of confidence in its ability to detect any evasion, the potential evader has to consider the risk of being detected, and may be deterred by a very small risk. Thus each side can find safety in the caution of the other side's bureaucrats, remembering, of course, that those bureaucrats might misestimate the probability of being detected or the probability that the other side will respond. When the mutual interest in compliance is strong, each nation may even view verification as a way to demonstrate to the others that it is not violating the treaty; the political standard takes into account this assurance role of verification. In the Biological Warfare Convention, for example, each party accepts a duty to cooperate in UN investigations to verify compliance. An accused but innocent nation is likely to make every effort to show its innocence; politically, hesitation amounts to an admission of guilt.

The desirable level of verification can become a battleground between the supporters of arms control and the opponents. The United States, perhaps thinking of Pearl Harbor, has tended to overemphasize verification, forgetting that the history of arms control shows few examples of a successful secret evasion.[8] In the German violations of the Versailles agreement or the possible Soviet violations of SALT I, the problem did not lie in a lack of detection; rather, it lay in the threatened nations' will to respond or in the ambiguity of the agreement. It would be unwise, however, to go to the opposite extreme and dismiss the need for verification. An authoritarian, closed society such as the Soviet Union is the type of society with the greatest political and bureaucratic ability to evade a treaty.

At the same time that the United States, the nation most concerned with verification, has shifted its preference from the juristic standard toward the strategic, the technical ability to discover violations by such means as satellites has improved dramatically.[9] The result has been a nearly irresistible pressure to use intelligence systems rather than formal inspection arrangements to verify arms control agreements. This reliance upon intelligence generally requires that the process of verification be secret, in order to protect the intelligence techniques from compromises that might help an opponent conceal its activities. Hence the executive of each nation may have to guard the verification information; and unless there are leaks, the public may then have no grounds for confidence that the other party is complying. In the United States, those privy to the intelligence who have doubts about arms control are almost certain to leak information showing Soviet violations. Even then, however, the facts can easily become lost in political controversy, as happened in the case of the 1974 allegations of Soviet SALT violations. Thus the issue of verification may turn out to have little influence on a political balance shaped by broader political issues.

Secrecy also lowers the confidence of third parties that the signers of the treaty are complying with it. There may be a shared interest by the American and Soviet governments in minimizing some SALT violations; thus other nations may not be sure SALT is being honored. Should these other nations depend on American and Soviet compliance, as they might if a European arms control agreement were concluded, the problem could become serious and even create tension between these nations and the great powers. This makes it particularly difficult to broaden U.S.-Soviet arms control to include nations that lack a comparable intelligence capability.

As an alternative, multilateral verification avoids some of

these problems but brings others. The prime example of multilateral verification is the inspection by the International Atomic Energy Agency (IAEA) of national nuclear facilities. The agreement setting up this inspection was a major international accomplishment, and the agency does help safeguard nuclear power. Some of the nations that vote on the IAEA inspection budget, however, have not signed the Non-Proliferation Treaty and may be less than convinced of the importance of verification. For this reason, the level of inspection is necessarily set by political compromise and may not be adequate to deal with a particular nation or region. Moreover, the IAEA keeps its inspection data just as secret as national governments do. Probably the underlying problem is that nations fear an international agency will pay little heed to the political factors likely to be entwined with any violation or near violation. The nations therefore weaken the agency's independent authority to act on the information it discovers. In addition, international arrangements lack the flexibility of national intelligence operations, although the renegotiation of inspection rights in response to political or technological change is always conceivable.

One possible future arrangement is an international system of verification by satellite. This could be based on existing national capabilities or on internationally financed and controlled satellites. The costs of such a system, however, would be significant and the organizational difficulties great. It might be particularly difficult, for example, to decide what geographic areas to observe, since objections could be raised that the information would be used by nations for their own military or economic purposes. Nevertheless, the primary barrier is probably political: neither of the superpowers, which control most of the technology, has been willing to admit for the record that it is using such satellite systems to observe other nations or to claim that such systems are used against it. The political cost of breaking the silence is probably overrated; low-resolution satellite photography, including pictures of other nations, is already available to the public for mapping, meteorological, and scientific purposes. Should arms control proceed further, an international system of verification will probably become essential for meeting domestic political demands for the verification of multilateral agreements.[10]

Normally, verification requirements need not limit arms control more severely than the political requirements discussed in Chapter Four. The exceptional cases occur in connection with relatively technical details of agreements, particularly in the strategic nuclear area. In most contexts, verification is more an extrinsic political issue than an intrinsic logical one; the debate about verification becomes a surrogate for debate about the desirability of arms control itself. Should new agreements cut more deeply, however, and should new nations enter the arms control framework, the problems of bad faith and military imbalance may become more serious than they are now. In that case, verification may prove vital to an agreement, and the need for an international system may become overwhelming.

CURRENT SANCTIONS

In spite of the heavy political emphasis on verification, there has so far been little public discussion of what to do after a violation is detected. Historical examples of the violation of treaties show that the issue of response is the critical one: the violator anticipates—usually correctly—that there will be no response. Only one existing arms control agreement even includes a formal sanction. The Non-Proliferation Treaty, together with the IAEA Statute, permits the withdrawal of nuclear materials from a nation violating the agreement; the IAEA may also make a report to the Security Council. These arrangements have never been applied and may prove even weaker than they sound. Although the shipment of new materials to a nation that violates the treaty may well be ended, no old nuclear materials are likely to be physically removed. And Security Council action may be thwarted by the veto.

The only sanctions available for today's arms control agreements, then, are those implicit in the general framework of international politics and in the fact of agreement itself. The strongest practical sanctions are for innocent nations to terminate the agreement, to resume the building of weapons forbidden by the agreement, and to undertake any other military and diplomatic countermeasures that might help compensate for the violation. A weaker response is simply to slow down or freeze the negotiation of further agreements with the violator. Finally, there may be very little response at all. In response to arguable, relatively technical Soviet violations of the Limited Test Ban and the SALT I agreement on offensive forces, the United States probably protested diplomatically; but the basic American reaction was an increased determination to be careful in negotiating with the Soviet Union. Arms control agreements usually turn out to be highly resilient, likely neither to be seriously violated nor to be abrogated in response to violation.

For arms control agreements of the settlement pattern, this is because all the forces working toward compliance also encourage each nation to overlook as much as possible any violations on the other side. It seems pointless to upset an agreement in response to a minor violation when, even after abrogation, it would still be in both nations' interest to negotiate a similar new agreement (presumably modified to prevent the repetition of the violation or to compensate for it). It is likely to seem more rational merely to protest diplomatically and to hope that the opponent's interest in maintaining the agreement prevents it from acting so flagrantly that termination cannot be avoided.[11] Thus a treaty that is in the common interest can sometimes be violated rather extensively without actually collapsing; even the weakened treaty might be preferable to none at all.

The political and psychological forces behind compliance

also make nations reluctant to apply sanctions in connection with settlement agreements. Leaders committed to an agreement find it difficult to accept the possibility that the agreement is being violated, and even more difficult to impose the sanction of abrogation. For instance, those who looked to the Paris Accords as a long-desired end to the Vietnam War tended to disbelieve the evidence showing North Vietnamese violations, and were absolutely unwilling to send troops to Vietnam in response. Similarly, Secretary of State Kissinger minimized the evidence of Soviet violation of SALT, and as a result the evidence did not become a political topic until there was a much broader debate on détente. It is only when a clear violation produces a sense of betrayal that the political forces reverse themselves and create a climate favoring countermeasures. Sometimes a leader may create such a climate by making a persuasive public argument, as President Kennedy did by releasing U-2 photographs of Soviet missile sites during the Cuban missile crisis. Those who wanted a response to German violations of the Versailles Treaty were unable to do as well.

With legislative arms control agreements, the politics of a response to a violation are rather different. Public opinion, concerned with the evil condemned by the agreement, is likely to favor a response that is substantial but short of abrogation. A government, however, is concerned with its general diplomatic relations with the violator and is therefore hesitant to respond at all. Only a nation that feels especially threatened by a violation or has obvious and relevant leverage is likely to act. The response to the Indian nuclear explosion—although that explosion was not a breach of a formal arms control agreement—shows these phenomena quite clearly. World public opinion (outside India) was quite troubled. Most governments, however, refused to act, and many were silent. Pakistan, which felt directly threatened, spoke out strongly. Canada, which had supplied the nuclear materials and felt especially mocked by the explosion, was the one nation that reacted immediately by cutting off further nuclear material and technology to India.

It is often easier to respond, as Canada did, with leverage, rather than with abrogation. The exercise of leverage does not call into question the benefits of the agreement; nor does it present the psychological difficulties of abrogation for the agreement's sponsors. There may be domestic political barriers to applying leverage—Canadian exports suffered from Canada's action—but these barriers are generally weaker than those to abrogation. The effect of the leverage on the violator is more problematic. If the leverage is too artificial or is unrelated to the violation, the violator may become psychologically defensive and may reinforce its commitment to the violation. This is the typical reaction to economic sanctions. By contrast, if the leverage is very carefully tailored so as to make further violation difficult, it may be effective. Few arms control agreements, however, offer the opportunity for such carefully tailored leverage.

Since more elaborate responses to violations can be awkward, the parties to a treaty have sometimes established procedures for discussing problems and alleged violations. An example is the U.S.-USSR Standing Consultative Commission, which was created to consider problems arising under SALT. This commission can help minimize the risk of erosion, and can perhaps serve as a forum for the private warnings that are likely to be more effective than public warnings. But the secrecy of the discussions, like that of the satellite surveillance, could cause problems. The public could lose confidence in the treaty, for example, or the commission could establish a pattern of interpretation different from that presented to Congress and the American public at the time of ratification. To be sure, there are strong arguments favoring secrecy in such consultations. For one, the discussions might involve sensitive intelligence data (of course, it is the public, not the opposing government, that is denied the information). Also, the public discussion of possible violations might create dangerous domestic controversy, unnecessarily discredit the agreement, or make it harder for either side to back down. If the discussions were made public, they might be used for propaganda rather than conducted in a spirit of cooperation. In the short run, these arguments may outweigh the need for public discussion. In the long run, a significant system of arms control cannot be stable in democratic nations unless its workings are shared with the public.

In the light of the characteristic political motivations for the evasion of a treaty, it is clear that the sanctions currently available are so limited that they can play only a minor role in the enforcement of arms control. A nation contemplating the violation of a legislative agreement may be deterred by the possibility of losing technical, economic, or military assistance. The threat of abrogation, however, is likely to be nearly irrelevant to a nation that commits a violation after a coup d'état or some other major change in its circumstances. Such a violator, by virtue of its ideology, is likely to dismiss the costs of any sanctions and political opprobrium the nation may suffer. Thus Germany, in violating the Versailles Treaty in the 1930's, had only contempt for its treaty partners.

The effectiveness of any system of verification and response is basically captive to the general political relations between the parties to the treaty. Verification and the possibility of some response do indeed contribute to the stability of an arms control regime that remains generally consistent with the interests of the parties. Moreover, to help ensure that an agreement will actually serve the goals of self-interest, each party may find it desirable to estimate in advance whether its security could be preserved by abrogating the treaty in response to an opponent's violation. But it is this mutual self-interest, not the formal arrangement for sanctions, that is the prime guarantor of an agreement.

THE IMPACT OF LIMITED ARMS CONTROL

The themes developed in this and preceding chapters can now be assembled so that we may estimate the actual impact of arms control. As this chapter shows, violation is only rarely a severe problem for agreements since the Second World War. The shared interest in maintaining the arms control, together with the existing verification system, usually ensures that a treaty will be honored. The problems come mainly from changes in national regimes, which can produce a reevaluation of national goals, and from erosion by repeated minor violations. In general, however, today's relatively weak agreements are likely to be observed.

It follows, then, that these arms control agreements will usually achieve their "agreed" effects: the demilitarization of the Antarctic, the reduction of atmospheric testing (but not of underground testing or the development of nuclear weapons) under the Limited Test Ban, the restriction of the ABM (but not the end of the strategic arms race) under SALT I. The impact of arms control is therefore primarily influenced by the limitations of the process of reaching agreements and by the way the possible agreements affect the mechanisms of war.

For two nations or alliances of roughly equal strength, an agreement of the settlement type can be beneficial. Many useful "agreed" effects can be achieved: the limitation of forces or deployments that might otherwise cause diplomatic incidents or encourage preemptive attack, perhaps the slowing of some technological change. These effects help decrease the risk of a diplomatic war. The likelihood of a popular war between the parties to such a treaty is rarely increased and can usually be decreased. The agreement will symbolize a détente between the parties and may give the public on the two sides some confidence in each other. This confidence will endure so long as neither side seriously violates the treaty or otherwise takes advantage of the other. Within the framework of arms control, there is little incentive for such disruptive action.

But the arms control treaty is a captive of broader political forces. When these forces work toward conflict, as they did between the United States and the Soviet Union in the mid-1970's, the politics of the arms control relationship sours as well. Any agreement may impose costs on both sides. The power of the leaders is likely to grow, and the agreement process can become simply a tool for the joint management of arms competition. The weapons levels may even be increased by the use of bargaining chips and the like. Nevertheless, unless the agreement process inadvertently directs the construction of weapons in a particularly dangerous direction, arms control appears likely to decrease the risk of war, if only slightly.

Where equality between the sides is lacking, a settlement agreement to reduce forces can rarely be of much help. It is very difficult for two parties of unequal strength to negotiate arms control. If they do reach an agreement, it will at best be weak; and at worst, it will intensify the risk of a later popular conflict. Multiple parties will seldom be able to define politically acceptable force balances. An agreement on force levels, therefore, is not likely to help prevent diplomatic war in the case of a risky and complex regional balance of power.

Legislative agreements, however, may still be possible in these situations, since they require symmetry only in the form of the agreement, rather than in the actual level of forces. The politics of these agreements favors further agreements, and thus offers the hope of building a structure of some significance. Each agreement of this sort, however, is necessarily concerned only with marginal military matters, not vital ones; therefore, these agreements should not be expected to provide dramatic short-term results. Moreover, though these agreements are stable in normal times, they can collapse under severe pressure, like the entire arms control structure negotiated during the 1920's. These agreements are an ineffective way to restrain a radical government or to curb the dynamism of a nation showing newly acquired strength. These are precisely the types least likely to enter into an arms control agreement and most likely to repudiate an existing agreement. Legislative agreements might, however, eventually help keep some nations from starting down the path of dynamic expansionism. In complex regional disputes, the avoidance of dangerous incidents and the exchange of data under legislative agreements can be particularly important. Even the negotiating process itself can contribute to the goal of preventing war.

With respect to transition agreements, however, greater pessimism is advisable. These agreements are the most likely to create resentment, and for this reason the most likely to be violated. Except in rare cases, then, they may contribute more to the risk of war than to peace.

On balance, it is clear that arms control agreements and even negotiations can produce benefits. Yet these benefits have often been oversold. Neither popular war nor situations of strategic inequality can be significantly affected by arms control. The direct numerical limitation of arms, applicable only between equals and often marked by bargaining chip phenomena, is seldom the most effective form of arms control; the prevention of incidents and preemptive attacks is likely to be much more significant. Finally, arms control, especially that in the settlement pattern, is not normally a significant step toward a general disarmament. The achievement of a just arms control treaty only rarely makes the political situation more favorable to later agreements sharply reducing forces.

In planning for the future, it is important to recognize that many patterns of arms reduction could help preserve peace and maintain the security of all parties if they were not politically impossible. The obvious response is to attempt to change the political structure of arms control negotiations in order to make these reductions possible. Several approaches are worth considering: a shift to less formal arrangements based on consultation; a modification of the economic pressures that favor the manufacture and transfer of arms; and the development of international methods of enforcement that might make asymmetric agreements more feasible. The last of these approaches, which is the most far-reaching of the three, is discussed in the next chapter.[12]

6. Multilateral Techniques of Enforcing Arms Control

THE TRADITIONAL concept of arms control enforcement, such as that embodied in the general and complete disarmament proposals of the early 1960's, is that an international police force would punish a violator. This concept, here called the "collective sanction," closely resembles the original 1945 United Nations concept of collective security, under which war would be waged against a nation that the Security Council determined to be a threat to the peace. The intended effect of the collective sanction is that the threat of military action will deter the initial violation or act of aggression. This concept is an extension of traditional alliance and balance-of-power diplomacy, but it has greater legitimacy.

The United Nations found the collective concept hard to apply and shifted to "peacekeeping": a use of limited force and an international presence, with the consent of at least some of the nations involved and without the designation of any nation as an aggressor. This suggests a second concept of arms control enforcement, here called "limited intervention," that avoids the punitive character of the collective sanction. Instead, it shapes the military intervention to achieve a specific, limited end such as the containment of the effects of a violation. Possible examples of this might be a guarantee, either unilateral or multilateral, to defend a border or to embargo the transfer of certain arms to a violating nation. Limited intervention can also usefully be understood to include a negative guarantee such as the promise of nations outside a region not to use nuclear weapons against the members of a regional nuclear free zone.

Finally, there is a third approach to enforcement, here called "direct intervention," in which the traditional sovereignty of the violator is ignored and direct action is taken against the fruits of the violation or the individuals involved in it. Such intervention could take many forms. For example, an international criminal court to try individual treaty violators has sometimes been proposed. Another idea is the use of international raids to suppress incipient nuclear weapons facilities.[1]

THE COLLECTIVE SANCTION

Under the collective security concept of the UN Charter, the Security Council would meet in the event of war to define an aggressor. The great powers would then use collective military force to end the aggression. This pattern was modeled on the alliance against Germany in the Second World War, which had posed unconditional surrender as its objective. In the light of this history and in reaction to the appeasement of the 1930's, the duty to participate in an enforcement action was emphasized in the UN.

The UN fully applied the collective security concept only once, in Korea in 1950, at a time when the USSR had walked out of the UN and thereby not exercised its veto in the Security Council. The failure of collective security is generally, and with some justice, attributed to the Cold War and to the Security Council veto. As will become apparent, however, Cold War antipathy is not the only force that weakens the collective sanction; its range of useful application to arms control is very limited.

The guarantor's ability to apply the sanction. The nations seeking jointly to punish a violator must have both adequate force and the will to use it. Against a major nuclear power able to defend itself by nuclear deterrence, no amount of force is adequate; the collective sanction is therefore useless. If the great powers are divided so as to be likely to intervene on opposing sides, the sanction also fails. But the limitations of this pattern are greater still. The Western nations did not use their power against Hitler in the 1930's and only a few helped in Korea in 1950, in spite of arguments as strong as will ever be offered in favor of intervention. The difficulty is that this sanction amounts to war, and can be as costly to the intervenor as to the violator.

This difficulty is particularly great in the enforcement of arms control. In that area, any intervention would have to be in response to the violation of a treaty, an action much less provocative than outright aggression. An act of aggression tends to evoke a strong popular response;[2] but only an exceptional case of treaty evasion, such as the starting of a nuclear weapons program in defiance of world denuclearization, might seem serious enough to justify immediate large-scale military action.[3] Instead, politics encourages temporizing in the hope that the violation will cease without leading to further trouble.

The growth of public involvement in foreign policy makes it even harder to use the sanction of military intervention. Public pressure influences which guarantees can be honored; and this pressure tends to be shaped by such factors as the outcome of previous intervention and the closeness of the historical and cultural ties with the other nations involved. Nations cannot today be expected to act with the cold rationality that marked the execution of guarantees in the eighteenth century. In the wake of the Vietnam War, for example, the American willingness to intervene in support of an arms control arrangement in Korea is questionable; intervention in support of a significant arrangement in Europe would be more likely, but still politically difficult. To favor intervention, the public would have to feel it was making a major contribution to world order, if not actually defending its own homeland. Political leaders, at the same time, would make sure that any act of intervention was consistent with their conception of the balance of power.

The same political factors make it hard to extend any guarantee for arms control in the first place. The diplomat applying cold strategic logic will favor a guarantee only when the benefits to the security of the arms control agreement outweigh the risk of having to honor the guarantee. Moreover, the public generally fears foreign entanglement. Since the Second World War, these pressures have generally restricted guarantees to treaties aimed at containing a particularly threatening nation, such as the alliances against the Soviet Union. It is also possible that some guarantees might be extended in order to help settle a regional conflict like that in the Middle East. The hope is always that the guarantee will be so effective as to make actual intervention unnecessary. Even in the creation of the North Atlantic Treaty Organization, the approval of the U.S. Congress rested on the expectation that the guarantee would stabilize Europe and never have to be honored.[4]

In the face of the various barriers, there are only two models of arms control in which a guarantee of a collective sanction is politically plausible. One is a regional agreement among fairly weak nations. Because such an agreement is necessarily a form of settlement, the parties to it are likely to expect the settlement to be successful. Hence outside powers might be able to extend bilateral or multilateral guarantees to enforce the agreement, provided conflict between the great powers is not prohibitive and the region is one to which the guarantor nations have close cultural or political ties. The other conceivable application of the sanction is in a legislative arms control agreement that the broad public regards as highly beneficial. This situation is more problematic. The arms control agreement would have to permit intervention before the violator became very strong; a later intervention would be so costly as to be politically prohibitive. And since the violator's identity could not be known in advance, it might be impossible for cultural factors to give support to intervention. A multilateral guarantee by all nations will be possible only when a consensus of citizens and governments regards the violation of the treaty as a heinous offense against mankind.

The deterrence of the potential violator. For a sanction to be effective, each potential violator must be deterred by the likelihood that a violation will be met with overwhelming force. Not only must the potential violator fear the guarantors will act; it must also calculate that the military balance favors the guarantors. The careful strategist planning to violate a treaty, like Hitler in the 1930's, will therefore build up his forces in a series of small violations designed to elicit compromise. In this way, the violator can ultimately become strong enough that the sanction is difficult to apply wisely. A well-designed military balance and a very subtle decision-making structure are thus necessary to deter the careful violator.[5]

It is also crucial to a guarantee that the potential violator's calculations actually influence its national decision making. This will normally be the case when diplomats shape foreign policy; it is less likely when public pressure is decisive. Guarantees can therefore help deter diplomatic wars, but are less effective in preventing ideological wars. Since popular ideology sometimes impels the violation of a treaty, it is unrealistic to assume that the collective sanction will never have to be used.

The willingness to rely on a guarantee. It would seem that innocent nations would readily accept the protection afforded by an arms control treaty that called for sanctions against a violator. Nations protected by alliances, however, have often found such protection constraining, and a similar feeling is likely to arise in the context of arms control. The result can be tension of several kinds.

First, there is tension over policy. The guarantor is likely to attempt to influence the protected nation's policies to make sure they do not provoke conflict. The protected nation may find that it has to accept some of this control if the guarantee is to remain effective. Typically, the two disagree over the exact circumstances under which the guarantee will be enforced. In an arms control treaty, the definition of a violation may represent an agreement on the circumstances in which intervention is to occur; but the subtleties of decision making will continue to pose difficult political issues, especially in dealing with a careful violator.

Second, if a nation is protected by a guarantee, it must also accept a sense of dependence. The guarantor nation is likely to be more powerful, and it will normally have the stronger bargaining position. Psychologically, the relationship imposes a dependence that is hard to accept; a desire to avoid it, for example, may partly explain de Gaulle's challenge to the structure of U.S.-European relations. The dependence itself produces a sense of insecurity. In Europe, the effect of this insecurity is that the guaranteed nations demand increasingly strong reassurance of the guarantee's reliability. The guarantee becomes a psychological substitute for national defense, not just a supplement to it. In Israel, the effect of the insecurity (deriving from what is only an informal guarantee) takes a slightly different form: an intense, almost belligerent self-reliance.

Such psychological effects make it very difficult for a party to an arms control agreement to regard a guarantee as adequate compensation for its acceptance of a weaker force level. Both the guarantee and the weaker forces would require the guaranteed nation to accept a politically inferior status. Moreover, a serious question always remains whether the guarantee can be reliable. The psychological problems are perhaps less severe if the guarantee comes from a multilateral body such as the UN, but multilateral guarantees are likely to be less credible than those from separate powers. The result is that the collective sanction is only rarely politically acceptable as a way to guarantee an unbalanced arms control agreement. Again, the most likely use for such an arrangement might be as part of a settlement in a region that has come close to war. The settlement could thus offer the reward of peace along with the guarantee and its concomitant restrictions.

Military requirements for the collective sanction. The military technology best suited to the collective sanction is the kind that makes forces highly additive, in the sense that an alliance of two or three nations against one is almost certain to prevail. In order to avoid the political difficulty of a long war, it is also helpful if the larger force can be quickly decisive. The military technology of the Second World War probably met both of these requirements. Much of today's conventional military technology probably also meets them, though guerrilla strategy and such weapons as the new precision-guided missiles may shift the balance in favor of a violator's defense against an intervention force.

Nuclear weapons definitely work against the ability to apply the collective sanction. A nuclear ally is of little help in an effort to punish a major nuclear power, for the enforcement action is itself likely to be deterred. The costs of enforcement are so far out of proportion to the violation that the deterrent effect is nullified. The only conceivable military sanction against a strong nuclear power is a conventional action under the cover of mutual nuclear deterrence. In general, however, major nuclear nations are immune to the collective sanction. Such a sanction is militarily feasible only against weak nuclear nations and those without nuclear weapons.

Possible applications of the collective sanction. The various drawbacks of the collective sanction limit it to only two possible types of application in arms control. One is in the enforcement of regional arrangements, and the other is in the enforcement of especially significant global legislative restraints. In the first, a regional settlement might incorporate an arms control provision in order to forestall a preemptive attack or reduce military costs. The sanction could be applied by an international agency like the UN (which already has much of the necessary formal authority); alternatively, the great powers could be authorized to apply it, each presumably acting in favor of its traditional client. Once the fundamental will to reach a settlement has evolved, it should not be too difficult to work out the legal decision-making procedures, most likely in an elaborate package of side arrangements. The problem is in the fundamental will; all nations in the region would have to be committed to such a regional settlement, and all interested great powers would at least have to acquiesce in it. Only a very strong drive to reach a settlement would be able to overcome the political barriers to the establishment of guarantees, especially if there are asymmetries in the forces. The Middle East is the region that appears most adaptable to the collective sanction; and indeed, many of the proposals that are heard for guaranteed settlements in the region amount to arms control of this type.

The other conceivable application of this sanction is to enforce a major global arms restriction that bears highly legal connotations—perhaps, for example, a future non-proliferation arrangement. Such an agreement would draw strength from the political thrust that has already created the substantial formal enforcement powers of the UN and of some regional organizations. Like the UN itself, the sanction may be politically feasible only in the wake of a war or some other major crisis. Otherwise, unless arms control can attract a strong global constituency, any such arrangement will probably have to rely on the enforcement powers already conceded to world and regional security organizations.

The collective sanction supports the status quo; the nuclear powers would necessarily play a major role in the operation of such a system of enforcement, effectively dominating it. If the system were to work, radical political change would thus probably be difficult. It is the harshness of the sanction, however, that raises the most serious difficulties for this pattern of enforcement. It is hard to believe that many people would view punitive warfare as an appropriate response to any but the most serious violation of arms control. A practical means of enforcement, therefore, must be less drastic and more flexible.

LIMITED INTERVENTION

To meet the problem of maintaining international peace, the UN has shifted from collective security to peacekeeping. Instead of conducting an international war against an aggressor, the UN forces now typically try to settle a dispute, as in the Middle East, by supervising a negotiated truce with the consent of the contending nations.[6] The advantages of this method are manifold. The intervention is less destructive and therefore more feasible politically. The effect of a deadlock between the great powers is minimized, for a great power is much less likely to veto an interim settlement involving a client state than to veto an enforcement operation against the same state. There are also disadvantages. In general, the consent of both sides in a war is required; but the nation winning a conflict is likely to obstruct the application of peacekeeping, either by denying its consent or by obtaining the veto of a friendly permanent member of the Security Council. Moreover, a truce may leave the underlying disputes unsettled. Repeated peacekeeping operations have not yet brought any settlement to the Middle East or to Cyprus; if they do so, it will only be by stabilizing the conflict until a new political generation takes power.

For enforcing arms control, nevertheless, limited intervention appears to offer substantial possibilities. Since the intervention is limited, it is easier to carry out, more credible, and more adaptable to the magnitude of the threat posed by a violation of an arms control agreement. Among the many possible patterns of limited intervention are: allowing threatened nations to rearm in specified ways in the event of a violation; applying an international arms embargo at the borders of a violator; terminating military guarantees to a violator; and actually guaranteeing boundaries by means of defensive intervention. The problems of the veto and of obtaining the consent of the parties could be avoided by appropriate commitments made at the time of agreement. The technique of limited intervention respects the tradition of national sovereignty in that there need be no intent to punish a national government or to exert control over territory or population.

The guarantor's ability to apply the sanction. The intervenor's motivations in a peacekeeping operation differ radically from those under collective security. It has been neutral nations such as Sweden and India that have staffed peacekeeping operations, in contrast to the nations strongly committed to one side that have participated in collective enforcement operations such as that in Korea. The connotation of collective enforcement is that of vindicating the international order and defending one's own nation. The connotation of peacekeeping is that of helping to maintain a truce already accepted by both sides. Collective enforcement entails dangerous warfare; peacekeeping requires only a substantially less dangerous policing operation with a strong moral appeal.

The limited intervention that could be used to enforce arms control may lie almost anywhere between these two extreme patterns. In some cases, such as the imposing of an international embargo or the maintaining of a symbolic border defense force during peacetime, it would be much like peacekeeping. In other cases, such as a war designed to expel an arms control violator from a nation it has invaded, the intervention would be closer to collective security.

In the less dangerous cases, the traditional peacekeeping motivations would probably be sufficient to spur nations to participate in an embargo or to contribute military forces. The mission of the intervention would be to support world order and to uphold a significant arms control agreement; this combines the appeals of both peacekeeping and collective security. The more dangerous cases, however, involve war, which might last a long while and might be demoralizing to the intervenors. They would be limited to maintaining a static defense line, rather than seeking the total victory implicit in the collective sanction; besides, they would lack the consent of both sides that characterizes peacekeeping. The traditionally neutral country might hesitate to risk the lives of its youth; the nonneutral country might chafe at the military restrictions that preclude total victory. One may hope that the psychological force of the commitment to world order together with the strong human incentive to respond to outright aggression would sometimes outweigh these negative factors. Fortunately, the favorable political impulses are strongest in the case of arms control agreements providing for substantial force cuts, precisely the agreements that need arrangements for intervention the most.

To gain the participation of relatively neutral nations and to avoid escalation, the intervention must appear just.[7] In traditional peacekeeping, the peacekeeper's neutrality serves this function; it helps elicit world political support, ensures that the intervention narrows rather than broadens the conflict, and attracts support for any associated offensive military actions. Sometimes, however, neutrality is nearly impossible. When the underlying conflict is one that divides the world politically, intervention favoring one side may induce counterintervention on the other; even a defensive form of peacekeeping could become a process of choosing up sides for a general war. This problem could be avoided in today's world simply by not having peacekeeping operations; but peacekeeping cannot be so easily dispensed with in the context of arms control. As a result, it becomes essential in arms control that any associated political settlement appear just to the world community. Otherwise, any peacekeeping might be dangerous. The technique of peacekeeping, for example, would probably be much more feasible in Latin America than in southern Africa (assuming that some sort of arms control agreement were possible in southern Africa).

The deterrence of the potential violator. The fundamental motive for violating a treaty is to gain the ability to exert power against other nations; the goal of peacekeeping is typically to deprive the violator of this benefit. This goal may not appear as forceful as the total victory proposed by the collective sanction. It is, however, equally likely to affect the calculation by the potential violator of its national interest. Moreover, the limited intervention is inherently more credible, since it is more likely to be applied. As a means of deterrence, limited intervention is also psychologically superior. A violator may well be ideologically motivated, in which case the threat of intervention contemplated by the collective sanction could unify the nation around its government. In that event, the collective sanction might work only if pursued to total victory. In contrast, the construction of an alliance to make the violation pointless would tend to encourage negotiation, rather than to radicalize the violator further.

The key drawback of limited intervention is the problem of timing. Limited intervention is most likely to succeed with minimal invasion of the territory of the violator; it is more a form of protection for innocent nations than a threat against the violator. In the face of defensive guarantees, then, a violator might undertake a large-scale arms buildup but not launch an attack until it thought its forces the equal of any likely intervention. The right to intervene would not accrue to other nations until too late. This danger depends on the military technology involved. With nuclear weapons, for example, it is serious; with conventional forces, it is less likely to be serious. In some cases, the danger might be met by tailoring an embargo so as to weaken the nation's military potential. In other cases, however, a stronger form of intervention would have to be designed into the arms control agreement.

The willingness to rely on the sanction. Limited intervention is probably much more effective than the collective sanction as a way to persuade nations to accept arms reductions that may leave them in an inferior position. This is mainly because a guarantee of limited intervention is more credible. But in addition, the intervenors are likely to be more nearly neutral, which decreases the affront to the guaranteed nation's sovereignty, the risk that guarantors will control its policies, and, most of all, any sense of dependency.

In a regional context, a guarantee of limited intervention could facilitate the entry into political settlements and accompanying arms control arrangements that might otherwise be impossible. The basic requirements for an agreement are a sufficient desire for it by the parties and the possibility of correction from the outside of any regional military imbalance. It is the will to reach a settlement that is usually most in doubt, but this limitation is less severe than in agreements backed by the collective sanction. Even failing a full settlement, an interim "truce" in such matters as border stabilization can sometimes be worked out with the aid of both limited intervention and arms control.[8] As the experience of the Middle East has shown, arrangements can even be negotiated in the midst of a serious ideological dispute.

The application of this sanction to legislative agreements is more complex. One problem arises in the case of a nation driven by internal expansionist forces. Such a nation seems particularly unlikely to accept this form of arms control enforcement, viewing it as an instrument of domination by the superpowers. The guarantee of limited intervention or an embargo might still be adequate to reassure the neighbors of such a dynamic nation, but a potential great power may fear any restriction on its ability to expand and to operate in a global theater. Moreover, a worldwide agreement may be possible only within a legal framework, which has some inherent bias toward a punitive sanction rather than a protective intervention. Nevertheless, there still might be situations in which protective intervention could be negotiable, such as in agreements on advanced conventional weaponry.

Military requirements for limited intervention. The form of limited intervention most like war—border defense—is like the collective sanction in requiring that large forces be able to overcome small ones. Unlike the collective sanction, however, limited intervention requires that the defense be dominant. The defense was not dominant with the technology of the Second World War, but it may be achieving supremacy with the emergence of the conventional warfare technology of precision-guided munitions and electronic surveillance of battlefields. The munitions tend to give a small unit, such as an infantry squad, a power comparable to that of such traditional offensive tools as tanks and aircraft. And the electronic surveillance greatly facilitates positional warfare. Thus, for conventional warfare, it is likely that limited intervention will be militarily feasible for some time.

The defense against a guerrilla force, however, may well be beyond the capability of limited intervention. Campaigns against guerrillas are usually lengthy and dangerous, often tempting the defender to take the sort of repressive action that would cause an internationally sanctioned intervention force to lose its legitimacy.

The presence of nuclear weapons does not absolutely preclude the use of limited intervention. It is conceivable that nuclear nations could conduct a conventional conflict, restrained by the fear of escalation; a nation is unlikely to use its nuclear weapons unless the conventional conflict threatens its national existence. Limited intervention, unlike the collective sanction, avoids threatening total defeat, and may therefore sometimes be feasible against a nuclear power. The intervenors would need to have some potential for nuclear retaliation, but this could well come from implicit understandings with nuclear nations.

Limited intervention can take a variety of forms other than border defense. Each form poses its own military issues. For example, a direct embargo against the international movement of arms to a treaty violator is probably an increasingly feasible military operation, especially if satellite reconnaissance is available. The rights and duties pertaining to intervention might be designed to increase military feasibility, as for example by allowing an intervention force under some conditions to attack certain categories of target within the violating nation. In designing such rights, it would be essential to avoid the political risk of escalating an internationally supported "neutral" operation into a general war.

The problem of ending an intervention is likely to be particularly subtle in a limited intervention. The collective sanction, if it fails to deter a violation, can conceivably—despite political obstacles—directly weaken the treaty violator. In peacekeeping and limited intervention, however, the intervention may have to continue indefinitely without necessarily weakening the violator's forces. Such an operation is likely to be both expensive and demoralizing. In that event, the best outcome would probably be a negotiated truce permitting some readjustment of arms levels. Even this prospect, it may be hoped, can sometimes still deter the potential violator.

In summary, limited intervention does not directly solve a conflict, nor does it directly punish a violator. What it does, and does much more credibly than the collective sanction, is create a significant deterrent to any policy involving the violation of an arms control agreement. It is more effective and easier to use than the collective sanction. It permits regional settlements that would otherwise be impossible. On the other hand, although it may be able to deter a minor nuclear weapons program, it cannot directly deter a major one. Nor is it likely to be very helpful in curbing dynamic nations that aspire to world power. It may sometimes require reinforcement by other forms of sanction; and it shares with collective security a bias toward the status quo. Nevertheless, limited intervention is a tool that could be extremely useful in the development of arms control to reduce regional conflict.

DIRECT INTERVENTION

In the two sanction patterns just discussed, the potential violator is conceived of as a single decision maker to be deterred. In this sense, both sanctions respect the traditions of national sovereignty. Direct intervention, the third pattern, ignores the national government and applies international power against the violation itself or against the individuals involved in the violation. For example, international forces might seize a specific nuclear facility[9] or bring to trial the director of an arms development program.[10] Thus the international authority, like a government, would exercise direct and specific powers over persons or things; to this extent the violating nation's sovereignty would be ignored. The rights of the intervenor could, however, be carefully delineated beforehand in order to reduce this infringement on sovereignty. Moreover, the military and human costs of such an intervention would usually be much lower than those of the other forms of international enforcement.

Several parallels to this concept of direct intervention already exist. The Nuremberg trials, though in many respects a form of "victor's justice," set a precedent for an international criminal court. The European Economic Community offers an example of an international entity that successfully enforces its decisions by judicial means in a number of politically charged areas. In Cyprus and the Congo, UN peacekeeping forces have had an authority similar to that of conventional police. Finally, the concept that the international ownership of nuclear facilities helps prevent the misuse of these facilities is ultimately based on a sense of respect that societies have for such an international presence. The task in this section, then, is to estimate whether these patterns of international authority can be extended to provide effective enforcement for arms control.

Forcible intervention. At one extreme, direct intervention could mean the establishment by an international organization of a raiding force empowered to seize or destroy nuclear materials, conventional weapons, testing facilities, or other contraband that violates an agreement. Such an action would resemble a covert operation or a police raid. The force would be prepared to confront local guards, but the operation would escalate to actual warfare only if there were broad resistance. The designers of such enforcement will clearly face the difficult choice of whether to emphasize military surprise or an orderly hearing before any action. One choice gives the intervening force the tactical benefit of surprise, and is perhaps preferable when the goal is to occupy or seize rather than to destroy. The other choice gives the offending nation a greater opportunity to explain its behavior, and is clearly preferable when there is doubt about the violation. In either case, an international decision-making body would have control over the action, which would probably be announced publicly as soon as it was executed. The international authority would require a small standing force, perhaps distributed around the world. It would also require excellent intelligence data.

Forcible intervention of this sort radically infringes on the traditions of national sovereignty. It is politically conceivable only if backed by a highly legitimate and enormously beneficial legislative agreement. The enforcement action would have to eliminate the violation directly and effectively, yet harm other interests as little as possible. Such sanctions could probably be used only in the control of weapons believed particularly heinous, such as nuclear and biological weapons. Moreover, the agreement being enforced would have to restrict all nations uniformly. This would be difficult in the nuclear area, except in regional agreements, because the risk of escalation might inhibit action against a major nuclear power.

Although this kind of enforcement has a certain appeal because of its potential effectiveness and its low military cost, it is politically unlikely. One political force that might favor its use, however, is the fear that stronger nations would conduct such raids unilaterally (à la Entebbe) if there were no available multilateral technique. Also, the concern about nuclear proliferation might possibly lead to support for a highly specialized international raiding force, say, to seize plutonium stockpiles under certain conditions. Nevertheless, in the foreseeable future these pressures are unlikely to override the strong barriers to the creation of raiding forces.

Judicial intervention. At the other extreme of this pattern of direct intervention, an international agency might seek to enforce arms control agreements by applying criminal sanctions directly against the individuals who violate a treaty. The court proceedings could be international; or, in the style of the EEC civil enforcement process, national courts might hold the hearings under the legal supervision of an international court. The prosecutorial responsibility could be assigned to an international authority.

Clearly, such arrangements are likely to be very weak. As in the case of the 1980 International Court of Justice decision to free the American hostages in Tehran, it would most often be physically impossible to enforce the decision within the offending nation. And in any event, a decree would be ineffective against a unified, highly motivated nation bent on the violation of the treaty. In the face of these weaknesses, no nation could rely on this means of enforcement to protect itself against a serious imbalance in forces.

Nevertheless, judicial intervention has a number of important political strengths. First, this form of enforcement gives a nation an easy way to terminate a violation. A judicial decision, unlike the 1980 Hague decision on the Tehran hostages, could place the responsibility for a violation on individuals rather than on a nation; perhaps this could stimulate domestic politics and diplomacy to generate pressure for concessions. For similar reasons, judicial techniques can handle minor or technical violations in ways less likely to evoke considerations of national prestige.

Second, the judicial technique can strengthen and build on those domestic political forces that oppose violation. Scientists, for example, might refrain from participating in illegal action because they respect the court or fear the possibility of court action. With such an international legal arrangement, domestic political pressures might lead a government to prosecute illegal terrorist activity it would otherwise support. Or data developed in an evidentiary hearing might strengthen domestic opposition to a violation.

Third, there may be ways to make the decrees effective despite a nation's unwillingness to comply. Foreign suppliers might be directed to cease sending materials to a nation that has disobeyed a decree. Foreign corporations might be required to direct their subsidiaries to comply. Accused individuals might be brought to trial when they travel outside the country.

Fourth, judicial techniques are the only ones that can offer any promise of coping with major nuclear powers and with heavily ideological conflict. For instance, a Middle East settlement that successfully dealt with the terrorist and irregular forces would almost certainly require judicial arrangements enforced in national or international courts. Finally, the only visible way that the United States and the Soviet Union can move toward agreements requiring sanctions is to create institutions or laws that gradually develop constituencies in each nation.

To develop such arrangements, it is first essential to recognize the difficulty of applying the criminal law in political areas. When a crime is regarded as political, a judicial sanction poses the dangers of creating a martyr and of arousing popular opposition from a wide variety of cultural and legal viewpoints. The problems of a politically oriented criminal law are difficult to overcome. Even in federal systems, the central government is often loath to try the leaders of a province or state. The criminal law is thus most likely to be useful in arms control when the legal goal is broadly shared by the international public. It may often be better for the international authority to forgo the criminal approach and instead to enjoin specific acts or to direct the forfeiture of specific objects.[11]

These judicial techniques are likely to be most effective in areas subject to many international economic linkages or to an overwhelming public opinion. This may be seen in areas related to arms control in which judicial enforcement arrangements are evolving: nuclear energy, where it is legally possible to cut off supplies, and terrorism, where a legal network is developing to provide for extradition and prosecution. Judicial intervention might also be an effective way to keep technical agreements from eroding under the pressures of technological change and minor violations. Judicial sanctions cannot now, however, be depended on as the primary means of enforcement in agreements whose violation would be strategically serious. Their main use would probably be in the control of research and in connection with legislative or regional agreements governing less significant weapons.

In spite of the immediate weakness of the judicial sanction, it could offer great benefits in the long run. If it could be successfully applied, its legitimacy and authority and, in turn, its effectiveness would increase. Its prospects are linked to a politics that could radically change the existing international order, by turning peoples and governments against specific evils, rather than one nation against another.

CONCLUSIONS

The use of sanctions adds somewhat to the range of arms control agreements that are politically conceivable. Particularly in regional cases, sanctions can sometimes make it strategically and politically possible for nations to accept agreements that impose moderately asymmetric force levels.

Several situations, however, are beyond the capability of arms control even with sanctions. Sanctions are too weak to force the acceptance of severely asymmetrical agreements. Sanctions are nearly helpless against most forms of popular, ideologically motivated warfare and against dynamic, expansionist nations. Finally, no formal international sanction of the traditional type is likely to be effective against a major nuclear power. These are the ultimate limits of arms control as it is currently conceived.

The sanctions that are useful in arms control are generally unlike that of an international police force. The most useful sanction is limited intervention, which is particularly applicable to regional settlements. For new forms of legislative arms control, the world must look to new forms of sanction, primarily the judicial. This sanction is based on the interpenetration of legal (and conceivably administrative) systems in such a way that it can gather political strength from within the nations involved. Closed societies like the Soviet Union will presumably resist the development of such sanctions, as may many of the newly independent nations of the developing world. Yet these sanctions, the only ones ever likely to be effective in important areas of legislative arms control, may become irresistible as economic and social interrelationships grow.

7. SALT and the Control of Bilateral Nuclear Deterrence

IF THE ANALYSIS in the preceding chapters is correct, it should satisfactorily explain the status of current negotiations and should suggest useful directions for arms control in the future. Moreover, by defining the limits of arms control, it should also suggest areas in which other kinds of policies are needed, and should give some hints of the desirable shape of such alternative policies.

SALT

On May 26, 1972, the United States and the USSR signed the SALT I accords:[1] a treaty to limit antiballistic missile systems to two on each side and a less formal agreement substantially freezing the number of offensive strategic nuclear missiles on each side. This agreement on offensive forces was supposed to last five years pending the negotiation of a more formal arrangement on offensive forces. Both agreements were to be verified by "national technical means," that is, by the technical intelligence systems of each nation. The parties undertook not to interfere with such systems operating "in a manner consistent with generally recognized principles of international law."

The SALT I negotiations can be traced back to a proposal for a strategic freeze put forward by President Johnson in early 1964, shortly after he took office. At the time, the United States was well ahead of the Soviet Union in offensive systems. It was proceeding with the deployment of 1,056 land-based missiles and 41 missile submarines, each carrying 16 missiles; the USSR had approximately 200 missiles and 120 submarine-launched missiles. It was four years before the two sides were ready to announce the beginning of negotiations; the announcement was then cancelled in the wake of the 1968 Soviet occupation of Czechoslovakia. After the Nixon administration, elected in the fall of that year, had extensively reviewed the United States position, the negotiations finally began in November 1969. They lasted another two and one-half years.

By the time the agreements were reached, the strategic positions of the two powers had shifted significantly from those obtaining in 1964. The USSR deployed large offensive forces in the 1967–72 period, reaching a total of over 1,500 land-based missiles and 29 missile submarines.[2] The United States did not increase the number of its missiles, but did increase the number of warheads by dividing the payload of each missile into "multiple independently targeted reentry vehicles" (MIRV's), which could be separately aimed at different targets.

The central compromise of the 1972 interim agreement on offensive forces was thus one in which the Soviet superiority in number and payload of missiles was balanced by the American superiority in number of warheads and in uncontrolled systems, such as long-range bombers and shorter-range aircraft able to attack the Soviet Union from aircraft carriers and bases abroad. The United States also gained a halt to the rapid Soviet deployment. For the five-year period, there could be no serious imbalance, because the USSR was well behind in MIRV technology and the number of larger Soviet missiles was specifically limited by the agreement. The five-year term of the agreement presumably reflected the Soviet fear of American advances in uncontrolled systems and the American fear of a Soviet conversion of its large missile payload into MIRV's.

The ABM treaty was meant to be more enduring and was

therefore more formal. The USSR had started to place an ABM system around Moscow in the 1960's, but had slowed work on it. In 1969, after several false starts and an extremely close Senate vote, the United States also approved the construction of ABM systems around several strategic American missile sites. The U.S. Congress had been swayed by the argument that the plan for the deployment of ABM's could be a useful bargaining chip in SALT. Later, however, the government concluded that the ABM was at best a marginal investment, and that its deployment might speed up the arms competition. The Soviet Union may have reached the same conclusions; and it also felt that the United States had a lead in ABM technology. The obvious compromise (short of no ABM system at all) would have been one ABM system on each side, but this was viewed as impractical because ABM systems defending cities differ strategically from those defending offensive missiles. The ABM treaty of 1972 compromised by allowing each side to have one of each kind. This treaty was readily ratified. Congress never authorized the city-defense system allowed by the treaty, and in 1974 the two nations agreed on a protocol—by then not controversial—under which neither would build the second ABM system.[3]

The offensive force agreement, however, gave rise to substantial controversy in the United States. The numerical inequality between the United States and the Soviet Union dismayed Senator Jackson (who may have been supported by President Nixon). The upshot was an amendment to the congressional resolution of approval requesting "the president to seek a future treaty that . . . would not limit the United States to levels of intercontinental strategic forces inferior to the limits provided for the Soviet Union."[4] Moreover, although the key compromises in the final negotiations had been made by the president and by Kissinger, nearly all the key American SALT negotiators and Arms Control and Disarmament Agency staff were replaced soon afterwards.

Negotiations proceeded with a view to converting the offensive forces agreement into a permanent treaty, but Presi-

dent Nixon was unable to achieve any significant arrangement before being politically weakened by the Watergate
scandal. President Ford could do little more; he achieved a
potentially significant outline agreement at Vladivostok in
late 1974,[5] but was unable to convert it into a treaty. Under the
Vladivostok accord, each side would have been permitted a
stated, large number of strategic delivery vehicles, of which a
stated number could carry MIRV's. Thus a formal parity
would be restored, but at a very high level. Many arms controllers objected because these force levels represented no
significant reduction. And many from the U.S. military
feared that the Vladivostok accords would allow the Soviet
Union to place high-accuracy MIRV's on enough large missiles for it to be able to destroy most of the American land-
based missiles on a first strike.

Not only did the outline accord fail to attract strong American support; it posed many specific difficulties for the
negotiators. The key difficulty was probably the cruise missile, a small unmanned aircraft with a very sophisticated
guidance system. The cruise missile can be launched from
sites as unobtrusive as a submarine's torpedo tube and it can
fly a great distance with high accuracy. Since the United
States was well ahead in the technology of the cruise missile,
a strong constituency formed to back the weapon. Thus the
United States argued that the Vladivostok accord permitted
the development and deployment of the cruise missiles,
whereas the Soviet Union took the opposite position. Political
difficulties emerged as well, the result of several factors: allegations that the Soviet Union had violated SALT I; a much
more rapid advance of the permitted Soviet strategic technologies than anticipated; the Soviet intervention in Angola
and later in the Horn of Africa. Congress hardened its position in a reaction against the entire concept of détente. Not
surprisingly, the Nixon-Ford administration was never able to
put together a treaty package acceptable to both Congress
and the Soviet Union.

With the offensive force agreement's 1977 deadline nearing, President Carter attempted a radically different approach during his first year in office. He offered the Soviet Union a choice of two proposals. One would sharply cut strategic forces and restrict the cruise missile as well. The other would be essentially a holding arrangement based on the Vladivostok accord, but with the cruise missile unrestrained, presumably to be maintained as a bargaining chip for later substantial cuts. The Soviet Union angrily rejected both proposals. It was already troubled by the new administration's emphasis on human rights and by the public way in which the proposals had been presented. In addition, although the details of the proposals were clearly subject to negotiation, the proposal for cutting forces was spelled out in such a way as to place the Soviet Union at a serious disadvantage.

After both sides had cooled off, the two nations agreed on the outlines of a three-part compromise package. The most formal part would be a treaty following the Vladivostok pattern but leaving the cruise missile and the corresponding Soviet systems uncontrolled. By a protocol, these systems would be restricted for a short period of two or three years. The final component of the package would be a statement of principles favoring more severe arms reductions. The United States would thus retain the ability to resume the full cruise missile program as a bargaining chip to achieve substantial reductions in subsequent negotiations. In view of the progress toward the assembling of this package, both sides were willing to continue honoring the SALT I agreement, even after its formal expiration.

President Carter and Chairman Brezhnev finally signed the entire package on June 18, 1979.[6] The package followed the anticipated pattern of compromise. The central treaty was an elaborate document embodying many common understandings and agreed statements that defined comprehensive limits and a number of sublimits on offensive strategic systems. Of these limits, only the comprehensive ones, based on the Vladivostok accord but due to fall by about 6 percent at the beginning of 1981, would require any actual elimination of existing forces (this being a small reduction of Soviet forces). The protocol, to be in effect until the end of 1981, restricted the deployment of mobile ICBM's and sea-based or land-based cruise missiles with longer than a specified range. The restriction on the corresponding Soviet system, an aircraft whose effective operating range was subject to dispute, was contained in a letter given by Brezhnev to Carter stating that the production rate of the aircraft would not be increased. The entire package reflected unusual candor in describing each nation's forces and in stating the code names and current force levels of each weapon.

The U.S. administration had prepared well to meet the early technical arguments on such issues as verification. Moreover, it supported the construction of an elaborate new missile system, the M-X, to replace components of the Minuteman, the silo-based system that was becoming increasingly vulnerable as Soviet missiles improved. Nevertheless, many in the Senate still called for reservations to the treaty, some of which would have made the package unacceptable to the USSR. Floor debate in the Senate was continually postponed. The administration took a rather defensive posture, arguing less that SALT II was desirable in itself than that SALT II would prevent a greater buildup. But the position of the administration was shaken by an unexpected leak of information concerning the presence of Soviet forces in Cuba, which raised questions of Soviet good faith and evoked the usual fears in the Senate.

Supporters of SALT argued that the value of the treaty did not depend on Soviet behavior outside the strategic area. Though this argument against "linkage" was strategically accurate, it did not reflect the political realities. At the end of the year, the attention of the United States shifted to the Iranian hostage crisis. The effect of that crisis on SALT was unclear, except that the situation increased American support for military preparedness. At the same time, the Soviet Union turned its attention to the decision by NATO to deploy cruise missiles. One Soviet commentator, discussing the cruise missile issue, dismissed SALT II on the ground that "it would fail to be ratified and, even if approved, would not constitute an advance in Russian-American relations."[7] It was no surprise when President Carter withdrew the treaty early in 1980 in response to the Soviet invasion of Afghanistan.

THE MOTIVATIONS UNDERLYING SALT I

The history of SALT I confirms many of the views presented in this book regarding the political requirements for arms control. There was a need for parity. As long as the United States had a clear superiority, no agreement was possible; only when the USSR had roughly caught up was an agreement achieved.[8] The agreements restricted only those developments that neither side wanted—each side had essentially built as many missiles as it wished and had grown doubtful about ABM technology. MIRV technology, the new direction that interested both sides, was not restricted, which demonstrates the difficulty of stopping a technology-intensive arms competition.

Nevertheless, the SALT I agreements are among the most politically significant arms control agreements ever achieved. For this reason, it is desirable to examine the different motivations behind these agreements. One, arguably, is a strategic theory, the theory of deterrence, by which each side would gain from joint limitations. Another, still more arguably, is a desire to reduce the economic costs of the strategic arms competition. Finally, the crucial motivation comes from the coalescence of broad but different American and Soviet political goals.

The strategic theory, more strongly held in the United States, begins with the premise that no nation will launch a major nuclear attack (the first strike) if its target nation has the credible capability to retaliate (the second strike) after absorbing the attack. The risk that the second strike would unacceptably damage the attacker's homeland deters the initial attack. When a nation has such a second-strike capability, it effectively holds the other side's cities as hostages against an attack on its own cities. It follows that a military balance would be unstable if either side could possibly attack in a way that would prevent the other from retaliating. This might be possible, for example, if the target nation's strategic force consisted entirely of unprotected missiles that could readily be destroyed. If both sides' forces were vulnerable, either might be tempted in a crisis to make a preemptive strike.

By making agreements designed to avoid these instabilities, both participants gain security against nuclear war and against the need for continued weapons construction. Moreover, for some analysts the credible ability to make a second strike is all that is needed strategically. The strategic theory thus offers a doctrine of sufficiency, a reasonable way to define the minimum necessary force levels. Above this minimum, any restraint in building forces need not be viewed as endangering national security.

For many American analysts, the ABM agreement of SALT I was intended to increase strategic stability in this manner. The ABM is not effective enough to stop all attacks; if it were, the principle of deterrence could be replaced by a stability based on an invulnerable defense that would dominate the offense.[9] Even an imperfect ABM might, however, threaten the stability of deterrence, because it is relatively more effective against small attacks than large ones. Against a first strike, an ABM system would probably be saturated. In a second strike, however, the number of incoming missiles would be much smaller and more commensurate with the capability of the ABM. If the introduction of ABM's created instability, each side could respond by increasing the number of its offensive missiles; but an intense arms competition would then be the result. In severely restricting the ABM, both sides would gain by avoiding the choice between instability and further arms construction.

Some Soviet strategists may now accept a similar logic; but any such acceptance came rather late, possibly even during the SALT negotiations. Soviet strategists have historically been oriented toward defense, and at one time may have believed in the naive doctrine that defensive systems are harmless and offensive systems are threatening. The Soviet Union may also have wanted to discourage competition in an area in which the United States seemed to be ahead. But even if this was the Soviet motivation for the ABM agreement, it encouraged a result consistent with American strategic theories.

The ABM treaty has been described as the unprecedented decision by two nations not to defend their populations, a decision with enormous political implications. (Most commentators believe that the remaining ABM's have a trivial strategic effect.) And to the extent that deterrence theory is correct, the agreement does reduce the risk of war. By preventing a competition between ABM systems and technologies designed to penetrate these systems, the treaty may also restrain the growth of nuclear forces and help avoid destabilizing technological surprises.

In the offensive forces agreement, the theory of deterrence is much less clearly applicable, particularly because Soviet strategic theory is so murky. The Soviet decision makers are probably as horrified as anyone by the specter of nuclear war. The Soviet military planners probably recognize the desirability of maintaining a second-strike capability. But the Soviet strategists seem less convinced than many in the United States of the adequacy of either a second-strike capability or a force level defined according to a second-strike criterion. Thus, in respect to offensive weapons, there is neither a strategic consensus nor a confluence of different strategic theories favorable to agreement. This is part of the difficulty in the offensive area that has arisen in both SALT I and SALT II; it is also part of the reason for the continued Soviet development of offensive weapons that are permitted by SALT I.

On the American side, the economic motivation was probably unimportant in SALT I, except for the hope symbolized by SALT that strategic expenditures might ultimately be reduced. SALT may have slowed or even prevented some procurement of weapons. But in the short term, it encouraged other military expenditures, for in seeking the support of the military for SALT I, the administration made commitments to support the development of the Trident submarine and the B-1 bomber.[10] The administration argued to Congress that these weapons were needed as bargaining chips for SALT II, just as the ABM had been defended as a bargaining chip for SALT I. The economic issues, however, received little consideration in the SALT debates.

On the Soviet side, though the evidence is weak, the economic motivation may have been more important. The Soviet government may have felt itself under substantial economic pressure,[11] facing a severe need to transfer resources from the military and heavy industry sectors to the consumer sector, as well as to expend resources against China. It is possible that in 1971 the Soviet leaders decided on a new policy of importing science and technology from the West and of normalizing relations with the West toward this end.[12] Some Western analysts have suggested that SALT was essentially the Soviet quid pro quo for the West's willingness to liberalize trade. Or SALT can be seen as part of a general détente that less explicitly permitted the liberalization of trade. Even if this economic analysis of SALT I is correct, however, the powerful position of the military within the Soviet bureaucracy suggests that arms control may prove as ineffective in slowing Soviet arms expenditures as it has been in slowing them in the United States. Perhaps arms negotiations are in effect simply a way to coordinate the demands to be placed on the two nations' taxpayers.

Clearly, strategic and economic motivations do not adequately explain the SALT accords. President Nixon chose to emphasize different motivations in presenting the agreements to the American public: "These agreements open the opportunity for a new and more constructive U.S.-Soviet relationship, characterized by negotiated settlement of differences, rather than by the hostility and confrontation of decades past. These accords offer tangible evidence that mankind need not live forever in the dark shadow of nuclear war. They provide renewed hope that men and nations working together can succeed in building a lasting peace."[13]

In 1972, after a quarter century of cold war and a widespread disillusion with the Vietnam War, almost any symbol of détente appealed to much of the American public. Arms control had become especially popular by 1972. Many Americans had come to believe that coexistence with the USSR was possible. They preferred the hope of friendship to the continuation of rivalry. In this context, the president presented SALT as a symbol of détente.

The American desire for détente was reflected in Kissinger's global strategy, as well as in public opinion. Kissinger apparently believed that the Soviet Union was still a growing, dynamic power and that relations with the Soviet Union were the most important aspect of American foreign relations. To counter the Soviet Union, the Kissinger strategy tried to build a network of relationships that would encourage Soviet restraint and give the United States leverage to help maintain that restraint. This policy included efforts to get the Soviet Union to accept explicit formal restraints, and efforts to develop an especially close working relationship with the Soviet leaders.

Thus, in the Basic Principles of Relations agreed upon in 1972 at the same summit meeting as SALT I, the two nations agreed that "in the nuclear age there is no alternative to conducting their mutual relations on the basis of peaceful coexistence." They declared that "efforts to obtain unilateral advantage at the expense of the other . . . are inconsistent with [their] objectives," and that the "prerequisites for maintaining and strengthening peaceful relations between the USA and the USSR are the recognition of the security interests of

the Parties based on the principle of equality and the renunciation of the use or threat of force."[14] These principles are
quite close to the traditional concept of spheres of influence.
The two nations were to seek to coordinate their policies, in
effect exercising a dual hegemony based on diplomatic ties
between the two leading nations. The nuclear balance would
be shaped so that neither power would be seriously tempted
to use nuclear threats to influence regional political crises.

The USSR, too, was interested in peaceful coexistence and
in normalizing relations with the United States. The Soviet
press laid great emphasis on the American acceptance of
peaceful coexistence in the Basic Principles.[15] The Soviet desire for détente may have derived in part from the economic
motivations already discussed, and in the eyes of the Soviet
leaders it may have been merely a tactic. But with high probability, there was a long-term underlying Soviet desire to
maintain a bilateral power system in the world.[16] The USSR
clearly wants to ensure that China does not become the equal
of the two superpowers or challenge the Soviet leadership of
the world Communist movement. Although the relationship
between the Soviet Union's SALT policy and its China policy
is not clear, the two policies are almost certainly linked in the
minds of the Soviet leaders. Several commentators have
noted that the announcement of SALT coincided with the
opening of Sino-Soviet negotiations on border questions.[17]
Later, Kissinger's opening to China was an important element
in the SALT I bargaining. From the Soviet point of view, there
were also indications that SALT became possible only after
the Non-Proliferation Treaty had strengthened the barriers to
Germany's becoming a nuclear power.[18] In general, the Soviet position on SALT probably rested on a judgment that the
USSR could have more power as one of two world leaders
than as one of perhaps five. The Soviet Union may eventually
seek superiority over the United States; but in the 1970's, its
goal was to codify both its newfound parity with the United
States and the superiority of the two over all challengers.

These Soviet motivations dovetailed with Kissinger's strategy. A major U.S.-Soviet bilateral agreement would help confirm the special status of the two nations and the special relationship between them. SALT gave the Soviet Union a symbol of its parity and shared hegemony, and it gave the United States a restraint on Soviet power. Building further on the Soviet Union's economic motivation, Kissinger entered into an alliance with the Soviet leaders to help stabilize the Soviet system economically. In return, he would acquire another form of leverage over the Soviet Union. SALT I was the paradigm of a settlement agreement.

SALT II AND THE FUTURE OF SALT

SALT I left a clear agenda for SALT II: the conversion of the numerical freeze on offensive forces of SALT I into a full treaty. In the time since SALT I, however, technology has evolved. And more significantly, the political framework shaped by SALT I generated only a weak thrust toward SALT II.

The key new strategic issue is missile vulnerability. This problem derives from the development of very accurate guidance systems that make it possible to use strategic missiles effectively to destroy fixed, land-based missiles. Even a small nuclear warhead is powerful enough to destroy any missile silo if the warhead explodes close enough to the silo. Because guidance technology is likely to advance more rapidly than silo-hardening technology, any missiles in fixed positions can be expected to remain vulnerable. In fact, they are becoming obsolete.

The vulnerability of land-based missiles does not necessarily mean that the United States and the USSR have lost their second-strike capability and are therefore vulnerable to a preemptive first strike. Even if all land-based missiles were destroyed by a first strike, the submarine and bomber-based systems can be expected to remain capable of retaliation. A few experts deny this, however, pointing out that these mobile systems can also become vulnerable.[19]

In the United States, a more sophisticated and controversial point is being widely argued. According to the argument, the Soviet Union, after equipping its large missiles with many high-accuracy warheads, might be able to attack and destroy most U.S. missiles without greatly harming the cities. The remaining U.S. missile systems, such as those on submarines, would be accurate enough to destroy Soviet cities but not Soviet missiles. But the United States would be deterred from attacking the Soviet cities by the fact that the American cities would still be at stake. Thus, after its intitial strike against the American missiles, the USSR could dictate terms based on a massive strategic superiority. This argument ignores the doubts that decision makers are likely to have about the effectiveness of such massive but controlled destruction; and it ignores the deterrent effect on decision makers of the prospect of any kind of strategic nuclear war. Moreover, it may be technically impossible to conduct the initial antimissile attack without doing so much harm to cities as to make retaliation a political necessity.

Nevertheless, it is understandable that each side might want to prepare for a situation in which deterrence has failed. What each seeks is a "war-fighting capability," the ability to conduct a nuclear war on a restricted scale that emphasizes military targets, rather than on an apocalyptic scale that emphasizes civilian targets. The difficulty is that any such capability also appears to the opponent as a first-strike capability; a nation can hardly deploy a system designed to preempt in the middle of a nuclear war without raising the possibility of a preemptive first strike. The war-fighting capability necessarily threatens an opponent's retaliatory forces, and thus calls deterrence into question.

The war-fighting concept also shatters the ceilings on force levels that are logically feasible under the deterrence theory. Under the classical theory, the only necessity is an assured second-strike capability; larger forces are irrelevant. But for war-fighting, larger forces might be useful. Some also argue that a superiority in the level of forces increases the diplomatic bargaining power available in times of crisis. The side with the larger nuclear force is more likely, under this argument, to be able to persuade the other to back down and to persuade third parties to accede to its wishes. Proponents of this position point to the Cuban missile crisis of 1962, in which the Soviet Union, then the nation with the weaker nuclear forces, did back down; critics argue that it was not the strategic superiority of the United States that shaped the Cuban outcome, but the greater availability of American conventional forces.

Thus, beyond making deterrence more difficult to maintain technically, the issue of missile vulnerability undercuts—in the eyes of many—the ability of either side to accept any inferiority in missiles. The emergence of this problem coincides with the development during the SALT period of large Soviet programs for the construction of offensive missiles. Moreover, it is possible the Soviet strategists lean more toward a war-fighting theory than a deterrence theory. As a result, it becomes easy to argue that the USSR has insidious motives in SALT, and that it is laying the groundwork for a preemptive MIRV capability or for an increase in its diplomatic power.[20] At the same time, the United States has strategic programs and theories that give Soviet strategists grounds for a similar suspicion.

It will not be easy for SALT to resolve this issue of missile vulnerability. The unratified 1979 SALT II agreement left the issue essentially unaffected, and also left the United States moving toward the deployment of the M-X, a high-accuracy missile system with special basing arrangements to reduce its vulnerability. Although it might be possible to define a future balance of forces that satisfies each side under its different strategic criteria, it seems more likely that future agreements will leave war-fighting capabilities uncontrolled or only indirectly restrained. A more dramatic resolution of the problem of the vulnerability of land-based missiles might be to abolish land-based missiles altogether. This may be the only strategically logical solution; but the bureaucratic politics of this move would be extremely difficult, for the Soviet Union has been investing heavily in such missiles. When President Carter moved toward this approach in his early proposal for a major reduction in forces, it drew an angry reaction from the Soviet Union.

The cruise missile poses quite different strategic questions, but these questions will be no easier to resolve. This weapon has the range and accuracy required for an attack against missile sites, but is currently slow enough that many doubt its usefulness for a first strike. The cruise missile can be based and launched in many ways, and can thus be made relatively invulnerable to attack and even undetectable by verification. Moreover, the weapon is relatively cheap.

In the maintenance of a bilateral strategic arms control system, these properties of the cruise missile could be helpful. The weapon could be the core of an invulnerable second-strike capability. Though it provides a war-fighting capability, the worst aspect of that capability—the accompanying capability for a first strike—might be avoidable, perhaps by prohibiting the development of supersonic cruise missiles. Moreover, the weapon could conceivably be effective against a missile silo even by using a nonnuclear warhead; this might prove significant, though no one has yet shown how this property could be used to help decrease the role of nuclear weapons in deterrence. But what causes very serious complications is that this weapon is impossible to verify except by highly intrusive means. Understandably, the Soviet Union wants either to acquire the cruise missile technology, in which it lags, or to obtain a commitment by the United States not to develop the technology further. Many in the United States, however, enchanted by the military potential of the weapon, are hesitant to give it up. The 1979 Protocol, reflecting these pressures, prohibited the deployment of the cruise missile for about two and a half years, but did not prohibit the testing of it.

The most significant impact of the cruise missile technology, apart from the verification problem it poses, is that the weapon can be important to other nations besides the two superpowers. France decided on a cruise missile development program as early as 1977.[21] The cruise missile, even without nuclear warheads, might eventually give emerging great powers of the Third World some strategic capability against the United States or the Soviet Union. This potential of the cruise missile is clearly important to the problem of nuclear proliferation and to North-South arms control in general.

In the context of SALT, the cruise missile has special relevance to Europe. Precisely because the cruise missile offers lesser powers a strategic potential against the superpowers, Western Europe is looking to it as a way to counterbalance the SS-20's, deployed by the USSR in the 1970's—the SS-20 is an intermediate range ballistic missile capable of reaching targets in Western Europe. In the SALT II negotiations, the Soviet Union sought to insert a clause prohibiting the United States from transferring technology to its allies. The "non-circumvention" clause actually negotiated, however, is not interpreted by the United States as prohibiting it from making arrangements to place NATO cruise missiles in Western Europe; and indeed, such arrangements were agreed to at the end of 1979.

The issue of the cruise missile is not clearly resolved. Western Europe has generally urged the ratification of SALT II in the hope that there will be a SALT III to cover this "gray area" of nuclear systems in the USSR and Europe targeted on each other's territory. If SALT resumes, the Western European interest can perhaps be represented in side negotiations between the United States and its allies while the United States alone negotiates with the Soviet Union. In the long run, however, it may be necessary to expand SALT to include a number of European nations. This is desirable because the "gray area" systems involved probably present a greater threat to peace than the traditional strategic systems. But it is also difficult. It would make the negotiations more complex, and would pose some risk of creating discord within the Western alliance.[22] Clearly, the talks would have to work toward a European nuclear settlement rather than toward a special relationship between the United States and the USSR. The bilateralism that appeals so greatly to the Soviet Union would be lost, and perhaps with it some of the exchange of strategic information between the two superpowers.

The economic factors that may have contributed to SALT I have also become weaker. At the end of the 1970's, the United States was both more inclined to increase its military expenditures and more sophisticated in evaluating the economic impact of arms control than it was earlier in the decade. Over the same period, the Soviet Union also showed a willingness to increase its military expenditures significantly. The possibility that economic pressure will favor SALT is further diminished by economic and technological asymmetries between the United States and the Soviet Union. From the Soviet point of view, the Soviet Union gained a form of parity by means of SALT I, and then lost it as a result of the American technological advance in cruise missiles. To the Soviet Union, technological parity may be as important as numerical parity; after the United States acquired MIRV's, for example, the Soviet Union insisted on its being able to develop MIRV's too. Other comparable issues are likely to arise as long as the basic Soviet approach to arms development is to improve existing weapons incrementally and the basic American approach is to develop radically new concepts. The United States seeks to maintain its technological superiority; the Soviet Union seeks to gain numerical superiority. Technology may be out of control.

Finally, and most important, the political framework underlying SALT has radically changed. From the Western standpoint, détente has all but collapsed. The Soviet Union's intervention in Africa and Afghanistan, its continuing violations of human rights, and its near violations of SALT I have made many in the West suspicious of the Soviet relationship. It is in large part this suspicion—a reaction against both the Soviet Union and against Kissinger's policies—that has made the Senate so wary of SALT II. Nor did the détente policy turn out particularly well for the Soviet Union. The USSR received relatively little technology from the West under détente, and it lost politically in both the Middle East and Eastern Europe. At the same time, the West became unwilling to accommodate the international interests that had moved the Soviets toward SALT I. It seems clear that Carter preferred a much broader diffusion of power through the world, rather than the centralized hegemony that Kissinger and Brezhnev had sought.

This international political problem was reflected by the Soviet domestic politics. In a sense, the Kissinger strategy was to permit the Soviet leadership to stabilize its domestic economy in return for SALT. Any possible negative consequences for Soviet dissidents were viewed as unfortunate short-term side effects. Carter's human rights policies, however, were directed against the Soviet leaders' position. Conceivably, this strategy might increase the pressure on the Soviet leaders to enter into further arms control; more likely, it will harden them against reaching agreement. The strategy must ultimately depend on the emergence of new Soviet leaders who are more liberal and more willing to enter into a genuine détente based on a broader domestic political consensus.

From this review, it is hard to be very optimistic about the future of SALT. As Chapter Four implies, an overall numerical limitation on arms is generally an ineffective way to terminate a technological arms competition. More broadly, the political factors that make for a settlement agreement only rarely encourage further agreement; it is hard to settle a conflict twice. Although a resumption of SALT may help avoid instability caused by some particular deployment, its actual benefits in arms reduction are likely to be minimal. Moreover,

SALT has focused the attention of the two superpowers on relative arms levels, and this is not necessarily the best focus for their relationship to have.

ALTERNATIVES TO SALT

Long before the withdrawal of SALT II from Senate consideration, some commentators had already concluded that SALT could no longer be expected to work toward explicit restrictions on the U.S.-Soviet strategic arms competition. Instead, they urged that the negotiations be redirected. One new approach is to emphasize controls on "missions," rather than on weapons.[23] The idea is that the nations might, for example, give up the mission of attacking each other's land-based strategic forces. Another approach is for SALT to become a forum for coordination and discussion; this might help the two sides avoid the sort of strategic planning that creates serious unintended provocations or misinterpretations. Negotiations aiming at the reduction of forces have proved nearly counterproductive; but consultation still might be desirable.

The first approach may be responsive to technological problems, but it seems likely to pose many of the same political problems as past efforts. The second approach probably goes too far. In a few areas, the United States and the Soviet Union may usefully pursue fairly traditional ideas of arms control when their relations improve again. One is the control of strategic technical developments that may spread to the rest of the world. The U.S.-Soviet strategic arms competition has proved to be an engine for generating new concepts in weaponry that sometimes upset military stability elsewhere. The cruise missile is the obvious current example; the thermonuclear weapon is an example from the past, and there may be other examples in the future. There is no doubt that the two superpowers will always find it difficult to control military research.[24] As other nations increase their power, however, the diffusion of military technology may become a serious enough threat to both great powers that the two will be driven to success in the control of new technologies.

An equally useful—but very difficult—approach is to work toward the designing of regional confrontation so as to reduce the risk of nuclear escalation. Strategic theory has often conceived of strategic stability without much attention to diplomatic situations in which strategic weapons might actually be used. If nuclear war comes, it will almost certainly be by the escalation of a regional crisis, rather than by a deliberate attack in a time of little tension. To analyze the process of escalation is extremely complex, however. The differences in the structure of the deterrent forces on either side—such as whether or not either has a war-fighting capability—are likely to be significant in the risk of escalation. Escalation is perhaps more likely if strategic forces are based in areas where conventional military action is conceivable. Likewise, the risk seems higher if there are missiles like the cruise missile that can be used with either conventional or nuclear warheads. These are only hypotheses, for the theory in this area is much weaker than in the area of abstract global stability.

One can conceive of useful agreements dealing with these issues. The agreements could affect the deployment of tactical nuclear weapons, the level and characteristics of nuclear weapons based in or committed to certain regions, the command and control doctrines associated with these weapons, and perhaps even the strategic doctrines for their use. The negotiations of such agreements would be extremely difficult, because there would be divergence between the United States and its allies, as well as between the United States and the USSR. Moreover, so long as the defense of Europe and Japan depends on a threat to use nuclear weapons, any efforts to preclude nuclear war may increase the risk of conventional war. Some agreements, therefore, might be feasible only if a political settlement in the region were also reached; and parallel agreements dealing with the balance of conventional forces might also be needed. Despite these difficulties, this direction is probably the most useful one to take for actually preventing large-scale nuclear warfare; it is therefore one to be seriously considered should SALT resume.

Other first steps—more limited but still useful—might be taken to protect regional stability. In Europe, for example, a multilateral military forum might be helpful, as might a European role in either the U.S.-Soviet Standing Consultative Commission or a follow on to SALT. Agreements designed to reduce incidents involving conventional forces might help limit the circumstances in which escalation can occur. The U.S.-Soviet agreement for the prevention of naval incidents has been called one of the most successful arms control agreements. A comparable arrangement is conceivable in a number of regions: Europe, the Middle East, and even Africa. If such incident-prevention agreements were made multilateral, the resulting restraints could be applicable to other nuclear nations as well.

Such steps as these, though worthwhile, are all that can be expected from an approach like SALT unless new Soviet leaders are much more cooperative. And in any event, these are weak substitutes for a major reduction in nuclear forces. In the short run, the risk of U.S.-Soviet nuclear war is small, and nuclear deterrence may be the only possible interim response to the existence of nuclear weapons. But a long-term reliance on deterrence can bring enormous costs if a decision maker dealing with nuclear weapons fails to act wisely. And there is a real risk that some such decision maker will, in fact, act erroneously or madly. The constant responsibility for a hair-trigger nuclear response may warp the judgment of decision makers. A messianically motivated decision maker may not be restrained by the prospect of retaliation. Moreover, the concept of nuclear hostages, although perhaps redeemed by the greater immorality of its alternatives, is fundamentally immoral. For these reasons, the control and reduction of nuclear weapons remain a desirable long-term goal.

To plot a politically conceivable strategy for nuclear reductions, it is useful to begin by imagining a world in which such reductions have already substantially occurred. Nuclear technology would not be forgotten, so there would always be a nuclear deterrence of a sort: nations would deter one another from the construction of nuclear weapons, as well as from the use of existing ones. This deterrence at the production stage is likely to be unstable in the face of such threats as concealed stockpiles and covert development programs. Moreover, deterrence is generally unstable at low force levels, because at those levels the statistical probability is relatively great that all the opponent's weapons will be destroyed by a first strike.* Although there are arguments both ways, this instability might also spill over into conventional war, perhaps less likely to be deterred by the possibility of escalation. These risks would probably not be significant unless forces were greatly reduced,[25] but they would ultimately have to be faced.

Except perhaps as a reaction to nuclear war or to a horrible crisis, it is unlikely that an agreement of the settlement type could lead to a world like that just described, and impossible for a settlement to be stable in such a world. No type of formal, nation-to-nation enforcement would be adequate. Instead, legislative restraints are needed, built on broad support within each nation. These domestically supported restraints might apply to either the use or the construction of nuclear weapons. The only plausible sanction for these restraints is direct enforcement. The world is currently far from any such restraints or any effective enforcement techniques. But the tasks of building these restraints and laying the political groundwork for enforcement structures are the tasks to which strategic arms control can most usefully turn.

---

*Suppose the probability that a single missile can destroy an opponent's missile is 0.8. If each side had ten missiles, there would be only about a 10 percent chance of destroying all the opponent's missiles with a preemptive attack (0.8^{10} or 0.107), and a 90 percent chance that at least one missile would survive for retaliation. On the other hand, with only two missiles on a side the chance that no missiles would survive an attack is 64 percent. The deterrence is much more effective in the first case.

Controls that restrict the *use* of nuclear weapons, and not just the *existence* of them, are probably an essential part of any ultimate arrangement. In theory, controlling the use of the weapons could solve the problem of instability at low force levels. It would contribute to strategic stability, for example, if all nuclear firing circuits were routed through an international control point.[26] If the goal were the elimination of nuclear weapons, then, all firing circuits could be broken at once. Alternatively, some weapons might remain independent to give stability against any covert nuclear deployment, with the international control arrangements ensuring that the legitimately retained nuclear weapons not be misused. This approach to nuclear arms control suggests that the emergence of multilateral restrictions on use will be an essential concomitant of deep arms reductions, and possibly a source of political support for them. The use restrictions are precisely the kind of law that must begin to penetrate the nuclear nations for arms control to be politically feasible. The Soviet interest in such restrictions is dubious; but the Soviet government is perhaps more likely to accept first steps toward use restrictions, intended to prevent nuclear war, than to accept force level restrictions that require it to confront directly its powerful military-industrial complex. Thus there may be great value in reorienting negotiations toward use restrictions.

First steps toward use controls have already been taken, and have often received broad support. The "Hot Line" between Moscow and Washington is in some respects a use restriction; its creation contained at least the seeds of a mutual promise that nuclear weapons would not be used without prior consultation. In 1978 the United States went further, stating that save for exceptions designed to maintain a nuclear umbrella over Europe, it would not use nuclear weapons against nonnuclear nations. Such a commitment, like any use restriction today, is unenforceable; no one can be confident it will be honored. It may, however, provide some restraining force, and it does amount to the beginning of a law that could gain in moral authority. Moreover, it discourages national leaders from threatening to use nuclear weapons, and thus may weaken the incentive for other nations to acquire these weapons.

There is a range of further plausible measures toward use control that might contribute both to arms control and to the maintenance of peace in general. One idea is to use diplomacy to control the use of nuclear weapons, perhaps by a formal or informal agreement to consult with the Security Council before any use of nuclear weapons or to make a report to the council on any nuclear or near-nuclear incident. Observers from opposing nations might be stationed in one another's strategic force control room to provide a mechanism of reassurance in times of crisis; such exchanges would be a major political step toward more effective international authority over the use of nuclear weapons. Agreements to avoid provocative nonnuclear actions could also be beneficial.

Another direction that might be taken is to control nuclear weapons by domestic constitutional procedures. In the United States, even though nuclear war is the form of war likely to affect the public the most, it is the one form of war effectively exempt from congressional approval. If congressional approval were required for a first use of nuclear weapons (as opposed to a retaliatory use), it might be reassuring to foreign governments without weakening American security; and depending on how Europe evolves, it might add to world stability. It would be desirable if all nuclear powers were to impose comparable restrictions on themselves. The constitutional form these might take in the Soviet Union is unclear; Soviet policymaking has so far been securely insulated from outside lobbying. If any such domestic restraint were in effect in the Soviet Union, it would be a major step toward the application of international rules there; indeed the very suggestion of such an arrangement to the Soviet Union might set in motion the Soviet political forces needed to generate such a restraint. And experience with use controls and the evolution of constituencies supporting them might eventually permit the negotiation of agreements renouncing specific military missions.

The problems of penetrating Soviet society and building internal Soviet restraints are the most intractable obstacles to the development of an arms control rooted in both domestic and international political forces. In the face of the Soviet Union's resistance to external pressures, a policy something like President Carter's early policy is perhaps the only possible course. The object of this policy is to encourage the emergence of new Soviet leaders who will renounce the current Soviet pursuit of global hegemony. Conceivably, economic pressure and support for Soviet dissidents will eventually force a fundamental change in Soviet policy. But it may be more likely that outside pressure is irrelevant or counterproductive. The economic difficulties of the Soviet government and the advanced age of its current leaders suggest that new leaders and new policies will come in any event.

There may be other ways to encourage Soviet flexibility, however. One possibility is a limitation on military budgets, which has frequently been suggested at the UN. This idea poses many difficulties for negotiation and verification. Asymmetry would present particular problems; manpower costs, for example, probably take a larger part of the U.S. military budget than that of the Soviet Union. But serious effort to negotiate a budget limitation might impel the Soviet Union to reconsider its economic priorities, and might even rally an internal Soviet constituency opposing military expenditures. A similar approach was used in the 1979 SALT II agreement, in allowing each side only one major new strategic system; such a restriction might modify Soviet procurement patterns and encourage a constituency favoring arms control. Another approach is to make verification more open, perhaps with a UN satellite system such as that proposed by France. If any system of verification were to operate publicly in the West, it would probably result in the further spread of military knowledge to the Soviet public. This, too, could create additional support for Soviet leaders who favor reductions in military forces.

All these approaches are admittedly very weak. Strategic arms control is at a political impasse that can be broken only by a major change in Soviet goals. Meanwhile, the best we can expect is a series of minor agreements designed to control particularly threatening weapons or to face specific regional problems. We should, however, begin to open the way toward restraints on the use of nuclear weapons and perhaps toward greater internal enforcement of arms control. Although these quasi-legislative approaches offer little short-run benefit, they offer the best long-term prospects for the future of both arms control and nuclear stability. They should be made the focus of U.S. strategic negotiations with the Soviet Union when such negotiations next occur.

8. Regional Arms Control

A PARTICULAR regional context can often be especially favorable to the making of arms control agreements. The nations of a region may seek to avert the escalation of a specific political conflict. They may have a common culture that permits deeper and better enforced agreements than would be possible on a global scale. The great powers might give their support to regional accords in order to decrease the risk to themselves of being drawn into a future regional conflict. Or the regional powers might want arms control precisely as a way to limit pressures from the great powers.

At the same time regional arms control poses its own special difficulties. Regional agreements would normally govern conventional weapons. The tactical theory treating such weapons is poor, and this makes it difficult to draft arms control proposals that are militarily feasible. Moreover, though the interplay between great-power interests and regional interests may sometimes favor an agreement, that interplay also makes the negotiations complex and poses very sophisticated problems of enforcement. The political and military requirements of the great powers and the regional nations may differ substantially, narrowing the scope of an agreement and sometimes dividing the great powers from their respective allies. Finally, regional tensions nearly always reflect deep human concerns, so that regional arrangements interact strongly with domestic politics. This interaction can sometimes help create domestic constituencies for international agreements and even for international institutions; but national leaders are almost always extremely fearful of encouraging any political dynamic that might undercut their authority.

THE EUROPEAN EXAMPLE

The history of European arms control negotiations shows the force of these factors, both the favorable and the unfavorable. Explicit alliances and the heavy deployment of forces have supported the peace in Europe for over a generation. Arguably at least, the threat of war has diminished. Thus European arms control negotiations were undertaken in the 1970's with substantial public support. Although their outcome was unclear at the end of 1980, it appeared likely that the efforts to reach a settlement had failed; the effective formal restraints remained those deriving from the postwar controls on Germany and from the 1975 Helsinki attempt to define rules for European security.

At the end of the Second World War, invading troops from both East and West occupied Central Europe. It soon became clear that the Soviet Union intended to use its forces to control Eastern Europe's domestic and foreign policies. The Western governments looked to America for protection from this Soviet political offensive. Led by the United States, the West created an alliance, the North Atlantic Treaty Organization (NATO), to formalize this protection and to permit the controlled rearmament of West Germany as a key contributor to the defensive structure. The USSR, for its part, created the Warsaw Pact, an analogous alliance with the nations of Eastern Europe. Though the Eastern bloc maintained numerical superiority over NATO in conventional forces, the West's position was secure because the United States was effectively committed to using nuclear weapons in response to a conventional Soviet attack on Western Europe. At the time this commitment was made, it was clearly effective, since the Soviet Union then posed no nuclear threat to the United States.

During the 1950's, the Soviet-led East proposed a series of comprehensive European arms control packages. These proposals, emanating from the relatively liberal generation of Soviet leaders that succeeded Stalin, made substantial concessions in the direction of previous Western arms control proposals. But the packages were probably also designed to forestall the rearmament of West Germany and to obtain Western recognition of the division of Germany. For these reasons, and probably also because of Secretary of State John Foster Dulles's distrust of arms control, the West refused to give serious attention to the Eastern proposals.

While the Soviet Union was conducting this diplomacy, it was also building substantial nuclear forces. By the early 1960's, although the United States still had a much larger nuclear force, the Soviet Union had gained a second-strike capability. Thus the credibility of the American deterrent came into question; for the United States would risk losing its cities if it launched a nuclear strike in response to a Soviet conventional attack in Europe. Further, NATO was weaker in conventional forces than the East. Western diplomacy of this era therefore sought to deter a conventional attack by finding ways to sharpen the Soviet fear of nuclear escalation.

One idea, not successfully carried out, was to give NATO a formal role in the control of the American deterrent. Some argued that the American forces in Europe should be viewed as "tripwires," since the United States would be psychologically compelled to escalate to the nuclear level if these forces suffered serious casualties. And in 1963 tactical nuclear weapons were deployed with NATO forces. The United States, it was felt, would be less hesitant to use these nuclear forces than to use strategic ones. Using tactical nuclear weapons, then, would give the USSR a warning of the West's determination to use strategic nuclear weapons, besides perhaps helping to win any ground engagement.

Nevertheless, France began the construction of its own nuclear deterrent, often using the argument that an independent nuclear force controlled by a European nation would deter more effectively than the American strategic force. But it was clear that General de Gaulle was also challenging the United States' leadership of the Western alliance, and seeking to establish a new European framework for negotiations to resolve the division of Europe. De Gaulle pursued this policy by withdrawing his forces from NATO in 1966.

What received little serious attention was the possibility of improving the balance of conventional forces in Western Europe so that there would be less need to rely on the threat of nuclear escalation. As has been said of the Western European nations, their hearts have rarely been in the effort to make a land war costly to the USSR. This may have resulted from a generation gap and a public opinion gap. Though most Western defense and foreign ministry officials were acutely concerned with the Soviet threat, much of the public, and particularly the youth, tended to consider the threat overblown if not absurd. It was therefore difficult in the West to secure parliamentary approval for large conventional forces. But the problem was also between the United States and Europe: each looked to the other for leadership in making the hard decisions, and each was "inevitably schizophrenic" about the relationship between the nuclear guarantee and the defense of Europe.[1]

By the late 1960's, new leaders had come to power and were seeking to terminate the Cold War. Under Willy Brandt's Ostpolitik, West Germany moved to normalize relations with Eastern Europe. Over the next several years, West Germany ratified treaties with its major Eastern antagonists; by 1974, even the United States recognized East Germany. These arrangements resolved most of the lingering symbolic questions such as the division of Germany and its boundaries, typically by yielding to the East. By the early 1970's, there was a sense of détente in Europe.

The United States and the USSR were cementing a détente of their own during this period, which was also marked by SALT I. Both superpowers had reason to pursue arms control in Europe. In the United States, the Vietnam War had produced in Congress a deep mistrust of stationing troops anywhere abroad; indeed a proposal to recall American troops from Europe failed in the Senate by only a few votes. The United States administration wanted to have negotiations with the USSR in order to neutralize this congressional pressure or alternatively to obtain a Soviet quid pro quo. The USSR, deploying enormous land forces on the Sino-Soviet border, probably wished to stabilize its western flank. It may also have feared that a unilateral reduction of U.S. forces in Europe would encourage Western Europe to assume a more militaristic posture. In sum, the constellation of events seemed favorable to arms control. The tension in Europe had dissipated, and nearly everyone had reasons to capitalize on the situation by reducing its forces.

Once certain key decisions had been made, the path to negotiations was relatively direct. The East had frequently called for what would become the Conference on Security and Cooperation in Europe (CSCE), a conference to settle the outstanding disputes in Europe. The West had traditionally rejected such a conference, fearing that any ensuing agreement would legitimize the Soviet-effected changes that were part of the European status quo. The typical response of the West had been to call for arms control discussions, centering on Mutual and Balanced Force Reductions (MBFR). The East had traditionally rejected this proposal, presumably judging that the weaker West would attempt to negotiate for parity. With arms control in the air, and with Germany less fearful of making symbolic concessions, the West offered to proceed on both proposals. In 1971 both the force reduction talks and the security conference were scheduled.

The CSCE negotiations reached a conclusion in 1975 with the issuance of the Helsinki Final Act, a statement of general principles of cooperation that the signers had agreed would not be legally binding. At first, conservatives in the West criticized the Final Act because of its recognition of the European status quo, including the division and postwar borders of Germany. Brezhnev had very much desired this recognition, and the West undoubtedly weakened its own position at the MBFR talks by granting the recognition before an MBFR agreement had been reached. But the CSCE Final Act gave the West an important group of provisions concerning human rights and the improvement of communications between East and West. Dissidents in Eastern Europe seized upon these provisions. A radically new politics emerged there, not, it must be admitted, reflecting actual freedom in Eastern Europe, but at least vindicating the West's interest in a movement toward that freedom. As an effort to define rules of conduct in Europe, the CSCE also included legislative arms control provisions designed to reduce tensions, mainly by requiring advance notification of military maneuvers.

The MBFR negotiation, in contrast, was seriously stalemated, at least until the end of 1980. Part of the problem was that many of the various political goals of the parties were satisfied by the mere existence of negotiations, irrespective of the success of the negotiations. Thus the USSR was interested in negotiations as a way to divide the United States and Europe and to make Western European force levels an area of legitimate Eastern interest.[2] Western Europe and the U.S. executive branch were hopeful that the negotiations would blunt the drive in Congress for unilateral American force reductions.[3] Success in the negotiations, therefore, was not important for the achievement of either side's goals.

The key problem in the negotiations, however, was the asymmetry of the force levels. The West sought to reduce Eastern forces relatively more than Western forces, with the goal of moving toward a balance. The East, in contrast, sought proportional reductions that would prolong its numerical superiority. The depth of this difference was suggested by the fact that the two parties even disagreed over the name of the negotiations, the West seeking to include the word "balanced" and the East rejecting it. In 1976 the West submitted a compromise proposal, in essence offering to trade some of its tactical nuclear weapons for Soviet tanks. And in 1978 the East made a proposal that moved somewhat toward the Western concept of balance; but probably because of this proposal's assumed current force levels, the West immediately rejected the proposal.[4] The Soviet Union also substantially increased its Eastern European ground forces during the period, although some of this increase reflected a military tradition of retaining obsolete equipment while new equipment is deployed. But it was the Soviet deployment of SS-20's, intermediate-range missiles targeted on Western Europe and given high political visibility by the SALT discussions, that led to renewed European concern. For a while, Western Europe hoped that these weapons might be controlled by further SALT or MBFR negotiations. But though the asymmetry stimulated Western interest in negotiation, it did not so readily produce agreement. At the end of 1979, NATO decided to deploy its own nuclear missiles, and Foreign Minister Gromyko responded by declaring that the basis for negotiations was destroyed.[5] Although there were indications in 1980 that the Soviets might discuss SS-20 reductions, these were probably directed at slowing the West's planned deployment of new nuclear missiles. The difficulty of negotiation in the face of unbalanced force levels was apparently unresolvable: superiority was too important to the Soviets and restoring a balance too important to the West.

In the late 1970's, moreover, the international political atmosphere became less conducive to agreement. At Belgrade in 1977 and 1978, the American efforts to discuss human rights in the Soviet Union led to angry recrimination. The Soviet Union placed an increasing emphasis on arms. Western diplomats grew more concerned about the Soviet conventional force buildup, though paradoxically the West gained in self-confidence as Eastern Europe faced severe economic problems and as the Western human rights initiative sparked a response among the people of the East. In spite of Western

Europe's interest in avoiding the deterioration of détente, there emerged no political dynamic, analogous to the détente underlying SALT or the concern for human rights and border recognition underlying CSCE, that could bring about a major European arms control.

The failure of European arms control is another illustration of the problems discussed in Chapter Four. Despite a great opportunity, no agreement was reached, because the asymmetries outweighed the thrust toward settlement. Moreover, the European balance rested so heavily on the use of nuclear weapons that no significant outside enforcement procedures could be added to the existing nuclear guarantees. Europe is also a demonstration of the way a regional agreement depends on the expected evolution of political forces. Any multilateral agreement is a gamble in which each party estimates how the agreement will cause political forces to evolve. Thus in CSCE the Soviet Union gambled, incorrectly, that the political settlement would outweigh the increased freedom of communication. The West gambled, correctly, on the opposite position. There are many conflicting political tendencies within Europe; the various nations will make different estimates of the strength and desirability of each of these tendencies. These evaluations can become the real motivating forces behind agreement. They can also block agreement; this has been the effect of the West's concern over the stability of its alliance and the East's concern over the position of its satellite nations. Major arms control agreements could be highly beneficial in Europe; but they have not been achieved, and they are unlikely to be achieved in the near future.

Should there ever be an effective MBFR, it would best provide for major arms cuts, because there can probably be only one full settlement agreement in a political generation. Such an agreement should also deal substantially with the deployment patterns of the two sides. Either because the Soviet leaders have not ruled out an attack or, more likely, because the Soviets view a quick thrust as offering them the greatest chance of victory, the Soviet forces are deployed in an offensive pattern.[6] The NATO forces are also deployed in an offensive pattern, partly deriving from an unthinking continuation of the Second World War pattern and partly from the political need to appear unwilling to accept a deep Soviet penetration into West Germany. Thus the postures of the East and West are mutually threatening, which creates a needless military tension and an unnecessary risk of escalation. The direction of reform is obvious.

Though the problem of asymmetry is real, the Western strategic position is probably stronger than is commonly assumed. Ultimately, the West is stronger than the East, despite the Soviet buildup. Moreover, the West can strengthen itself tactically, as several serious military commentators have suggested,[7] in a number of possible areas: logistics, depth of deployment, and deployment of antitank weapons, for example. The short-range precision-guided missile, whose effectiveness was shown in the 1973 Middle East war, can give small units a high chance of destroying tanks or aircraft. Should these missiles be useful in the more overcast climate of Europe, they may give an advantage to the tactical defense over the tactical offense for the first time since the development of tank warfare.[8] The West, therefore, almost certainly has the technical ability to establish a much more effective defense, although perhaps at the cost of predicating the defense on some Soviet penetration into West Germany. A great improvement in NATO forces, such as has been begun, might restore the balance needed to make arms control negotiable in a more politically propitious time. If there were a balance of conventional forces, the elimination of regional nuclear forces would probably also be a desirable arms control objective, and one with great public appeal. It would have to be mutual, however, and would be very difficult to achieve under the best of circumstances.

Unless the Soviet government dramatically changes its policies, the immediate goals of arms control are probably limited to the establishment of arrangements for preventing incidents and perhaps also arrangements for facilitating consultations. Either would be beneficial. There are many opportunities for dangerous incidents in Europe: a Soviet effort to put down an uprising in a satellite country, Eastern and Western jockeying for position in Yugoslavia, the spread of a Middle Eastern or Mediterranean conflict, and a Soviet intervention in an intra-NATO controversy like the Greek-Turkish dispute. Conflicts such as these, which are likely to lead to war, pose special risks if the states directly involved have their own nuclear weapons or access to the nuclear weapons stored on the continent by NATO and Warsaw Pact forces. Both superpowers, and Europe as well, have a great stake in containing such conflicts.

The best way of doing this would be by a limited withdrawal of forces, enough to disengage the forces of the two sides and increase the warning time for each. This may not be politically feasible; if it is not, there are other options. Warning systems such as observers and mutual reconnaissance and intelligence arrangements might often be useful. Limited agreements, at least dealing with the security of command and control arrangements for nuclear weapons, could help prevent unintentional escalation, and perhaps also contribute to future legal restrictions on nuclear weapons.

Probably the most important possible arrangement, since it would be needed in the event of any substantial European arms control agreement, is the creation of new consultation procedures. The West has traditionally objected to such procedures, fearing the Soviet Union would use them to encourage dissension among the Western allies. In the MBFR and CSCE negotiations, however, the West was able to maintain unity. And in the future, the Western nations could certainly use their own procedures to assist them in developing a unified position, in interpreting the side guarantees that would undoubtedly accompany any major security arrangements, and in exchanging intelligence data on Soviet compliance.

New East-West consultation arrangements, then, could be available to help avoid the escalation of incidents, to prevent the misinterpretation of particular military deployments, and perhaps to encourage the designing of forces in less provocative ways. Conceivably, such arrangements might increase the restraints on the Soviet Union. They would create an additional channel of East-West contact through which new ideas could reach Eastern Europe, and could nourish the sense of European unity. Though it is not clear which of these measures are the most feasible, they are generally likely to be more acceptable than numerical force reductions.

REGIONAL SETTLEMENTS OUTSIDE EUROPE

A number of diplomatic arrangements have already been made that amount to regional settlements with arms control provisions. After the Cuban missile crisis, the USSR effectively agreed to limit the forces it would supply to Cuba. Several Middle East truces have significantly restricted the deployment of forces, some providing also for UN supervision. Each region is unique, but these and other plausible areas for future regional arms control generally share several characteristics that differentiate them from Europe. The probability of conventional war in the regions is relatively high; but plans for war do not call for nuclear weapons, and the great powers share a fear of nuclear escalation in connection with the region. Because of a recent or threatened war, the local interest in negotiated arrangements may be high. In the case of the Middle East, for one, alliances with the great powers are not so sharp as to leave no space for new enforcement procedures. But all the regional arrangements, as in Europe, require complex negotiations linked very closely to domestic political evolution.

Such regional settlements are particularly important in the developing world, where the risk of diplomatic war is especially high. The international borders are often remnants of an imperial era that reflect little strategic or cultural logic. Frequent border wars have resulted: in the Andes from the nineteenth century down through the 1930's, along India's borders, in Southeast Asia and Indonesia, and in the Middle East. Regional powers, by suggesting that they might respond to great-power influence, have often themselves manipulated the great powers. Thus they have obtained arms from the great powers, established alliances with dissident groups in neighboring countries, and waged international guerrilla warfare. This is the pattern of warfare common in Africa and Southeast Asia. More important, as suggested in Chapter One, newly developing nations may express their dynamism in military preparations that can easily carry over into expansionism; this has already happened with India, Indonesia, and Vietnam. The mechanisms of diplomacy are weak in the less developed regions. In areas like the Persian Gulf, where arms levels have been increasing rapidly, the tradition of communication between the nations is weak, and there is relatively little shared understanding of the constraints needed to support a local balance-of-power system.

Popular conflict, which is inherently less amenable to arms restrictions, is also a problem. The central governments of developing nations often are relatively weak and have difficulty in exercising effective authority over their entire territory. This lack of authority, combined with a major ideological conflict, affords the opportunity for armed intervention. An obvious example is South Africa; most of the developing world regards white majority rule as a threat to the peace that justifies intervention. For different ideological reasons, other nations such as Israel and Taiwan are similarly denied legitimacy. Thus popular warfare on a regional scale is both possible and likely.

Traditional arms control settlements. The traditional formal arms control, when negotiable, can assist in preventing regional wars. As in Europe, forces can usually be redesigned to make a border or a cease-fire line more secure against a preemptive attack or an unintended escalation. The acquisition of interceptor aircraft rather than attack aircraft could be required, or antitank weapons rather than tanks. The new tactical technology of precision-guided missiles may favor a defensive tactical stability. To enforce any cease-fire arrangements, UN forces could be placed along the lines to give each side greater confidence that the other side is honoring restrictions on deployment. Or the superpowers could promise to pass on intelligence data indicating preparations for a surprise attack. There are limits to traditional arms control: popular warfare cannot be stopped by regulating force levels, and the small arms that are the key to guerrilla warfare are unlikely ever to be effectively controllable. Nevertheless, regional arms control agreements could significantly reduce the probability of some forms of war, and perhaps buy time for dealing politically with the other risks.

Most of the agreements so far achieved, however, deal only with one specific type of situation: the stabilization of a border following a major incident. The reason for this is that neither great powers nor regional powers have yet been strongly interested in arms control except in time of war or its aftermath.

During peacetime, on the contrary, the great powers have been more interested in supplying arms. Though the great powers could reasonably exercise their control over the supply of arms so as to impose a kind of arms control, seldom have they taken wise advantage of this opportunity. This is only in part because of the fear that an economic or political rival will supply the arms anyway. Suppliers tend to think that arms will never be used, and therefore give little attention to the design of forces; U.S. decision makers dealing in arms seem to have thought primarily in terms of an abstract political influence. The opponents of supplying arms, meanwhile, have often focused their attention on the dollar volume of the arms, without arguing seriously about what particular weapons are supplied. (The USSR is perhaps an exception here. For example, the air defense weapons it supplied to

Egypt before the 1973 Middle East war were chosen and placed so that Egyptian forces could operate effectively in the western part of the Sinai, but could not go further east without losing their protection against Israeli aircraft.) In general, the great powers have wanted to retain the freedom to supply weapons. They tend to view this freedom as a way to shape regional politics and to dissuade nations from obtaining nuclear weapons. In some cases, the maintenance of regional tension may be useful to a superpower, as it sometimes has been for the USSR in the Middle East. Until there is war, therefore, the supplying of conventional arms appears to be a useful, low-cost diplomatic tool.

During and immediately after a war, however, this perception changes and the great powers are likely to become more interested in arms control. A war brings suffering, tension, and a psychological feeling of pointlessness (for war can seldom be decisive). Limitations may be put on arms supply to help halt the war and to define postwar borders; the UN may enforce any arrangements. Since the stability the great powers seek usually requires some limitation on arms and deployment, arms limitations rather than arms supplies become the medium of great-power influence. The cease-fire line, typically shaped by this influence, usually becomes a long-term boundary as a result of an elaborate settlement, which may be carefully labeled as an interim arrangement. The negotiations are never easy; the settlements abound in ambiguous language and secret side understandings. Nevertheless, minor powers are sometimes so confident that this sort of settlement will be imposed by the great powers that they design their military action to evoke the expected intervention.[9]

Minor powers find it much easier to negotiate arms control in a time of actual conflict. In peacetime, which may be a time of fearful preparation for a future war, they tend to view arms restraints as an intolerable infringement on their sovereignty and national security. But in wartime they may look for a guarantee, a stable settlement. As discussed in Chapter Four, it is the postwar period, here telescoped into the process for terminating a war, that is most conducive to settlement negotiations.

Extensions of the pattern: guaranteed regional settlements. In some regions, the traditional limitations on arms control might be breaking down. The entire pattern of regional military balances and great-power intervention is evolving profoundly in ways that may encourage the search for new security systems. In this context, regional settlements might gain in appeal as a component of this new regional security, and could conceivably bring significant arms control.

The great powers may become interested in regional security because they are losing their ability to shape the outcome of regional war. They already find it difficult to control guerrilla warfare and terrorism. The number of nations able to manufacture sophisticated weapons is increasing, so the great powers are also likely to lose their leverage over military supplies. Great-power military intervention, typically based on naval or aerial forces, is likely to become increasingly vulnerable to precision-guided missiles. And soon, developing nations with cruise missiles may be able to threaten the great powers themselves. Of even greater importance, the proliferation of nuclear weapons may be beyond control by restrictions on technology. It has thus become necessary to design security systems that weaken the incentive to acquire nuclear weapons, or else to face the horrible risks of regional nuclear war and its escalation. As the great powers lose their military influence, they may be readier to cooperate with each other in the more humane diplomatic approach of preventive arms control in peacetime.

For the regional powers, this approach has the appeal of a more stable security structure. Although enmeshed in regional disputes, they also have reason to be concerned about possible nuclear escalation. At the same time, the technology that may make great-power intervention difficult may also make defensive guarantees and arms control enforcement militarily feasible. Thus the regional arena is the most appropriate place for applying the concepts of defensive enforcement described in Chapter Six. The task is to find ways to stretch the limits of both arms control and defensive guarantees to their utmost, presumably with the aid of the UN and of regional organization, so as to legitimize the role of the great powers where necessary but to avoid domination by them.

The UN already has the formal powers necessary to enforce arms control agreements. A serious violation of an arms control agreement is almost certainly a "threat to the peace" that calls for mandatory Security Council action. Moreover, a violation poses a question "relating to the maintenance of international peace and security"; this allows the General Assembly to make recommendations such as for particular governments to take enforcement action.[10] The authorized means of enforcement include indirect military action and embargo; probably, various forms of direct military and economic intervention are also permissible.[11] Although there is a UN Charter provision against intervening in domestic affairs, this does not apply to enforcement action; and the argument that arms levels are not purely a domestic matter is becoming increasingly reasonable.

Formally, then, the UN already has nearly all the authority it needs to enforce arms control arrangements. Politically, however, it is seldom able to use this legal power. An obvious difficulty is the veto, by which any permanent member of the Security Council can prevent mandatory action. This problem is not simply a legal one; it reflects a political reality as well. The permanent members are all major nuclear powers, and this could deter any enforcement action that threatened their national interests. The Third World nations' voting dominance, on the other hand, shapes the General Assembly deliberations and frequently makes the great powers fearful of UN involvement in an issue. Moreover, this voting dominance makes the UN generally reluctant to authorize the use of force for any purpose, and particularly reluctant to infringe those aspects of national sovereignty related to the possession of arms.

These limitations imply that no nation can confidently expect the UN to step in, unprepared, in the face of a treaty violation. Thus detailed arrangements for enforcement would have to be made, probably outside the UN, at the time any treaty is negotiated. There would have to be specific promises by specific nations to intervene under specific conditions. In the Middle East, for example, relevant guarantors such as the United States, the Soviet Union, and Saudi Arabia would have to promise, at the time of an arms control agreement, to intervene in specified ways in the event of a violation: to terminate military or economic assistance to a violator, to increase military sales to an innocent party, or to intervene defensively on behalf of an innocent party. Such strong advance commitments are currently the only way to give credibility to the threat of intervention.

Such agreements would also have to specify the procedures for resolving various disputes, perhaps even setting up special decision-making organs. Most likely, these organs would be given some status within the UN, perhaps by being formally created or approved by a UN resolution. But their decisions would be carefully controlled by the parties to the agreement so as to make sure a Security Council deadlock would not block intervention. Alternatively, the parties might make advance arrangements to eliminate UN legal barriers so that they might use the Security Council. For example, the parties could irrevocably give their advance consent to UN enforcement within their boundaries.[12] Or the permanent members of the Security Council might agree in advance not to exercise their veto.[13]

These are not the only ways to adapt the UN to arms control enforcement. In a much weaker way, the United States, Britain, and the Soviet Union promised in support of the

Non-Proliferation Treaty to seek immediate action by the Security Council to assist any nonnuclear signatory that might be attacked with nuclear weapons. But much is gained by stronger links between the UN and the enforcement apparatus. The UN can make intervention both more feasible and more legitimate. It can help assure the fairness of the decision-making structure, and can protect the Third World from improper intrusion by great powers. Moreover, it may be politically easier for a nation contemplating regional arms control to concede the right to operate on its territory to international forces than to concede it to foreign national forces.

It would be naive to suggest that such elaborate regional arms control settlements could be widely applicable. Nevertheless, if military technology continues to evolve in the direction described at the beginning of this section, such settlements can offer the benefits of arms control in a number of serious situations, primarily in Africa, the Middle East, and South Asia. In these areas the use of the UN or a comparable regional organization could facilitate negotiation and permit the bilateral guarantees that are politically essential to asymmetric settlements.

Shorter-term approaches. Since these full settlements will only rarely be possible, it is useful to consider less comprehensive approaches that might be more readily negotiable. The most effective such approach is probably to establish a mechanism for consultation, designed to encourage tacit accords and restraints.[14] Ideally, a mechanism of this kind would create political restraints on military assistance, arms procurement, and arms transfer, and would encourage opposing nations to look to mutual restraint as preferable to increased arms levels. Consultations might produce informal rules for peacetime military operations; such rules might reduce the risk of escalation by preventing provocations and incidents. Consultations could also be extremely helpful in preventing regional diplomatic war, for ease of communications could add to the stability of a balance-of-power arrangement.

Finally, the most important impact of improved consultations might be in the creation within a region of the sense that force levels are not purely a domestic concern, but are a reasonable concern to neighboring countries as well.

For the UN or another international organization to establish a series of consultation procedures on regional armaments is a more likely political possibility than full arms control. If properly designed, these procedures would enable the nations to avoid some of the great-power influence likely under less formal consultation procedures. The dangers of consultation—that it will be used for deception, intelligence collection, or increased arms procurements—can be minimized by careful design. The delegates could be a well-prepared combination of both military and civilians. The discussions could be kept confidential to discourage demagoguery, but public reports might be required in order to ensure that the consultations are actually directed toward force reductions promoting stability. These forums might work in conjunction with arrangements for sharing intelligence—perhaps an international satellite system—to give warning and to reduce the risk of deception. An international system to provide military advice might also help nations to design their forces free from the influence of the great powers.[15]

Regional legislative arms control. In the regional settlement pattern, it is the great powers that are particularly interested in reaching agreement and the regional powers that are likely to be reluctant. Regional legislative arms control, however, is more likely to be negotiated at the primary insistence of the nations of the region, with the great powers reluctant. The reason is that legislative arms control often builds on a regional interest in excluding great-power interference. The great powers may acquiesce in this exclusion, provided all great powers are excluded.

The closest traditional analogue to this kind of arms control is the doctrine of neutrality, which is intended to prevent intervention by outside nations. By promising not to threaten other nations and not to help either side during a war, a neutral nation hopes that no outside nation will attack it. In a typical pattern of mutual self-interest, each belligerent power may refrain from attacking the neutral as long as it expects others to refrain too; all will thus forgo the strategic benefit of occupying the neutral nation. To be neutral may, as in the case of Switzerland, require a substantial military force, to raise the costs of any foreign military intervention; but the neutral's forces usually do not have to be nearly as large as would otherwise be required. In Sweden, for example, neutrality has provided the strategic and political resources that make possible a policy against the construction of nuclear weapons.[16]

The contemporary arms control proposal that most clearly reflects the motivation of excluding outside powers from a region was the proposed Indian Ocean Zone of Peace. The main objective of the proposal was to keep great-power naval activity out of the Indian Ocean. For the region, the proposal was a reaction to the Soviet naval presence dating from 1968 and to the parallel U.S. naval presence, particularly the construction of the Diego Garcia base and the movement of warships into the Bay of Bengal during the Bangladesh war. The United States and the Soviet Union might at one time have been willing to accept the neutralization of the area; but most likely, this possibility is a casualty of the Soviet invasion of Afghanistan in 1979. Moreover, the legislative content of this Zone of Peace concept would have weakened the legal tradition of free navigation for naval vessels on the high seas; and both the United States and USSR, as well as Japan and the European nations, were very dubious about creating such a precedent.

The Latin American Nuclear Free Zone, already in force, combines an exclusionary motivation with an effort to restrain future regional conflict.[17] The agreement includes a protocol to be signed by the nuclear powers in which they promise to respect the zone. The treaty is not binding on the nations of the region until all nuclear powers have accepted this protocol, although a nation of the region can, by a waiver, bind itself anyway. In the developing world, many viewed the commitment by the outside nations as central to the concept of the nuclear free zone. One Indian commentator wrote:

"The essence of any agreement on denuclearization is the assurance of all nuclear powers that they would sincerely respect the juridical status of the zone. Ever since the concept of denuclearization was put forward, there has been concern among the nonnuclear powers that the renunciation of nuclear arms in their territory might endanger their security or they might be subject to the threat of a nuclear blackmail. Therefore, it is considered that there is a moral obligation on nuclear powers to undertake to respect the juridical status of the nuclear free zones."[18]

In addition to this exclusionary motivation, there are other broad motivations that might support regional legislative arms control.[19] Although the time is probably over when nations like India can see themselves as the custodians of a moral pressure for arms control and disarmament, there is still some idealism in the developing world. A regional spokesman described the Latin American Nuclear Free Zone as a "Latin American contribution to the military denuclearization of a zone of the planet," and "a model for the establishment of other similar zones."[20] Moreover, there is some sense in the developing world that arms supplies from the developed nations amount to a form of imperialism designed to absorb funds and to ensure that their wars will be fought by proxy. And there is always the hope of avoiding the waste of resources on arms.

These political motivations will not be strong enough to create regional legislative arms restrictions, unless they are coupled with specific military goals. The most important weapons agreements might thus entail a regional renunciation of particular offensive weapons in exchange for a great-power renunciation of the use of the same weapons against the region. Nuclear weapons are the obvious candidates, and nuclear free zones are understandably and properly a common proposal. Perhaps equally important weapons, because of the way they might spread regional conflicts, are cruise missiles, supersonic aircraft, and certain naval forces.

Regional arms control, like most other kinds, may often be more readily negotiated in the areas of mutual nonintervention and the restriction of military actions that might lead to incidents. Narrowly defined rules with specific purposes could be very useful to solve problems like incidents at sea, conflicts over the use of straits, and military overflights. The commitment of the great powers not to intervene in particular regions could be very important. There are already tacit rules of this sort that have some force, such as the generally respected understanding that it is in the common interest of all African nations not to attack the inherited colonial boundaries, no matter how irrational these lines may be. Such rules become a form of law that might help slow the growth of military forces and would almost certainly add to the legitimacy of future law.

To encourage such legitimacy, it is particularly desirable if these rules are negotiated or applied within a regional organization. The Organization of American States (OAS) could play a greater role in preventing inter-American conflict. Conceivably, the Organization of African Unity could help to enforce a principle against the foreign supply of military forces, a principle that might help the continent free itself from its current troubles. Because many regional organizations are designed to help protect a region from outside pressures, these organizations play a political role fundamentally different from that of the UN. They are easier to create than global organizations, and may have greater power.

In some cases, regional legislative agreements could provide for enforcement, but the enforcement would have to be very different from that of settlement agreements. Unlike nations accepting outside guarantees as part of the settlement of a dispute, the nations of a region would agree to forgo a particular weapon and to accept international guarantees or international enforcement to assist them. Because the impetus for the agreement is highly legal, the enforcement mechanism is also likely to be legal. It might take the form of direct intervention, such as the seizure of a plutonium stockpile or the embargo of specific chemicals to a nation producing chemical warfare agents. Early on, however, the enforcement would probably be judicial. Though judicial approaches are weak in much of the world, they might be adequate when a government is still debating whether to proceed with a violation, when ambiguity threatens to destroy an agreement, or when a judicial decision is used to stimulate more forceful diplomatic responses. A large part of the world is already moving toward the judicial approach with the "extradite or prosecute" response to terrorism, a concept that uses national courts to enforce an international norm. It would be a surprisingly short step to establish judicially enforced restrictions on biological warfare or nuclear development. Perhaps judicial procedures could build as much on the safeguarding of peaceful programs as on the prohibiting of military ones.

There are of course major barriers to regional legislation. Many developing-world governments appear unwilling to accept any restrictions; indeed the Latin American Nuclear Free Zone itself has serious limitations of this sort. The great powers, for their part, are generally unwilling to accept a duty not to intervene. Thus legislative approaches are more likely to succeed in a region where the great powers are not in conflict; Latin America has been more successful than Asia in this respect. Perhaps only Latin America and Western Europe are sufficiently homogeneous to accept the judicial approach. There is also a risk that regional legislative arms control will become a mechanism of regional hegemony; nonintervention has traditionally been the cry of the nation that is weak in a broad context but strong in a narrow one. The United States used the Monroe Doctrine, in form a rule against intervention, to gain hegemony in Latin America, even though, as a world power, the United States was weak at the time. Regional organizations have also sometimes served to assist a dominant nation to enforce its control. The OAS provided a cover for U.S. intervention in the Dominican Republic; a concept of socialist unity provided a nearly equivalent cover for the Soviet intervention in Czechoslovakia. The neighbors of such regional powers as India and Brazil may fear a similar use of nonintervention arrangements.

Regional legislative agreements to reduce arms or to restrict provocative behavior could have important long-term consequences. By their nature, these measures shade over into new security arrangements, and it is precisely new security arrangements that are needed for effective arms control. As they evolve into a pattern of security consultation, military restriction, and regional organization, these arrangements, far more than settlement arrangements, have the political potential to help transform international military conflict into transnational political conflict. In such a transformation, the level of arms would be only one aspect; the economic and political aspects would be just as important, shaping both the motivations and the institutions.

Even the shorter-term proposals in this chapter presuppose a world that, at least in some regions, is becoming much more internationalized. The ultimate political goal of the weakest proposal, the establishment of regional forums, is to make national arms procurement a matter of international concern. This goal is currently heretical, particularly in the developing world. Yet an approach presuming such a political evolution, as well as the imposition of formal restrictions, is essential for preserving peace in an increasingly nuclearized world. The developing world will find it necessary, moreover, to strengthen regional arrangements to meet the threat of great-power intervention. For though the great powers may be losing their ability to control the developing world, they probably will continue to try, since the role they have played in the past has often been useful to them. There is an obvious tension between settlement approaches built around the possibility of intervention and legislative approaches intended to exclude intervention. If the developing world is to gain stability without being dominated, it will need new regional political and security arrangements. Some of these arrangements could be compatible with intervention that is under international control. Others, which help resist outside intervention, are possible only if new political forms can be developed that work toward integration.

9. Global Arms Control

REGIONAL approaches may help to slow the proliferation of nuclear and other high-technology weapons, but these weapons that affect the global balance of power can be fully confronted only at the global level. They pose nearly intractable problems for traditional arms control. By extending the concept of arms control, however, it is possible to define extremely important approaches that build on a genuinely global politics.

THE WEAKNESS OF TRADITIONAL ARMS CONTROL

The use of traditional arms control to halt nuclear proliferation and the spread of conventional arms raises all the problems of negotiating in the face of deep asymmetry. Not surprisingly, efforts of this sort have had little success.

Until well into the 1960's, the United States encouraged the export of peaceful nuclear technology. To be sure, there were safeguards, at first bilateral in form and later supervised by the International Atomic Energy Agency (IAEA). The United States also attempted to build nuclear strength in Europe, at the same time opposing proliferation elsewhere.[1] Finally, in 1967, after negotiations that focused on the question of transferring nuclear arms to Europe, the USSR and the United States reached agreement on a draft Non-Proliferation Treaty (NPT) and urged the nonnuclear nations to accept it.[2] Under this treaty, nuclear nations would promise not to help nonnuclear nations build nuclear weapons, and nonnuclear nations would commit themselves not to build nuclear weapons and would submit to IAEA safeguards.

To the United States, the usefulness and bona fides of the treaty were obvious: the treaty was a holding action that would prevent or delay proliferation and allow time for further negotiations. A world with few nuclear powers appeared per se less dangerous than a world with many. The Soviet support of the treaty probably rested on similar judgments, but the USSR understandably also had the strong specific motive of strengthening treaty barriers to Germany's becoming a nuclear power.[3]

The two superpowers may have expected other nations happily to accept the agreement. Only four years earlier, almost all nations had readily signed the Limited Test Ban Treaty. But in 1967 the reaction proved quite different; many nonnuclear nations were decidedly unenthusiastic. They argued that the treaty was unequal because by not placing any real restraints on the nuclear powers it only protected the existing nuclear status quo. The treaty would offer no protection against nuclear nations. Nor would it assure nonproliferation, since the right to withdraw from the treaty was so broad. Some nonnuclear nations even argued that the treaty was a scheme to maintain a great-power monopoly over peaceful uses of nuclear energy, as well as military uses.[4]

The superpowers responded by modifying their draft. They committed themselves to negotiate "effective measures in the direction of nuclear disarmament." This would reduce the disparity between the commitments of nuclear and nonnuclear nations. The nuclear powers also agreed to make peaceful nuclear technology available to nonnuclear nations without discrimination. The term of the treaty was limited to twenty-five years, and a review conference was to be held every five years. As a step toward meeting the nonnuclear nations' stated desire for protection from nuclear attack, the superpowers promised to seek immediate Security Council action if such an attack occurred.[5] With these modifications, the treaty eventually went into force. Nevertheless, many of the most important potential nuclear nations have either not signed it or not ratified it: Israel, Egypt, India, Pakistan, Brazil, Argentina, and South Africa.

The follow-up diplomacy has been only a little more effective. Shortly after India's 1974 nuclear explosion, a number of the nuclear supplier nations organized a continuing secret conference, the London Supplier's Group, at which they negotiated a series of restrictions on the export of those peaceful technologies that might be useful in making nuclear weapons. President Carter sought to expand these restrictions so as to prevent the use of separated plutonium, a nuclear weapons material, anywhere in the normal nuclear power fuel cycle; he also initiated an international discussion of ways to operate that fuel cycle more safely.[6] The U.S. Congress went even further, directing the negotiation of nuclear supply agreements to tighten the controls on the peaceful nuclear fuel cycle;[7] this led to difficult bilateral negotiations. These negotiations, although they might slow some proliferation of nuclear capabilities, have been seriously complicated by national desires to preserve nuclear power options in the face of rising energy prices.

Politically, the NPT may also have failed. The first review conference, held in 1975, ended in a stalemate: the nuclear nations wanted to strengthen restrictions on the flow of technology, and the nonnuclear nations wanted more transfer of technology and more arms control by the great powers. The effort by the great powers to restrict technology may have deprived the NPT of what legitimacy it had. Some commentators have even suggested that the NPT, by focusing on the spread of nuclear weapons and the symbolic value of possessing them, actually increased the nonnuclear nations' interest in acquiring nuclear weapons.

In the area of conventional arms, no nation has yet seriously proposed significant restrictions. As pointed out in the previous chapter, few governments are disturbed enough by the spread of arms to give up the benefits they gain from this spread. The governments that acquire arms believe they gain in national security and prestige. The governments that supply the arms do so to affect the balance of power, to increase their influence with other governments, and to gain the economic benefits of foreign exchange and increased domestic employment.[8]

The flow of arms from the developed to the developing nations has therefore been enormous and increasing. In the 1960's the total value of these transfers averaged about $2.3 billion a year. By the late 1970's, the United States alone was selling over $10 billion worth of weapons a year, mainly to the developing world, and the Soviet Union was also making large transfers. Some of the arms being supplied were nearly as sophisticated as those used by the great powers themselves. And increasing amounts of arms were being manufactured in many more parts of the world.

There has been little progress toward controlling these transfers of weapons. The U.S. Congress has enacted a few restrictions on arms transfers, but these restrictions generally have many loopholes. President Carter stated a strong policy against arms transfers, but failed to carry it out. Several supplier nations have attempted to impose specific restrictions; the United States, for instance, sought to delay the introduction of supersonic aircraft into Latin America, and France and Sweden have doctrines against sending arms to active belligerents. During the late 1970's, the United States and the Soviet Union discussed joint restraints, apparently with some early agreement, but these discussions seemed likely to be shelved as a result of tension between the two nations. Several nations in the Andean area have discussed regional restrictions, but so far have produced no more than a statement of general policy. At the UN, Malta, the United States, and Denmark have proposed the publication or registration of arms transfers, but the proposals failed in the face of arguments that such a rule would discriminate against nations unable to produce their own arms.[9] The argument has been made that the sale of conventional arms amounts to a form of neo-imperialism, keeping the developing nations in a state of dependency and transferring balance-of-payments deficits to them; but this view has not yet gained broad support in the developing world.[10]

Diplomatic, economic, and security motivations have thus encouraged the transfer of arms and discouraged any significant restraints. In the short term, the transfer of arms has probably contributed in some measure to regional stability; but this stability has come at the expense of the more serious long-term global problem.

So far, then, the great powers have achieved significant global arms control agreements only in the case of nuclear proliferation, and with only limited success there. The disparities between developed and developing nations are too great for effective negotiations on the level of forces. The NPT itself is so unsymmetrical that it can only be considered a transition agreement; but the next step in the transition has not been defined. Moreover, the approach of the great powers has probably overemphasized technology at the expense of security. Trying to control the flow of technology is a politically poor approach: technology has great romantic appeal for nations, and constraints imposed by the supplier may even increase the appeal. At the same time, genuine security needs are often forgotten.

Arguably, the NPT was intended as only a holding action pending a very different kind of strategy: a succession of settlement agreements based on the ultimate broadening of nuclear arms negotiations. As SALT and détente stabilized relations between the superpowers, it may have been hoped, other nuclear powers such as France and China would change ideologically; eventually they would participate in expanded SALT negotiations for further nuclear force reductions. The NPT would keep the nuclear club from growing during this process, and within a generation worldwide nuclear control would be possible. This strategy, however, was destroyed by the 1974 Indian nuclear test and by the SALT impasse. Moreover, the timing of the strategy is probably flawed. Nuclear proliferation could well be rapid, yet the SALT process is so slow that there will probably never be a time when all nuclear nations are willing to participate in SALT-like arms control negotiations. It will always be necessary to wait for someone else. The strategy's implicit assumption that SALT will help slow proliferation is also subject to some doubt. SALT undoubtedly provides an element of political balance for the NPT. But SALT may also favor nuclear proliferation by institutionalizing the hegemony of the superpowers. SALT can give allies of the United States a reason to build nuclear weapons, on the argument that the U.S. guarantee is unreliable; and it can also give nations challenging the great powers a reason to arm themselves, on the argument that hegemony is bad.

THE NUCLEAR EXAMPLE

The strategy just described is clearly unable to cope with the realities of global weapons spread. The combination of asymmetry, economic pressure, and the varying attitudes toward technology makes traditional arms control settlements unnegotiable. To suggest alternative approaches, which have to be legislative and yet go beyond the traditional legislative pattern, it is useful to consider the example of nuclear weapons with some care, for this is the most important example.

The risks of nuclear proliferation. It is often argued that a world of many nuclear powers can be stable.[11] This may be true, but the stability is likely to be much more delicate than that currently existing between the United States and the Soviet Union. The basis of U.S.-Soviet stability is that each nation can maintain enough forces to produce unacceptable destruction when retaliating against an attacker. The Western European nations can perhaps reach this level of strength in relation to the Soviet Union,[12] depending on the evolution of Soviet capabilities in MIRV's, intermediate-range missiles, and antisubmarine warfare. But as the number of nuclear powers increases, the necessary level of forces to meet this criterion soon becomes astronomical, especially if each nation feels constrained to deploy enough forces to deter a coalition of other nations or to achieve a war-fighting capability against other nations.

Nations are therefore likely to modify the theory of deterrence in order to rationalize the lower level of forces they are in fact likely to maintain. They will probably build their forces only against those coalitions considered likely to occur. Nuclear deterrence will rest in part on the assumption that a nuclear war will escalate to include an attack by an ally's nuclear forces. There will be a complex analysis of the risks and expectations of conventional war, of whether the threat of nuclear escalation would support conventional military operations, and of how the use of nuclear forces would affect the relations between the combatants and third nations.[13]

French nuclear policy provides an example of these new approaches. Even if France had no nuclear force, a Soviet conventional or nuclear attack on France would risk provoking a U.S. nuclear reply. The French nuclear force increases the likelihood of such American action, if only because France has the ability to initiate nuclear hostilities. Moreover, the French nuclear force affects France's prestige and authority, especially in relation to the United States. Thus the French calculation of its nuclear policy requires both a diplomatic assessment and a complex analysis of possible American and Soviet nuclear behavior. This trilateral balance is probably not quite as stable a way to avoid nuclear war as is bilateral nuclear deterrence. But it probably does help deter a conventional attack on France, and it may do this even more effectively when U.S.-Soviet mutual deterrence is less stable.

A completely different pattern might well emerge in the case of two small opposing nuclear powers—say, India and Pakistan—loosely aligned with different superpowers. This pattern is clearly stable if the alliances with the superpowers are close enough that the nuclear forces of each small power are effectively controlled by the superpower. It is also stable if there is a stable balance between the small powers and the alliances are so loose that a local nuclear war would clearly not escalate. There might also be a kind of local balance resting on military estimates of both nuclear and conventional forces. But without a local balance, a small power's decision whether or not to use nuclear weapons is likely to be dominated by the likelihood of great-power intervention. If it appears that the great powers will act together—they may have stated, for example, that they would jointly retaliate against one small nation for a nuclear attack on another—a nuclear stability can probably be achieved with almost any relative force level among small nations. However, if the great powers are likely to oppose each other and seek to deter each other from intervening (or if the minor powers have the ability to attack the great powers, perhaps with nuclear cruise missiles), there is a serious danger that a local nuclear war will escalate. Thus the posture of the great powers can often be crucial.

With nuclear proliferation, it is not only the strategic logic that becomes more subtle; so does the very definition of a nuclear force. There are many stages in the development of a nuclear force: a peaceful nuclear program that creates the technological and material potential for building nuclear weapons; the research and knowledge needed to convert this potential into completed or nearly completed weapons; the revelation to the world, by open testing, that a nation has a nuclear capability; and finally, the construction of large numbers of weapons and delivery systems, of varying degrees of sophistication. Some of these stages are influenced by economic factors and the need for energy; others by explicitly political and strategic factors. Sometimes, as apparently for Israel, there may be strategic value in ambiguity about the existence of nuclear weapons.[14] One can expect to find a wide variety of nuclear relationships at different levels.

It is starkly clear that nuclear proliferation is dangerous. In a world of many nuclear or near-nuclear nations, though each nuclear nation would *generally* be deterred from a conventional or nuclear attack on others, the calculations would be much more subtle and the chance of error much greater than in U.S.-Soviet deterrence. Bilateral deterrence would no longer be adequate to enforce stability. Nor could a global stability depend on the traditional balance of power that worked with conventional weapons. The stability of such a balance depended on the military fact that several allies, by combining their forces, could become much more powerful than individual nations. Nuclear forces do not add together in the same way as conventional forces; they provide very little basis for a balance of power based on alliances.

The control of nuclear technology. The existence of Pakistan's program to develop nuclear weapons, using equipment readily available on the open market, suggests that the era when nuclear weapons can be fully controlled by restricting the flow of technology is coming to an end. Nevertheless, it may still be desirable to control nuclear technology as much as possible, in order to slow the rate of proliferation among smaller nations and nongovernment organizations. Such restraints, whether domestic or international, are helpful even when not completely effective.

The one-sided restraint on technology sought by the nuclear nations, if not already a failure, is likely to prove one. But restraints by the nuclear powers on nonnuclear nations are not the only way to control nuclear technology. In many nations, domestic pressure groups are already trying to control this technology; if such pressure groups could be replicated worldwide, they might well be successful. Especially after the Three Mile Island incident in 1979, peaceful nuclear power evokes a powerful public opposition based on its mystique, its safety and environmental hazards, and its associated risks of terrorism and diversion to military uses, all of which create a constituency favoring domestic controls. To the extent that similar constituencies arise in the developing world, they would assist in the domestic and international control of the nuclear industry, and as a by-product, of military nuclear technology.

The most obvious way both to encourage the evolution of such constituencies and to build on them is to give a reformed IAEA a substantial authority over these political aspects of nuclear power. The IAEA's handling of these issues could stimulate citizen interest in these issues in many nations; citizen interest, in turn, would focus on the IAEA and increase the agency's legitimacy. Ideally, the restructured IAEA would control the actual operation of fuel cycle facilities and guarantee the security of its members' nuclear energy supply. The barrier to the flow of technology would then no longer be between nuclear and nonnuclear nations. Rather, it would be between the international institution and the rest of the world, and this line would have much greater legitimacy, provided the nonnuclear nations were given a reasonable share of the control of the institution. Such a new structure would also provide a political basis for international or national judicial sanctions against terrorism or against the illicit diversion of nuclear materials. There are problems, such as ensuring that the institution does not become a long-term political advocate of nuclear power and designing appropriate arrangements for the flow of data within the organization. Nevertheless, the concept has promise, and could be usefully pursued even without the participation of the Soviet Union.[15]

Should the Soviet Union be willing to participate, there are several legislative arms control concepts that could replace the unequal obligations of the NPT with obligations that are equal for all. The comprehensive nuclear test ban, although often overrated politically, is symmetrical and creates a clear barrier to the testing of weapons. The most important new obligations, however, would be a verified commitment to produce no more nuclear materials for military purposes. In this fashion, the peaceful production and operation of reactors need not be hindered, yet all nations' military nuclear programs would be affected. All nations, whether they have nuclear weapons or not, would receive parallel treatment. The Soviet Union has traditionally opposed this concept, but the idea has been proposed several times by the United States and may be acceptable to some near-nuclear nations. It was probably acceptable to France when that nation was considering nuclear weapons in the late 1950's.[16]

Among the weaker but more available approaches would be the transfer of enough authority to the IAEA to help it build political support. Such authority might include that of giving technical assistance to developing nations in their bargaining with developed nations for reactors and supplies, assisting reactor operators in preventing the diversion of nuclear material to terrorists, assisting the developing nations in avoiding the environmental and health hazards of nuclear power, and perhaps supervising plutonium stockpiles. Still weaker approaches might be to encourage unofficial contact between North and South in the energy and environmental areas, to help build constituencies for the control of nuclear technology. It is clear that the task of forming such constituencies is critical, and that any interim arrangements should be measured by their likely contribution to it.

Reducing incentives to acquire nuclear weapons. As nuclear technology becomes more accessible, it becomes easier for any nation that wishes to acquire nuclear weapons to do so. Moreover, it will never be technically possible to eliminate all nuclear weapons. There is too much nuclear material in the world, and there are too many people who know or could invent ways to assemble the material into an explosive device. As early as the mid-1950's, the estimates of the amount of nuclear material produced were so uncertain that even the best inspection system could not create the confidence that all the material was accounted for.[17] The only effective way to slow the spread of nuclear weapons among the nations is to reduce the strategic incentive to acquire these weapons.

This is a problem that has only rarely been examined. Any step toward a peaceful and stable world or toward decreasing

the prestige value of nuclear weapons would clearly be beneficial. In large part, the task is one of finding fundamental
new security arrangements and of making the old ones work
better. Thus it is a task that requires a deepening of regional
organization, especially in Africa and Latin America, and a
more careful management of alliances, especially in Europe
and East Asia. The regional consultation forums discussed in
Chapter Eight might prove particularly useful interim steps in
helping nations avoid building nuclear weapons, in focusing
informal public opinion and diplomatic sanctions on those
nations that do build nuclear weapons, and in helping restore
regional security at as low a cost as possible after a nation has
built nuclear weapons. The growth of constituencies concerned with nuclear technology issues might also have the
side benefit of decreasing the prestige value of nuclear
weapons.

In these areas the role of the great powers is particularly
important. Other nations often rely on these powers to maintain global strategic stability, typically by providing positive
and negative assurances. In making a positive assurance, the
normally envisioned type of guarantee, the great powers
commit themselves to provide nuclear or conventional assistance to a nonnuclear nation that is being attacked by nuclear
weapons. If the great powers are not divided or vulnerable,
and if the commitment is to make a nuclear response, the
threat is likely to deter the use of nuclear weapons in a regional conflict. Such an assurance, however, violates very
strong feelings against the use of nuclear weapons, and these
feelings should not be weakened. Moreover, if the great powers are at odds, there is a serious risk of escalation; thus the
most effective tool is also the one most likely to bring a cata-
clysm if it fails. The promise of conventional assistance is only
a little more appealing; for all the reasons discussed in Chapter Six, it is generally less credible. Nuclear or conventional, a
positive assurance is difficult to sustain politically and may
become increasingly difficult to execute militarily.

The negative assurance, a commitment not to use nuclear

weapons against nonnuclear nations, is much more likely to be generally acceptable.[18] Such an assurance is seldom strong enough to persuade a potential nuclear power to commit itself to the NPT, but it may have the much more important effect of inducing such a nation to delay its actual construction of nuclear weapons. Since a negative assurance eliminates the right to make nuclear threats, it also reduces the prestige value of nuclear weapons. And it can be designed so as to avoid encouraging nations dependent on a nuclear power to develop their own nuclear weapons. The Chinese, for one, have long sought such a negative commitment.

The negative assurance both builds on and strengthens the existing inhibitions against the use of nuclear weapons. These inhibitions, stemming from the horror of these weapons and the fact that they are normally useless, are real; in spite of the availability of tens of thousands of nuclear warheads, not one has been used in combat since 1945. The goal of the negative assurance is to strengthen these inhibitions by giving them a stronger legal and moral status. Only by this approach, probably, can the concept of deterrence be rendered obsolete; and possibly this is the only way a world of many nuclear powers can survive.

Leonard Beaton has already suggested the creation of an international nuclear authority to control the firing links for nuclear weapons.[19] The international authority would be physically able to veto the use of the weapons. Participation in this system would be voluntary in the sense that each nation would have the right to withdraw from the international authority, and to regain exclusive control over its weapons after a reasonable time delay of perhaps 48 hours. This voluntary character is designed to make the concept somewhat more negotiable without significantly reducing its political benefit. Presumably, there could be techniques enabling nations to retaliate immediately for a nuclear attack. The main purpose of such a system—to increase the political inhibitions against use of nuclear weapons—would be achieved even if nations withheld some of their weapons. To the extent the system were honored, it would provide a cooling-off period during a crisis and give diplomacy additional time to work. This would also make it easier for nations with constitutional limitations on the declaring of war to impose these limitations on the use of nuclear weapons.

In the near future, probably the most that is feasible is an agreement among the nuclear powers to consult in the Security Council in the event of any use or threatened use of nuclear weapons. This could be a step toward a concept such as Beaton's. It also permits international consideration of whether nuclear threats should ever be used to deter a small nation from making a nuclear attack on another. Although the threat of conventional intervention may be preferable, nuclear deterrence may sometimes be more effective and more politically feasible. If either kind of intervention is not to escalate, the nuclear powers will need a consultative mechanism to coordinate—and ideally to approve or disapprove in advance—their response to a nuclear conflict, perhaps by laying down principles in advance or by consulting during an actual crisis. If the Security Council served as this mechanism, it could help prevent the coordination between the nuclear powers from becoming a global hegemony that would encourage further proliferation. The Security Council already has formal legitimacy, and it provides a mechanism for nonnuclear nations to participate in the decision making. Several immediate further actions might help support this function of the council: a commitment by nuclear nations not to use nuclear weapons (save in retaliation) without Security Council consultation; a standing UN policy that the Security Council or a subgroup must discuss the implications for stability any time a nation first builds nuclear weapons or significantly changes its nuclear deployments or policies; formal reports by agencies such as the U.S.-Soviet Standing Consultation Committee; and the creation of a Security Council subgroup or standing committee to consider issues of nuclear stability, command, and control.

The use of the Security Council for these purposes would

be difficult and sometimes pointless in an immediate controversy, but any development of an international component in nuclear decision making is valuable. It lays the groundwork for the more elaborate restrictions needed in order to impose serious limitations on the use of nuclear weapons in the U.S.-USSR confrontation. It turns diplomatic pressure against the easy expansion of nuclear guarantees. It gives the entire world a political focal point for efforts to achieve global nuclear stability. Moreover, it helps build a worldwide sense that the use of nuclear weapons is rarely useful and only permissible—if ever—with a special moral and legal authorization.

THE BROADER PROBLEMS OF ARMS TRANSFERS AND TECHNOLOGY

The nuclear weapon is but one of a series of major developments in military technology that also includes supersonic aircraft, MIRV's, cruise missiles, and genetic manipulation. A technological advance of this sort typically emerges from the U.S.-Soviet military competition and is soon shared by both sides. Ultimately it has only a limited effect on the U.S.-Soviet balance; but it may spread through the world and have much more important strategic effects, sometimes seriously destabilizing regional balances. Often the advance is associated with peaceful technology, as nuclear arms are with nuclear power. The negotiation of arms restraints is, therefore, affected by economics and by the developing world's interest in new technology, as well as by military considerations.

The economic framework is the most promising one in which to set up new international arrangements for the less advanced weapons. What is needed is to find ways that new economic arrangements (for which there is already a political motivation) can be made to include arms control concerns. This concept is significantly different from the existing proposals that the economic surplus generated by disarmament be dedicated to economic development, proposals that have failed to generate political support. The more effective approaches are likely to be more specific. For instance, can the trading partners of a nation like Japan that refrains from exporting weapons reward that nation in trade negotiations by accepting other exports more readily? Can the developed nations rationalize their defense industries so as to decrease the pressure to export arms, or can they develop better industrial adjustment mechanisms so as to have alternatives to arms exports when under balance-of-payments pressure? Can the developing nations shift their arms procurement to an open bidding system, in order to decrease economic costs and possibly to decrease covert influences and overprocurement? Is there a way to lower petroleum costs or to allocate the burden of these costs so as to reduce arms export pressures?

Some questions like these might be negotiable in broad packages. Global arrangements, however, are always difficult because of the asymmetries between North and South; nearly all the comparable North-South negotiations of the 1970's failed. Thus it may be better to attack components separately. The developing nations might, for example, find it in their interest to create an international competitive bidding system for arms supplies. The developed nations might find certain trade arrangements negotiable and economically beneficial, as well as conducive to arms control. Any formal arrangements might be accompanied by direct legal enforcement procedures to help build citizen support. At the same time, there are obvious informal measures, including both diplomatic and privately defined guidelines, for redirecting the economic pressures that support arms production. Conceivably, arrangements, both formal and informal, may be available even without Soviet participation. All could build on, and might strengthen, the existing constituencies against the expenditure of resources on weapons.

Questions of technology deserve a closer examination. The developed nations have been weighing two concerns in considering restrictions on the export of technology: security concerns, based on strategic risks of specific technologies, and economic concerns, based on a desire to protect the domestic economy against foreign competition. Although both of these concerns are disagreeable to developing nations hungry for economic development, the second is by far the more disagreeable. Only in rare cases, as in connection with some aspects of nuclear power, will any global agreement to restrain the flow of technology be possible—and even then it will probably be feasible only if cast in an international form like that discussed in the previous section.

Some restrictions on technology, however, may be negotiable by the developed nations alone. Even the United States and the Soviet Union have a common interest in avoiding the proliferation of dangerous technology, which parallels their interest in avoiding strategic instability. When such restrictions are negotiated or imposed unilaterally, they will be much more effective if the restrictors have a way to demonstrate that strategic concerns are paramount. Thus it might be useful to create neutral international institutions that could evaluate the balance between arms control goals and monopolistic economic goals in such specific restrictions on the flow of technology. The legitimacy of such evaluations could be further improved by the funding of research institutions to guarantee the supply of nonmilitary technology to the developing world.

In general, however, the best ways to control advanced military technology would be more oriented toward the strengthening and coordinating of public opinion and domestic legislation. Political forces that support the control of technology are emerging; and the national and international tasks form a continuum. The key need is probably for international expert advisory groups to discuss arms transfers and specific military technologies. Such groups, both formal and informal, could suggest useful unilateral policies, point out which technologies and weapons are likely to be especially dangerous, and begin to build political constituencies to control them. The advisory groups could thus counterbalance the official viewpoint within each nation, and help build a technological ethic to which scientists and engineers might respond directly. These groups could also seek to define and encourage alternative directions for technology. It is too often the military area that appears to be at the exciting "cutting edge" of technology.

As in nuclear arms control, the efforts to weaken economic motivations for transferring technology are much less important than efforts to weaken security incentives. The key task again is to help shape world security systems so that nations feel less need to acquire arms. The entire range of regional organizations, international forces, guarantees, and consultation is important; but two mechanisms appear especially relevant in the global context. Because these mechanisms are voluntary, without binding requirements, they ought to be relatively easy to negotiate, even in the near future. Nevertheless, even as voluntary arrangements, they can in the long run shift political relationships in favor of arms restraint.

The first mechanism is an international organization to give military advice, a concept already introduced in Chapter Eight. Such an organization, which could be public or private, could help nations plan their military forces as economically as possible and deploy them with as little threat to stability as possible. There are the obvious difficulties of deception and of secret information, and the obvious risks that the organization would become a proponent of increased arms levels. Nevertheless, the benefits of supplementing the opinions of interested arms suppliers and of helping to develop a common understanding of the capability of rapidly changing technology are almost certain to make the effort worth the costs.

The other important mechanism is an international satellite system. The lack of intelligence data often makes for insecurity that can lead to higher arms levels. Again, the difficulties are enormous, but the existence of adequate intelligence, available to all nations and possibly even to the public, could contribute to a climate in which arms procurement can more readily be forgone.

These rather diffuse voluntary approaches may not be as satisfying as the achievement of broad formal agreements, but they are more likely to be feasible in the short run and effective in the long run. The problem of controlling new technology for the public benefit has not yet been solved at the national level. International questions of technology will be even more difficult.

10. Conclusions

SUBSTANTIAL arms control, even if in the traditional pattern of defined numerical limits, could have many desirable effects. It could prevent some wars, and mitigate the evil of wars that do occur. It could help avert strategic instability, and help settle regional conflicts. It might particularly help prevent the wars that are almost inevitable if many nations engage in balance-of-power maneuvering. Conceivably, it could sometimes help forestall the emergence of expansionism in dynamic developing nations. Admittedly, arms control cannot prevent all war, because weapons are only part of the cause of war. No arms control arrangement in the world can prevent a radicalized nation from launching aggression with whatever weapons it has. Nevertheless, well-designed arms control has much to offer.

Despite these theoretical benefits, however, it does not follow that even the undeniably useful self-interest agreements will ever actually be negotiated. The appeal of arms control is vague and general. One cannot say with certainty that a particular balance of power will break down by a particular time in the absence of arms control. One can only say that high and rapidly changing levels of arms, especially if the arms are suited to preemptive attack or to diplomatic threats, will make it more likely for a balance of power to break down. And to limit arms for this reason is politically weak in the face of threats from neighboring countries that seem to make increased arms necessary. Arms control is usually feasible only when the motivation for it happens to be both strong and specific; a typical motivation of this sort is the desire to symbolize a settlement between two equals or to condemn a particular weapon. Otherwise, it is nearly impossible to overcome the political and bureaucratic barriers to arms control.

Thus most projections for arms control negotiations are quite pessimistic. In many critical military areas there is a significant asymmetry. The United States and the Soviet Union have deployed substantially different kinds of strategic nuclear forces; the East-West balance in Europe is being tested by new Soviet deployments; and the forces of advanced developing nations are growing rapidly enough to fuel aspirations to great-power status, but not rapidly enough to produce equality with the great powers. Negotiations have become highly complex, reflecting the asymmetry, the advances in technology, and in some cases the increased number of nations wielding military power. And political pressure appears to be working against arms control. Both the SALT negotiations and—indirectly—European negotiations are captive to bad U.S.-Soviet relations; and neither North nor South appears very interested in negotiations to slow the spread of weapons technologies.

AN ALTERNATIVE STRATEGY

If arms are to be controlled, it is necessary to develop a new political approach that avoids the barriers to traditional arms control. The crucial need is for popular attitudes in all nations to evolve toward a transnational politics that favors domestic and international arms restraint. The Soviet Union will have little concern for any substantial arms control until its public is both interested in arms control and able to affect the policies of its leaders. The developing world will cooperate little in the control of military technology until public opinion in the developing world demands such control.

This approach is different from that generally taken in discussions of the long-term goals and potentials of arms control. Most previous discussions have treated arms control as proceeding toward a substantially disarmed world that is politically organized much like the current world. Clearly, my approach assumes a parallel process of political change, so that ultimately citizens of nations would accept an international decision as unhesitatingly as residents of states and provinces today accept a federal government decision. The new international order would have to have legitimacy in the eyes of citizens of all nations.

There are several reasons why this dramatic change is required. The first is simply that the usual diplomatic strategy will not work. Certainly it can go further than it has; and in a period resembling, say, that after the First World War, it might produce politically significant agreements. Nevertheless, as the preceding chapters have demonstrated, arms control negotiations face severe political limitations as long as they envision government-to-government agreements enforced by arrangements that fail to penetrate national sovereignty. Moreover, settlement agreements between governments lack the potential to move step by step toward a deeper arms control; only the legislative agreements, with their citizen involvement, offer this potential.

Second, the most feasible long-term method of enforcing a deep arms control is by direct intervention. Ultimately, international arms control enforcement could take a form analogous to that of domestic police and marshals operating under legal safeguards and the supervision of courts. The alternative concept of an international army punishing an entire nation is an absurdity that would tend to produce a global war. A deep arms control is possible only if an international organization can attract enough loyalty from citizens that they would support specific, legally sanctioned international operations to terminate a violation. Only if this sort of loyalty grows can the great powers be controlled with any degree of equality. Such loyalty is also essential for imposing significant arms restraint on reluctant governments; this will often be necessary, for new arrangements will constantly have to be legislated if arms control is to keep abreast of technology. Moreover, the use of direct intervention is the most effective way to avoid a tyranny of the enforcer; this problem is one of the reasons ordinary military intervention forces are unlikely to be created.

Third, a substantially disarmed world would be unstable unless citizens had ways to participate and bring about change in the international order.[1] Rearmament, including nuclear rearmament, can never be made technologically impossible; the risk of competitive rearmament will always be present. Without alternative mechanisms for producing change, the demand for justice will turn into the demand for war. It follows that a major global centralization is a prerequisite for arms control, both to maintain stability and to provide a focus for the loyalty and political activity of citizens.

It would be a mistake, however, to pursue centralization only for the sake of arms control. Centralization is desirable only if it serves other ends as well. In the existing world order, it is precisely the independence of national governments that allows freedom and diversity. Usually, moreover, the national decision makers are successful in maintaining peace by means of diplomacy.

For freedom and diversity to be preserved in a centralized world, the central authority would have to be controlled either by cultural strictures or by a balance of political power. For such a world to be stable, there would have to be a broad willingness to submit to the central authority; and most political groups would have to value the maintenance of that authority more than the achievement of their own specific goals. Loyalty to the international order would have to be linked to the citizen's desire for order more than to actual compulsion. Although there would have to be a military balance between the central authority and local groups, the community consensus, which could survive for some time in the face of an imbalance of power, would be far more important.

The choice between world centralization and the current order depends on the ability of each system to prevent war and to provide justice. For preventing diplomatic war, the centralized system is clearly better. Under the prevailing state system, the strategic conditions for successful balance-of-power diplomacy can no longer be met.[2] Such diplomacy can be successful only if there is an international consensus on the policies to be adopted toward specific conflicts and if each nation values the continuation of the international community more than it values victory in any major confrontation. These were the political conditions that failed during the wars of the Reformation but were met in part by the "agreement to disagree" of Westphalia. Stability also requires that the major powers be able and willing to enter into effective alliances in order to maintain the balance of military power. It was this aspect of the balance of power that broke down in Europe in the 1920's and 1930's and that is in doubt today.

The conditions of world community and balance of power must both be satisfied. The political community component of diplomacy is often ignored in thinking about diplomacy. But without a broad sense of community, it is too easy for a single nation to seek supremacy or to ignore balance-of-power needs; without it, too, ideological division between nations is more likely. The Concert of Europe, the most successful example of a balance of power, probably succeeded as much because of its cultural community, established in opposition to the disturbing forces of democracy, as because of its realpolitik. Nor is it feasible to maintain peace by great-power hegemony; such hegemony is becoming unacceptable to weaker nations, and its military underpinnings are collapsing in the face of new tactical technology and newly acquired military power.

Under a greater international authority, by contrast, nations are likely to have less motivation to construct weapons, and national leaders might have more chance of assembling coalitions to deter aggression. Moreover, the chance seems to be greater that national political cultures will shift toward the acceptance of a centralized order than that they will maintain the more complex parallelism needed for a stable balance of power. This judgment may seem surprising. However, the wide differences between nations and the rapidly changing character of society make it unlikely that the separate political cultures governing international relations will move in parallel. To be sure, the Western-trained elites (including, in this context, Soviet-trained elites) found in almost every nation have imposed a sort of global pragmatism. But those elites are small, and the Western culture they represent is in disarray. The unity they provide, therefore, may disappear as new elites come to reflect local traditions. Despite these differences, however, there is a growing political sense that many problems require global solutions. This sense is probably the political force that can most effectively prevent diplomatic war.

To prevent popular war, the choice between the current world order and a greater centralization necessarily rests on the expected character of politics and the ability to provide justice under the two systems. An international authority may often find it as difficult as national authorities to resolve local problems in such areas as race relations and economic development. An international system could also split along cultural lines and, like sectionalism before the U.S. Civil War, contribute to popular war. Nevertheless, some of the problems that underlie popular conflict may be more amenable to international leadership than to national. This is clearly true of global economic issues. Perhaps it is also true of some human rights issues; apartheid, for example, has already entered the scope of international authority. Centralization might work if it rested on transnational political movements and offered ways for citizens to work at both the local and the international levels to produce change. Politics and conflict would doubtless remain, but in a form analogous to today's domestic governance rather than today's international governance. On balance, a centralized system is probably better for controlling popular conflict.

In summary, a world in which arms were controlled but in which international authority remained closely similar to that of the current UN would be a world too strongly oriented toward the status quo to accommodate necessary change. The demands of justice would too often be directly opposed to the demands of security. Such an order would be likely to collapse in the face of change like the world of the 1930's, which was marked by elaborate alliances, organizations, and arms control arrangements. A strategy aimed at a deep arms control cannot follow the current pattern; it must instead be built on direct citizen participation in a supranational system.

In a world order thus centralized, arms control itself would become less critical. Political conflicts could find political solutions, which would lead to fewer demands for military solutions and consequently to less pressure for keeping peace and controlling war. National governments could place much less emphasis on defense calculations. They might even voluntarily refrain from expanding their armed forces; this has been the pattern under the U.S. Constitution even though it expressly protects the states' right to build armed forces. At the same time, arms control would be more feasible. There could be mechanisms for reaching international decisions to prohibit or restrict arms by a less than unanimous consensus. Direct intervention could become the normal mode of enforcement. International action against a violation would be much easier to organize, and it might be possible to avoid the tyranny that otherwise seems likely to accompany arms control enforcement. Ideally, arms control would be for the most part a technical legislative problem of how to deal with the residue of the old order and with the side effects of new technology. The enforcement of arms control would, appropriately, be legal rather than political.

Only in a centralized world is a truly deep arms control possible. It is the only system in which the sanction of direct intervention is natural, and thus the only one affording a reliable, veto-free way to control dangerous new military technology. It is the only one that can ultimately permit effective sanctions against the current major powers. Most important, it is probably the only one that can offer the new mechanisms needed for peaceful political change. Finally, it is perhaps the only one that can be fully responsive to the political changes imposed by the invention of nuclear weapons.

THE TRANSITION PROCESS

The arguments just stated could easily lead one to despair, for national governments usually avoid giving international organizations the ability to build citizen constituencies. Western international law, for example, has long had a tradition rejecting direct contact between the individual and international law; this tradition is only now beginning to break down. Marxist regimes and the governments of newly independent developing nations have also persisted in maintaining exclusive national control over their citizens.

Nevertheless, limited precursors of an international authority can already be discerned, and there is already some sense of international community. The process of peaceful centralization has typically occurred in two phases. In the first, as reflected in the negotiation of the U.S. Constitution in 1789 and in the first two decades of the European Economic Community, the goal is a limited federalism that brings specific benefits obtainable only by cooperation. During this phase, local leaders view the central organization as their creature; thus they often encourage such centralization. Nevertheless, they carefully calculate the gains and losses accruing to each member. The negotiations essentially involve a bargaining to ensure that each member gains in the overall balance.

When such a process of integration enters the second phase, people focus on an organization that already exists, and seek to transfer power to it, typically to compel the members to behave in ways generally desired by the community.

The people look to the central authority to reform or replace the local governments. Thus the amendments to the U.S. Constitution following the Civil War gave the federal government new rights to intervene in state government. Similarly, the change to direct elections for the European Parliament rests in part on a sense that this will ultimately strengthen the EEC and give Europe a more forceful voice than it can gain by mere cooperation among the national governments. Indeed, many believe the increased integration of Europe will help maintain democracy in nations such as Greece and Spain.

In the United States the concentration of power followed a war in which victory gave a psychological legitimacy to the central government. War also marked much of the nation building in both Western Europe and Asia. To achieve on a global scale a peaceful transition like that now occurring in Europe will require the telescoping of the two historical phases. The immediate task is to work for contact between citizens and international authority at all levels—in short, to build a sense of world community.

In general, the traditional forms of arms control are unlikely to play a major role in effective world centralization; indeed, so far they have often reinforced the traditional system of a balance of power among nations. It is economic concerns and human rights that will attract the greatest political support. Nevertheless, when arms control deals with problems that command public constituencies, such as the control of technology, it can play a significant political role. Perhaps by stimulating the creation of international political institutions, arms control can also strengthen the political forces for centralization. For example, a successful UN procedure for enforcing regional arms control, even if only loosely linked to the UN, would both encourage citizens to look to the UN for such action and help overcome the common fear that arms control agreements are per se unenforceable. A UN role in verification, although less dramatic, would give the UN routine visibility apart from crises; such visibility could be especially important if verification findings were open to the public.[3]

New procedures for settling disputes related to arms control can also be important in building constituencies. For this purpose, the key requirement is that such procedures be judicial, or at least public. The lack of these attributes is the weakness of the Standing Consultative Commission (SCC), established by the United States and the USSR under SALT I. The SCC leaves authority with the separate national governments, and directs political pressure toward them. Such consultation as that in the SCC, although perhaps desirable as a practical, "second-best" approach to arms control because it is easier to negotiate, does not have the potential of judicial means either for building a framework for public reliance on international law or for stimulating the public interest in reshaping that law. The main political benefit of consultation is the important but weaker one of promoting the idea that arms levels are properly a matter of international concern.

Of all the ways to encourage centralization, the most important is probably the creation of a directly elected international parliament. This would help political parties to transcend national lines. It would also increase the citizen's sense of international community, much as the direct election of congressmen and senators in the United States encouraged the citizens to transfer loyalty from the various states to the federal government. A directly elected parliament would provide a way to supervise and control international organizations, and would thus permit more power to be transferred to these organizations with less risk to liberty. Ultimately, such a parliament could use international legislation to meet change without being hampered by national vetoes.

Though national governments are hesitant to create such a body, almost any sort of international elected group would be a major step toward a transnational politics of security; it would force statesmen to pay greater attention to global needs.[4] Such a group could raise new issues—including arms control—in ways favorable to international cooperation. Its delegates could be expected to form coalitions tantamount to international political parties, and to work for change at both the national and the international levels. Most of this would occur even if the elected assembly had no formal power, and little would be lost in the early phases if the membership were incomplete or if some elections were rigged by national governments.

Other conceivable arrangements are an elected international advisory body and a custom that nations include an elected member of their legislature in their UN delegation. Though very weak, such arrangements are likely to gain political force with the passage of time. What is essential is that from the outset any elected body of this sort be competent to deal with economic and social issues as well as strategic issues. Except in times of crisis, international security issues, and still less arms control, do not attract great public interest. Economic and social issues, however, have the political appeal both to give an organization legitimacy and to draw together transnational coalitions.

The design of broader politics of this sort is beyond the scope of this book. Nevertheless, it should be noted that such a politics is unlikely to emerge unless accompanied by a political theory dealing with issues such as democracy, justice, and peace on the international level, and suggesting appropriate roles for international organization in achieving these ideals. The widespread appeal of the Leninist theory of imperialism, in spite of its inadequacies in describing the world, is precisely that it attempts such a task. A more adequate theory that focuses on the emerging issues between North and South, for example, is crucial if there is ever to be effective international organization.

THE SHORT-TERM AGENDA

The analysis in this book suggests an arms control agenda substantially different from the current working agenda. The key point is that the most important steps in arms control will be those moving toward institutional reforms. It is not essential that all nations immediately support these reforms. Even if only some nations participate at first, most new arrangements can still be designed both to provide strategic safety and to have the beginnings of international political legitimacy. Any arms control institutions that are initially unattached to a centralized structure such as the UN could later be grafted onto such a structure; indeed, this may be the only way to effect a deep reform of the UN.

The most important of the immediately plausible institutional reforms are:

1. Establishment of an international, directly elected advisory group to deliberate on political, economic, and security issues.

2. Agreement by the nations with nuclear weapons to consult among themselves, preferably in the Security Council, in the event of any use, threatened use, or new construction of nuclear weapons.

3. Establishment, by the UN or by existing regional organizations, of regional military consultation forums to discuss military forces, procurements, and deployments affecting the region.

4. Creation of an international military advisory group designed to offer confidential assistance to any nation requesting such assistance in connection with decisions to procure weapons.

5. Establishment, privately or by the UN, of a panel of independent experts to consider the global stabilizing or destabilizing effects of specific new military technologies.

6. Reform of the IAEA conferring upon it new authority to define minimum standards for the safety, environmental, and antiterrorist aspects of nuclear power, and to give it or a new agency full authority over sensitive nuclear fuel cycle facilities.

7. Creation of a UN observation satellite system.

It is these institutional reforms that are most important and should take priority. Nevertheless, even in the face of the collapse of SALT, there is a useful immediate agenda for a more traditional form of arms control, an agenda that differs in part from the current one:

1. Regional settlement packages in areas such as southern Africa and the Middle East, incorporating arms control and guaranteed enforcement.

2. Reshaping of the international trade system (and of national economies and arms industries) so as to reduce the economic incentive for arms transfers.

3. Improvement of national restraints on the use of military force, the export of military goods, and the provision of military assistance.

4. International judicial arrangements to help in controlling terrorism.

5. A promise by all nuclear nations not to use nuclear weapons against nonnuclear nations (with appropriate exceptions for deterring war in Europe and Northeast Asia).

6. A comprehensive nuclear test ban.

In addition, there are several possibilities for negotiation that deserve very serious consideration, though particularly in tense times they may offer only a slight chance of success or carry a significant risk. Some of these proposals might reasonably be reserved for circumstances more favorable to negotiation, such as a period of détente or a time when the world is recoiling from a crisis. They are:

1. Global or regional rules restricting great-power military intervention and military assistance.

2. A global prohibition on the further production of nuclear materials for military purposes.

3. A revival of SALT, preferably focusing on arrangements to slow the development of new military technologies.

4. Regional discussions to improve the stability of regional deterrence.

5. Global or regional restrictions on specific destabilizing weapons and technologies.

Precisely because it is the sense of global community that is most important, the central need is less for formal new agreements and institutions than for discussion and political action by the world's unofficial international communities. At this time, the indirect approaches to arms control are more important than the direct ones.

Notes

Notes

CHAPTER 1

1. For a taxonomy and analysis of theories of war, see Kenneth N. Waltz, *Man, the State, and War: A Theoretical Analysis* (New York, 1959); and Quincy Wright, *A Study of War*, abridged ed. (Chicago, 1965).

2. See generally David N. Daniels, Marshall F. Gilula, and Frank M. Ochberg, eds., *Violence and the Struggle for Existence* (Boston, 1970); Konrad Lorenz, *On Aggression*, trans. Marjorie K. Wilson (New York, 1966), p. 47; and L. Harrison Matthews, "Overt Fighting in Mammals," in J. D. Carthy and F. J. Ebling, eds., *The Natural History of Aggression* (London, 1964), p. 23. For criticism, see Samuel S. Kim, "The Lorenzian Theory of Aggression and Peace Research: A Critique," *Journal of Peace Research*, 13 (1976): 253. I wish particularly to thank Peter Corning, who helped me significantly in my effort to understand evolutionary approaches to aggression.

3. For a review of the data on primates, see J. F. Eisenberg, N. A. Muckenhirn, and R. Rudran, "The Relation Between Ecology and Social Structure in Primates," *Science*, 176 (1972): 863. The view that aggression and authority are physiologically related is supported by evidence that the two behaviors derive from identical or contiguous brain areas. See R. Charles Boelkins and Jon F. Heiser, "Biological Bases of Aggression," in Daniels et al., *Violence*, pp. 15, 28–30.

4. See Hannah Arendt, *On Violence* (New York, 1969), pp. 39–40.

5. Stanley Milgram, *Obedience to Authority* (New York, 1974).

6. Andrew P. Vayda, "Hypotheses about Functions of War," in Morton Fried, Marvin Harris, and Robert Murphy, eds., *War* (Garden City, N.Y., 1968), p. 85.

7. See Roy L. Prosterman, *Surviving to 3000* (Belmont, Calif., 1972), pp. 141–46, for a summary of the evidence that prehistoric society was generally peaceful. See also Vayda, "Hypotheses." Robert L. Carneiro, "A Theory of the Origin of the State," *Science*, 169 (1970): 733, suggests that warfare occurred earlier in history than most scholars think. For a mixed position, see Wright, *Study of War*, pp. 33–42. For a suggestion of the complexity and variation of different

patterns of war and peace in traditional societies, see Keith F. Otterbein, "Warfare: A Hitherto Unrecognized Critical Variable," *American Behavioral Scientist*, 20 (1977): 693.

8. Even in animals, the genetic determinants sometimes provide only a set of possible response patterns whose characteristics are then shaped by learning. See Boelkins and Heiser, "Biological Bases," pp. 33–40. Such complexity certainly holds for humans as well. See also L. von Bertalanffy, "Comments on Aggression," *Bulletin of the Menninger Clinic*, 22 (March 1958), cited in Group for the Advancement of Psychiatry, *Psychiatric Aspects of the Prevention of Nuclear War*; *Reports and Symposiums*, 5 (Sept. 1964): 231; and Daniels et al., *Violence*, pp. 428–32.

9. Margaret Mead, "Warfare Is Only an Invention—Not a Biological Necessity," *Asia*, 40 (1940), quoted in Prosterman, *Surviving*, pp. 148–53.

10. Fred H. Willhoite, "Primates and Political Authority: A Biobehavioral Perspective," *American Political Science Review*, 70 (1976): 1110. For a criticism of this article by Phillip C. Chapman and a response by the author, see *ibid.*, 71 (1977): 1050.

11. See Isidore Ziferstein, "Psychological Habituation to War: A Sociopsychological Case Study," *American Journal of Orthopsychiatry*, 37 (1967): 457.

12. For a careful discussion of this era, see Charles Tilly, ed., *The Formation of National States in Western Europe* (Princeton, N.J., 1975).

13. See generally Kalman H. Silvert, ed., *Expectant Peoples: Nationalism and Development* (New York, 1963).

14. Compare Charles Burton Marshall: "Prestige is the faculty enabling a great power to avoid final, miserable choices between surrender and war. Prestige is the ingredient of authority in international affairs . . . that demands being listened to . . . and a nation suffers loss of it at great peril." *Cuba: Thoughts Prompted by the Crisis* (Washington, D.C., n.d.), p. 3, quoted in Alexander L. George, David K. Hall, and William E. Simons, *The Limits of Coercive Diplomacy* (Boston, 1971), p. 93.

15. See Charles R. Beitz, "Bounded Morality: Justice and the State in World Politics," *International Organization*, 33 (1979): 405.

16. See R. R. Palmer, "Frederick the Great, Guibert, Bülow: From Dynastic to National War," in Edward Mead Earle, ed., *Makers of Modern Strategy: Military Thought from Machiavelli to Hitler* (1941; reprint ed., New York, 1970), pp. 69–74, for a discussion of the disarray among strategic thinkers following Napoleon's development of an army in which he could rely on allegiance rather than force to motivate his troops in time of war.

17. For discussion of some of these variations, see John J. Johnson, *The Military and Society in Latin America* (Stanford, Calif., 1964).

CHAPTER 2

1. Richard A. Preston, Sydney F. Wise, and Herman O. Werner, *Men in Arms: A History of Warfare and Its Interrelationships with Western Society*, rev. ed. (New York, 1962), pp. 78–79.

2. For examples of the importance of finances in limiting military power in the eighteenth century, see Geoffrey Blainey, *The Causes of War* (London, 1973), pp. 87–91. Although this book's conclusions are oversimplified, it contains many useful insights. Armies did not become large until about Napoleon's time, as may be seen from the table in R. R. Palmer, "Frederick the Great, Guibert, Bülow: From Dynastic to National War," in Edward Mead Earle, ed., *Makers of Modern Strategy: Military Thought from Machiavelli to Hitler* (1941; reprint ed., New York, 1970), p. 57.

3. See Preston et al., *Men in Arms*, pp. 129–46.

4. *Ibid.*, pp. 176–83.

5. The wars in the nineteenth century were generally much more decisive than those in the eighteenth; see Blainey, *Causes of War*, p. 118.

6. Another major historical change, perhaps as great as that of the French Revolution, may have occurred around 1900. The supporting evidence is a break in the applicability of the theoretical models being developed by quantitative analysts of war. Thus the Singer group at the University of Michigan contrasted a balance-of-power model, under which peace among major powers is more likely to be associated with the presence of many relatively equal nations, with a preponderance and stability model, under which peace is more likely to be associated with dominance. Though neither model was strongly verified, the first fit substantially better in the nineteenth century and the second in the twentieth. The authors suggest that the change may have derived from the greater dependence of foreign policy on domestic politics starting around 1900. J. David Singer, Stuart Bremer, and John Stuckey, "Capability Distribution, Uncertainty, and Major Power War, 1820–1965," in Bruce M. Russett, ed., *Peace, War, and Numbers* (Beverly Hills, Calif., 1972), p. 19.

7. For a careful and much more detailed summary of these historical interpretations, see David M. Potter, "The Literature on the Background of the Civil War," in *The South and the Sectional Conflict* (Baton Rouge, La., 1968), pp. 87–150.

8. Russel B. Nye and J. E. Morpurgo, *A History of the United States* (Baltimore, 1955), 2: 381–82.

9. *Ibid.*, pp. 407–16.

10. Potter, *South*, pp. 137–38.

11. *Ibid.*, pp. 138–39.

12. On the importance of the fear of slave rebellion, see *ibid.*, pp. 77–80.

13. Kenneth M. Stampp, *And the War Came: The North and the Secession Crisis, 1860–1861* (Baton Rouge, La., 1950), pp. 13–19.

14. *Ibid.*, pp. 53–57.   15. *Ibid.*, pp. 84–85.

16. *Ibid.*, p. 216.   17. *Ibid.*, p. 90.

18. *Ibid.*, p. 133.   19. *Ibid.*, pp. 137–39.

20. See *ibid.*, pp. 204–62, for a careful review of Northern motivations, among which was the fear that allowing secession would lower public morality.

21. *Ibid.*, pp. 263–64.

22. Lincoln's motivation is subject to the predictable dispute; see *ibid.*, pp. 280–86, and Potter, *South*, pp. 142–43.

23. Stampp, *And the War Came*, pp. 290–91.

24. Charles Petrie, *Diplomatic History, 1713–1933* (London, 1946), pp. 229–31.

25. Charles Fisher, "The Changing Dimensions of Europe," in Walter Laqueur and George L. Mosse, eds., *1914 (Journal of Contemporary History*, 1 [July 1966]).

26. Petrie, *Diplomatic History*, pp. 239–41.

27. *Ibid.*, p. 238.

28. *Ibid.*, pp. 242–44.

29. Jonathan Steinberg, "The Copenhagen Complex," in Laqueur and Mosse, *1914*, pp. 25–28.

30. W. H. Langer, *The Diplomacy of Imperialism*, cited in A. Whitney Griswold, *The Far Eastern Policy of the United States* (New York, 1938), p. 37.

31. Petrie, *Diplomatic History*, pp. 306–8.

32. Norman Stone, "Hungary and the Crisis of July," in Laqueur and Mosse, *1914*, pp. 158–59.

33. Imanuel Geiss, "The Outbreak of the First World War and German War Aims," *ibid.*, pp. 80–82.

34. For good discussions of the issues, see Wolfgang J. Mommsen, "The Debate on German War Aims," *ibid.*, p. 47; Klaus Epstein, "Gerhard Ritter and the First World War," *ibid.*, p. 193; and Fritz Stern, "Bethmann Hollweg and the War: The Limits of Responsibility," in Leonard Kreiger and Fritz Stern, eds., *The Responsibility of Power: Historical Essays in Honor of Hajo Holborn* (Garden City, N.Y., 1967), p. 252.

35. See I. V. Bestuzhev, "Russian Foreign Policy, February–June 1914," in Laqueur and Mosse, *1914*, p. 93.

36. This definition is very similar to Professor Alexander George's "operational code" concept. See George, "The 'Operational Code': A Neglected Approach to the Study of Political Leaders and Decision-making," *International Studies Quarterly*, 13 (June 1969): 190.

37. John Whitney Hall, *Japan from Prehistory to Modern Times* (New York, 1970), pp. 327–28.

38. Compare Michael D. Wallace, "Status, Formal Organization, and Arms Levels as Features Leading to the Onset of War, 1820–

1964," in Russett, *Peace, War, and Numbers*, p. 49. In the short term, differing domestic and foreign evaluations of prestige would seem more likely to produce diplomatic war than popular war. But studies show relatively long time lags (up to fifteen years) between the perception of the inconsistency and the onset of war; these time lags would be likely to affect the mass political culture more than the diplomatic sphere. Some of the effect, therefore, may be best explained at the popular level.

39. Data are readily interpreted so as to be consistent with preconceptions about another society. See Frederic W. Ilfeld and Richard J. Metzner, "Alternatives to Violence," in David N. Daniels, Marshall F. Gilula, and Frank M. Ochberg, eds., *Violence and the Struggle for Existence* (Boston, 1970), p. 134.

40. A statistical study of violence between Israel and various Arab countries found that the violent actions on each side could "best be explained by the violent actions of that country's enemy." The action-reaction phenomenon was quite clear. Jeffrey S. Milstein, "American and Soviet Influence, Balance of Power, and Arab-Israeli Violence," in Russett, *Peace, War, and Numbers*, p. 139.

41. The Milstein study, *ibid.*, showed that the level of violence in the Middle East did not depend on either arms levels or the relative arms balance or imbalance.

42. The complexity of this description is substantiated by an empirical study of correlations over the period from 1820 to 1964, an era in which diplomatic war was dominant; see Wallace, "Status." The study found only a weak correlation between political concerns and war, though a tie between the two would be the heart of a pattern of escalation analogous to that of popular warfare. Instead, there was a strong correlation between political concerns and the formation of alliances, suggesting that the general fear of war is associated with diplomatic activity. Likewise, arms levels were closely related to war frequency and to alliance activity, suggesting that arms are procured to maintain the balance of alliances and in preparation for impending wars. Thus the diplomatic and military system may serve as a buffer and transmission link between political concerns and diplomatic war, precisely the pattern described in the text.

43. See Alexander L. George and Richard Smoke, *Deterrence in American Foreign Policy* (New York, 1974), pp. 572–76, for a careful discussion of misperception of diplomatic signals.

44. For examples, see Blainey, *Causes of War*, pp. 68–86.

45. See Thomas C. Schelling, *Arms and Influence* (New Haven, Conn., 1966).

46. Alexander L. George, David K. Hall, and William E. Simons, *The Limits of Coercive Diplomacy: Laos, Cuba, Vietnam* (Boston, 1971), pp. 215–28, develops further elements of diplomatic coercion, which are also somewhat difficult to achieve: strength of coercer's motivations, asymmetry of motivation favoring the coercer, clarity of

coercer's objectives, sense of urgency to achieve those objectives, adequate domestic political support, usable military options, opponent's fear of unacceptable escalation, and clarity concerning settlement terms.

47. *Ibid.*, pp. 8–15.

48. See L. Chester, G. Hodgson, and B. Page, *An American Melodrama: The Presidential Campaign of 1968* (New York, 1969), p. 28, cited in Michael P. Sullivan, "Symbolic Involvement as a Correlate of Escalation: The Vietnam Case," in Russett, *Peace, War, and Numbers*, p. 185.

CHAPTER 3

1. See for example Michael Barkun, *Law Without Sanctions: Order in Primitive Societies and the World Community* (New Haven, Conn., 1968).

2. This need for breadth of definition is also suggested in Kjell Goldmann, *International Norms and War Between States* (Stockholm, 1971), pp. 10–11.

3. See H. A. R. Gibb, "Constitutional Organization," in Majid Khadduri and Herbert J. Liebesny, eds., *Law in the Middle East* (Washington, D.C., 1955), p. 3.

4. For an elaboration of this point, see Leo Gross, "The Peace of Westphalia, 1648–1948," *American Journal of International Law*, 42 (1948): 20. The parallel changes in the theory of domestic politics are outlined in Leonard Krieger, "Power and Responsibility: The Historical Assumptions," in Leonard Krieger and Fritz Stern, eds., *The Responsibility of Power: Historical Essays in Honor of Hajo Holborn* (Garden City, N.Y., 1967), p. 1.

5. For elaboration, see J. L. Brierly, *The Law of Nations*, 6th ed. (New York, 1963), pp. 1–40.

6. See for example Hungdah Chiu, "The Nature of International Law and the Problem of a Universal System," in Shao-Chuan Leng and Hungdah Chiu, eds., *Law in Chinese Foreign Policy: Communist China and Selected Problems of International Law* (Dobbs Ferry, N.Y., 1972), p. 1.

7. Vattel recognized this point quite clearly; see his *The Law of Nations*, book 3, secs. 105–6, trans. Joseph Chitty (London, 1834), p. 233. The United Nations Charter's formal limits on war raise the same problem today.

8. C. John Colombos, *International Law of the Sea*, 6th ed. (London, 1967), p. 632.

9. W. S. M. Knight, "Neutrality and Neutralization in the Sixteenth Century—Liège," *Journal of Comparative Legislation*, 3d ser., 2 (1920): 98–101.

10. See for example Chr. Robinson, *Collectanea Maritima* (London, 1801), p. 25. These courts date from at least as far back as Edward III; see Colombos, *Law of the Sea*, p. 11.

11. For examples see Philip C. Jessup and Francis Deak, *Neutrality: Its History, Economics and Law* (New York, 1935), 1: 40–41.

12. Colombos, *Law of the Sea*, p. 479.

13. Robinson, *Collectanea*, pp. 83–104.

14. See for example the English Royal Instructions of 1512 directing the English Admiral to search "strange ships" (*ibid.*, p. 11) and the 1591 application of this doctrine to Dutch ships cited by Colombos, *Law of the Sea*, p. 753.

15. For example, the destruction or absence of a ship's papers creates an inference that the ship was violating the rules of neutrality. Jessup and Deak, *Neutrality*, pp. 226–46.

16. Carl J. Kulsrud, "Armed Neutralities to 1780," *American Journal of International Law*, 29 (1935): 423.

17. For a parallel approach reaching quite similar results, see Kenneth N. Waltz, *Man, the State, and War: A Theoretical Analysis* (New York, 1959), pp. 188–225. This analysis can readily be stated in game theory terms.

18. Article I of *Convention Relative to the Opening of Hostilities* (The Hague, Oct. 18, 1907).

19. Scholars seem unable to find any general policy in this area, leaving the initiation of a war to be defined as necessary for such varied purposes as interpreting war risk clauses in insurance policies and interpreting legal provisions authorizing executive actions only in time of war or emergency. Clyde Eagleton, "The Form and Function of the Declaration of War," *American Journal of International Law*, 32 (1938): 19; L. C. Green, "Armed Conflict, War, and Self-Defense," *Archiv des Völkerrechts*, 6 (1956–57): 387.

20. Compare Tom J. Farer, "Law and War," in Cyril E. Black and Richard A. Falk, *The Future of the International Legal Order* (Princeton, N.J., 1971), 3: 17–21.

21. Thus many authors describe international law as a form of "communication," which presumably assists in finding those balances that encourage restraint. See Nicholas Greenwood Onuf, "The Principle of Non-Intervention, the United Nations, and the International System," *International Organization*, 25 (1971): 209–27.

22. Compare Richard J. Barnet, "Toward the Control of International Violence: The Limits and Possibilities of Law," in Black and Falk, *Future*, 3: 385–90.

23. United States v. Curtiss-Wright Export Corp., 299 U.S. 304, 318 (1936).

24. For examples, see Sardino v. Federal Reserve Bank of New York, 361 F.2d 106, (2d Cir.) *cert. denied*, 385 U.S. 898 (1966) (seizure of property); and Korematsu v. United States, 323 U.S. 214 (1944) (internment of citizens of Japanese descent).

25. In *Ex parte* Milligan, 71 U.S. (4 Wall.) 2 (1866), the Court, after the Civil War, retroactively struck down a military conviction of a civilian under Civil War emergency legislation. During the Second

World War, the case was distinguished to permit curfews enforced by civilian courts, Hirabayashi v. United States, 320 U.S. 81 (1943) (a case on which Korematsu relied), and, in dictum, to permit detention by civilian authorities (as opposed to the military authorities of *Milligan*), *Ex parte* Endo, 323 U.S. 283, 297–302 (1944) (petitioner freed under interpretation of rules, but government authority to issue rules upheld). Then, after the war, wartime military convictions of civilians in Hawaii were set aside on the basis of the Hawaiian Organic Act; Duncan v. Kahanamoku, 327 U.S. 304 (1946). The military-civilian distinction may be valid, but one wonders.

26. The judgment is my own, based on the court's action in a number of recent cases, such as Nuclear Tests (Australia v. France) [1974] I.C.J. Rep. 253; Case concerning the Barcelona Traction, Light, and Power Co., Ltd. (Belgium v. Spain) [1970] I.C.J. Rep. 4; and Nottebohm Case (Liechtenstein v. Guatemala) [1955] I.C.J. Rep. 4. For a comment more sympathetic to the Court, see Julius Stone, *Legal Controls of International Conflict* (Sydney, 1959 ed.), pp. 146–52.

27. See Goldman, *International Norms*, pp. 22–23.

28. Michel Tournier, "Il y a vingt-cinq ans; Le tribunal international de Nuremberg condamnait à mort les principaux chefs nazis," *Le Monde*, Sélection Hebdomadaire (Sept. 30–Aug. 6, 1971): 6.

29. See for example Telford Taylor, *Nuremberg and Vietnam: An American Tragedy* (Chicago, 1970).

30. See Ryukichi Imai and John H. Barton, eds., *Arms Control II: A New Approach to International Security* (Cambridge, Mass., forthcoming).

CHAPTER 4

1. For such reviews, see the publications of the Stockholm International Peace Research Institute (SIPRI); see also John H. Barton and Lawrence D. Weiler, eds., *International Arms Control: Issues and Agreements* (Stanford, Calif., 1976).

2. Cf. C. Wilfred Jenks, *The World Beyond the Charter* (London, 1969), p. 167.

3. Chalmers M. Roberts, "The Road to Moscow," in Mason Willrich and John B. Rhinelander, eds., *SALT: The Moscow Agreements and Beyond* (New York, 1974), pp. 3–4.

4. For an example of this public strategy in the British system, see Laurence W. Martin, "The Market for Strategic Ideas in Britain: The 'Sandys Era,'" *American Political Science Review*, 56 (1962): 23.

5. Alton Frye, "U.S. Decision Making for SALT," in Willrich and Rhinelander, *SALT*, p. 76.

6. Cf. Fred Charles Iklé, *How Nations Negotiate* (New York, 1967), pp. 43–58.

7. Salvador de Madariaga, *Disarmament* (New York, 1929), p. 61.

8. Iklé, *How Nations Negotiate*, p. 2.

9. Cf. Roberts, "Road to Moscow," p. 4.

10. I am indebted to Professor Hisashi Maeda of Sophia University, Tokyo, for his articulation of the relationship between détente and arms control. Although détente must probably precede arms control, I must also admit that arms control may become so significant an aspect of a particular détente relationship (such as that between the United States and the Soviet Union) that the failure to negotiate arms control agreements may seriously hurt the relationship. Thus SALT and U.S.-Soviet détente may be mutually dependent, as is suggested by the Soviet invasion of Afghanistan while SALT II was in difficulty in the Senate.

11. Thus, if Israel does have nuclear weapons, it has been very careful not to admit it publicly. On tacit agreements generally, see John H. Barton, "Tacit Political Restraints as a Way to Control Conventional Arms," *Stanford Journal of International Studies*, 14 (1979): 29.

12. It is debatable, however, whether the U.S.-Soviet arms competition is in fact an action-reaction arms race or one driven by parallel internal pressures on each side. See Albert Wohlstetter, "Is There a Strategic Arms Race?" *Foreign Policy*, 15 (1974): 3.

13. See John G. Cross, *The Economics of Bargaining* (New York, 1969), pp. 12–14.

14. Thomas C. Schelling, *The Strategy of Conflict* (London, 1960), pp. 67–74.

15. On the use of the U.S. ABM program as a bargaining chip, see Frye, "U.S. Decision Making," p. 74.

16. G. B. Kistiakowsky and H. F. York, "Strategic Arms Race Slowdown Through Test Limitations," *Science*, 185 (Aug. 2, 1974): 403.

CHAPTER 5

1. Abram Chayes, "An Inquiry into the Workings of Arms Control Agreements," *Harvard Law Review*, 85 (1972): 905, 937–39, argues against this tendency, suggesting that a penumbra of activities near the agreement will be avoided. I would disagree, citing the course of experience: underground nuclear tests that vent, Soviet fractional orbital weapons systems, and Soviet actions under SALT I. The later edition of Professor Chayes' work weakens his point somewhat; see G. W. Rathjens, Abram Chayes, and J. P. Ruina, *Nuclear Arms Control Agreements: Process and Impact* (Washington, D.C., 1974), pp. 47–48.

2. This discussion draws heavily on Chayes, "Inquiry," which develops this argument extremely well.

3. Kissinger, quoted in Graham Allison, "Cold Dawn and the Mind of Kissinger," *Washington Monthly*, 6 (March 1974): 39, 45.

4. Chayes, "Inquiry," pp. 934–35, would argue that such a bad faith entry into a treaty is nearly impossible anywhere. He is quite correct in asserting that a widespread bureaucratic involvement

makes a bad faith entry unlikely for a government like that of the United States, but I think he underestimates the ability of senior officials to work their will on the bureaucracy in authoritarian countries.

5. John Whitney Hall, *Japan from Prehistory to Modern Times* (New York, 1970), p. 325.

6. Arnold J. Toynbee, ed., *Survey of International Affairs: 1936* (London, 1937), pp. 85–104.

7. For a hint of this difficulty, see the symposium entitled "Technological Change and the Strategic Arms Race," in William R. Kintner and Robert L. Pfaltzgraff, Jr., eds., *SALT: Implications for Arms Control in the 1970s* (Pittsburgh, 1973), pp. 118–22.

8. An interesting confirmation of the irrationality of attitudes toward verification is provided by the ready willingness of nations to rely purely on intelligence data in making the crucial decision whether or not to enter into an agreement. Conceivably, in some elaborate multiphase agreement of the future, on-site inspection might be necessary to obtain information on whether or not it is safe to proceed with a further phase of the agreement.

9. Ted Greenwood, "Reconnaissance and Arms Control," *Scientific American*, 228 (Feb. 1973): 14.

10. Alva Myrdal, "The International Control of Disarmament," *ibid.*, 231 (Oct. 1974): 21; see also the 1978 French proposal, French Mission note of May 30, 1978, addressed to UN Secretariat, UN Document A/S-10/AC.1/7.

11. One author argues that Britain's choice of such a strategy in the face of the German violation of the Versailles Treaty was deliberate, made in the expectation that Germany would construct fewer weapons if the treaty were not formally terminated. Arie E. David, *The Strategy of Treaty Termination: Lawful Breaches and Retaliations* (New Haven, Conn., 1975), p. 142.

12. I explore the concept of consultation in "Tacit Political Restraints as a Way to Control Conventional Arms," *Stanford Journal of International Studies*, 14 (1979): 29. An introductory exploration of the economic incentives approach is contained in Ryukichi Imai and John H. Barton, eds., *Arms Control II: A New Approach to International Security* (Cambridge, Mass., forthcoming).

CHAPTER 6

1. For a general review of international intervention arrangements, see Mark W. Zacher, *International Conflicts and Collective Security, 1946-77* (New York, 1979). Economic sanctions are not considered in this chapter. Experience has shown them too ineffective to be useful for deep-cutting arms control. They are often little more than a way to avoid action, and frequently they are counterproductive. The U.S. sanctions against Cuba, for example, have probably encouraged the Cuban population to support the offending policies. For studies, see C. Lloyd Brown-John, *Multilateral Sanctions in Inter-*

national Law: A Comparative Analysis (New York, 1975); and Margaret P. Doxey, *Economic Sanctions and International Enforcement* (London, 1971). Mr. Brown-John does find some economic sanctions successful; but his conclusion is severely qualified, and his standard of success is weaker than would be acceptable for serious arms control agreements. Ms. Doxey is much more negative.

2. See Hans Blix, *Sovereignty, Aggression, and Neutrality* (Stockholm, 1970), p. 35.

3. This problem of the lack of proportionality between the sanction and the violation has long been noted. See Roger Fisher, "International Police: A Sequential Approach to Effectiveness and Control," in Richard J. Barnet and Richard A. Falk, eds., *Security in Disarmament* (Princeton, N.J., 1965), pp. 240, 243–45.

4. See Robert Endicott Osgood, *NATO: The Entangling Alliance* (Chicago, 1962), pp. 40–45.

5. If a sanction is to support a substantial arms control, there must be confidence that the sanction will actually be imposed during the course of a military buildup. Thus an automatic sanction seems called for. In the case of the traditional UN sanctions against aggression, however, many commentators have argued that the imposition of the sanction must be discretionary, resting on an estimate of its potential military success. See Blix, *Sovereignty*, pp. 30–32. In arms control, of course, force levels can be designed to affect this chance of success.

6. The use of UN forces in the Congo and perhaps in Cyprus followed a somewhat different pattern, which will be discussed in connection with direct intervention.

7. The contradiction between the presumed demands of justice and the presumed needs of collective security explains such results as the failure of the UN to respond to India's annexation of Goa in 1961. See generally Herbert Nichols, "An Appraisal," in Lincoln P. Bloomfield, ed., *International Military Forces* (Boston, 1964), pp. 105–6.

8. For a series of examples, see James O. C. Jonah, "Peacekeeping in the Middle East," *International Journal*, 31 (1975–76): 100.

9. For suggested uses of this technique, see Richard J. Barnet, "Violations of Disarmament Agreements," Barnet and Falk, *Security*, pp. 157, 169; and Louis B. Sohn, "Responses to Violations: A General Survey," *ibid.*, pp. 178, 198–99.

10. For similar suggestions, see Sohn, "Responses," pp. 188–94; and Fisher, "International Police," pp. 254–59.

11. *Ibid.*, pp. 250–68. Fisher argues that it may be possible to develop a quasi-judicial procedure that turns the highly political question of general compliance with an agreement into the less charged question of compliance with a specific, well-designed legal decree. His position is likely to be correct when international sentiment strongly favors the decree; but it is probably too optimistic as long as

the nation-state system remains the central basis of political loyalty. One has to have a commitment to the international system to find even a narrow international decree forceful enough to demand compliance.

CHAPTER 7

1. *Weekly Compilation of Presidential Documents*, 8 (June 19, 1972), pp. 1026–42. For general discussions of SALT I, see William R. Kintner and Robert L. Pfaltzgraff, Jr., eds., *SALT: Implications for Arms Control in the 1970s* (Pittsburgh, 1973); John Newhouse, *Cold Dawn: The Story of SALT* (New York, 1973); and Mason Willrich and John B. Rhinelander, eds., *SALT: The Moscow Agreements and Beyond* (New York, 1974).

2. J. P. Ruina, "U.S. and Soviet Strategic Arsenals," *ibid.*, pp. 34, 52–55.

3. 1974 Protocol to the Treaty Between the United States of America and the Union of Soviet Socialist Republics on the Limitation of Anti-Ballistic Missile Systems, signed July 3, 1974, *Weekly Compilation*, 10 (July 8, 1974): 750–51.

4. Public Law 92–448, 92d Congress, H.J. Res. 1227, Sept. 30, 1972.

5. Joint United States-Soviet Statement on Limitation of Strategic Offensive Arms, issued at Vladivostok, Nov. 24, 1974, *Weekly Compilation*, 10 (Dec. 2, 1974); 1489. (The numbers were released later.)

6. [Draft] United States-Soviet Union Treaty on the Limitation of Strategic Offensive Arms and Related Documents, Vienna, June 18, 1979, *Weekly Compilation*, 15 (June 25, 1979): 1051–79.

7. Gyorgi Arbatov, quoted in Alan Wolfe, "NATO and the Atomic Furor," *San Francisco Chronicle*, Dec. 10, 1979, p. D-1.

8. In 1968 *Pravda* described the time as "one of those rare moments in history . . . when both sides are ready to admit equality in the broadest sense." Roman Kolkowicz, Matthew P. Gallagher, and Benjamin S. Lambeth, *The Soviet Union and Arms Control: A Superpower Dilemma* (Baltimore, 1970), p. 59.

9. For the counterargument, see D. G. Brennan, "The Case for Missile Defense," *Foreign Affairs*, 47 (April 1969): 433.

10. This is made quite explicit in the president's June 15, 1972, briefing of congressional leaders on the SALT accords; *Weekly Compilation*, 8 (June 19, 1972): 1043–45.

11. Kolkowicz et al., *Soviet Union*, pp. 6–7, provides a selection of economic pressures.

12. Marshall D. Shulman, "SALT and the Soviet Union," in Willrich and Rhinelander, *SALT*, pp. 101, 104–5; Seyom Brown, *New Forces in World Politics* (Washington, D.C., 1974), pp. 69–78.

13. The President's Message to the Senate Transmitting the ABM Treaty and the Interim Agreement on Strategic Offensive Arms, June 13, 1972, *Weekly Compilation*, 8 (June 19, 1972): 1026.

14. Basic Principles of Relations Between the United States of America and the Union of Soviet Socialist Republics, May 29, 1972, *Weekly Compilation*, 8 (June 5, 1972): 943–44.

15. Shulman, "SALT," p. 102.

16. Malcolm Mackintosh, "Moscow's View of the Balance of Power," *The World Today*, 29 (March 1973): 108; Kolkowicz et al., *Soviet Union*, pp. 54, 186. The closely related Soviet concern with proliferation was expressed as early as 1960 to Walt W. Rostow; see his "Introduction: The Politics of Arms Control or How to Make Nuclear Weapons Wither Away," in Kintner and Pfaltzgraff, *Implications*, pp. xv, xvi.

17. Chalmers M. Roberts, "The Road to Moscow," in Willrich and Rhinelander, *SALT*, pp. 3, 24; Shulman "SALT," p. 104.

18. Mason Willrich, "SALT I: An Appraisal," in Willrich and Rhinelander, *SALT*, pp. 256, 261–62.

19. See for example Roger D. Speed, *Strategic Deterrence in the 1980's* (Stanford, Calif., 1979), pp. 45–64.

20. Wynfred Joshua, "SALT and the Middle East," in Kintner and Pfaltzgraff, *Implications*, pp. 237, 238–42.

21. Jacques Isnard, "La France va mettre au point des missiles de croisière et des satellites d'observation," *Le Monde*, June 11, 1977, p. 1.

22. Consider the arguments made in the conventional forces context in "Reflections on the Quarter," *Orbis*, 16 (1973): 841.

23. Christoph Bertram, *The Future of Arms Control*, pt. 2, *Arms Control and Technological Change: Elements of a New Approach* (London, 1978).

24. But see G. B. Kistiakowski and H. F. York, "Strategic Arms Race Slowdown Through Test Limitations," *Science*, 185 (Aug. 2, 1974): 403, which argues for the limitation of testing as a way to make SALT more effective.

25. George W. Rathjens, "Future Limitations of Strategic Arms," in Willrich and Rhinelander, *SALT*, pp. 225, 239–40.

26. This example is based on Leonard Beaton's suggestion for "force commitment"; see his *The Reform of Power* (London, 1972), pp. 204–11.

CHAPTER 8

1. Christopher Makins, "Western Europe's Security: Fog over the 'Grey Areas,'" *The World Today*, 35 (Feb. 1979): 55, 56.

2. Christoph Bertram, *Mutual Force Reductions in Europe: The Political Aspects* (London, 1972), pp. 22–25. One commentator argues, however, that the USSR may have been finding its position in Eastern Europe extremely costly and been seeking a way to maintain its influence in Europe at a lower cost. Seyom Brown, *New Forces in World Politics* (Washington, D.C., 1974), p. 65.

3. Bertram, *Force Reductions*, pp. 4, 26–27.

4. See *The Economist*, 267 (June 17, 1978): 60.

5. Daniel Vernet, "Moscou souhaite devenir un interlocuteur direct de l'Europe de l 'Ouest," *Le Monde*, Dec. 12, 1979, p. 5.

6. See for example Steven L. Canby, *NATO Military Policy: Obtaining Conventional Comparability with the Warsaw Pact* (Rand R-1088-ARPA, Santa Monica, Calif., June 1973), pp. 24–31. See also Richard D. Lawrence and Jeffrey Record, *U.S. Force Structure in NATO: An Alternative* (Washington, D.C., 1974), pp. 9–12.

7. E.g. Canby, *NATO*, p. 59.

8. See A. Merglen, "Military Lessons of the October War," in *The Middle East and the International System*, pt. 1, *The Impact of the 1973 War* (London, 1975), p. 26; and Lawrence L. Whetten and Michael Johnson, "Military Lessons of the Yom Kippur War," *The World Today*, 30 (March 1974): 101.

9. Lawrence L. Whetten, *The Arab-Israeli Dispute: Great Power Behavior* (London, 1977), p. 25.

10. UN Charter, arts. 39, 11.

11. See D. W. Bowett, *United Nations Forces: A Legal Study of United Nations Practice* (London, 1964), pp. 266–74. The Security Council's legal powers are often interpreted quite broadly; see for example Jorge Castañeda, *Legal Effects of United Nations Resolutions* (New York, 1969), pp. 75–76.

12. For a discussion of associated legal problems, written before U Thant's 1967 withdrawal of the UN forces from Egypt, see Leon Gordenker, *The UN Secretary-General and the Maintenance of Peace* (New York, 1967), pp. 252–57; Bowett, *United Nations*, pp. 235, 311–12, 412–27, and especially pp. 421–22 on giving up the right to require withdrawal.

13. There is legal precedent for an agreed suspension of the veto power; *ibid.*, p. 540.

14. John H. Barton, "Tacit Political Restraints as a Way to Control Conventional Arms," *Stanford Journal of International Studies*, 14 (1979): 29.

15. Cf. Leonard Beaton, *The Reform of Power* (London, 1972), pp. 158–74.

16. An analogous argument often made in Japan against the acquisition of nuclear weapons is that they would increase the chance of being attacked. Although Japan is within the U.S. defense shield, its "low-profile" diplomacy is in many ways parallel to the "neutral" diplomacy of Sweden.

17. Treaty for the Prohibition of Nuclear Weapons in Latin America, 634 U.N.T.S. 281. For good general discussions, see Davis R. Robinson, "The Treaty of Tlatelolco and the United States: A Latin American Nuclear Free Zone," *American Journal of International Law*, 64 (1970): 282; Alfonso García Robles, "Mesures de Désarmement dans des Zones Particulières: Le Traité, Visant L'Interdiction des

Armes Nucléaires en Amérique Latine," *Recueil des Cours*, 133 (The Hague, 1972): 43; and Hector Gros Espiell, *En Torno al Tratado de Tlatelolco y la Proscripción de las Armas Nucleares en la América Latina* (Mexico, 1973).

18. P. K. Jha, "Treaty for the Prohibition of Nuclear Weapons in Latin America—1967: A Critical Appraisal," *Indian Journal of International Law*, 8 (1968): 63, 71–72.

19. See John H. Barton, "The Developing Nations and Arms Control," *Studies in Comparative International Development*, 10 (1975): 67.

20. Gros Espiell, *En Torno al Tratado*, p. 12.

CHAPTER 9

1. William B. Bader, *The United States and the Spread of Nuclear Weapons* (New York, 1968), p. 48. Parts of this discussion of the NPT are based on my review of Mason Willrich, ed., *International Safeguards and Nuclear Industry* (Baltimore, 1973), in *Ecology Law Quarterly*, 4 (1974): 169.

2. Bernhard G. Bechhoefer, "Historical Evolution of International Safeguards," in Willrich, *International Safeguards*, pp. 21, 40.

3. Chalmers M. Roberts, *The Nuclear Years: The Arms Race and Arms Control, 1945–70* (New York, 1970), p. 69. See also the 1960 Soviet arguments described in W. W. Rostow, "Introduction: The Politics of Arms Control or How to Make Nuclear Weapons Wither Away," in William R. Kintner and Robert L. Pfaltzgraff, Jr., eds., *SALT: Implications for Arms Control in the 1970's* (Pittsburgh, 1973), pp. xv, xvi.

4. For this history, see Senate Committee on Foreign Relations, *Hearings on the Non-Proliferation Treaty*, 90th Cong. 2d sess., July 10, 11, 12, and 17, 1968, and Feb. 18 and 20, 1969, especially pp. 251–57 (Letter of Submittal) and 450–61 (Charles R. Gellner, "The Conference of Non-Nuclear-Weapon States, 1968: A Survey of Views and Proposals"); Elizabeth Young, *A Farewell to Arms Control?* (Harmondsworth, Eng., 1972), pp. 1–130; Jean Klein, "Vers le traité de non-prolifération," *Politique Étrangère*, 33 (1968): 225; and William Epstein, *The Last Chance: Nuclear Proliferation and Arms Control* (New York, 1976).

5. Security Council Resolution 255 (June 19, 1968) and accompanying United States Declaration on Security Assurances to Non-Nuclear Nations, S/PV 1430 (June 17, 1968).

6. Address by President Carter to the Organizing Conference of the International Nuclear Fuel Cycle Evaluation, Oct. 19, 1977.

7. Nuclear Non-Proliferation Act of 1978, P.L. 95–242 (March 10, 1978).

8. See Anne Hessing Cahn, Joseph J. Kruzel, Peter M. Dawkins, and Jacques Huntzinger, *Controlling Future Arms Trade* (New York, 1977).

9. U.S. Arms Control and Disarmament Agency, *The International*

Transfer of Conventional Arms: A Report to the Congress Pursuant to Section 302 of the Foreign Relations Authorization Act of 1972 (P.L. 92–352), 83–84.

10. Speech by S. Rajaratham, Minister for Foreign Affairs, Republic of Singapore, at UN General Assembly, Sept. 29, 1976.

11. E.g. William R. Kintner, "Arms Control for a Five-Power World," in Kintner and Pfaltzgraff, *SALT*, pp. 167, 176–79.

12. Geoffrey Kemp and Ian Smart, "SALT and European Nuclear Forces," *ibid.*, pp. 199, 203–10.

13. This sort of scenario is suggested by Harry G. Gelber, "The Impact of Chinese ICBM's on Strategic Deterrence," *Orbis*, 13 (1969): 407.

14. George H. Quester, "Implications of SALT Outcome for Potential 'Nth' Powers: Israel, India, and Others," in Kintner and Pfaltzgraff, *SALT*, pp. 255, 257–63.

15. For an example, see Stanford Law School International Nuclear Fuel Cycle Working Group, *Evaluation of an Integrated International Nuclear Fuel Authority* (Palo Alto, Calif., 1978).

16. The Soviet problem was most likely the Soviet objection to the inspection; Bechhoefer, "Historical Evolution," p. 41. On France, see Wolf Mendl, *Deterrence and Persuasion* (New York, 1970), pp. 221–22. The U.S. history is given in *U.S. Arms Control and Disarmament Agency, Fourth Annual Report*, 5–6 (1965). Parallel, unverified U.S.-Soviet cutbacks were, however, worked out; Address by President Johnson and Statement by Premier Khrushchev, April 20, 1964, USACDA, *1964 Documents on Disarmament* (1965), pp. 165–68.

17. Bechhoefer, "Historical Evolution," pp. 25–27.

18. For a careful discussion of negative assurances, see Hedley Bull, "Rethinking Non-Proliferation," *International Affairs*, 51 (1975): 175, 187–88.

19. Leonard Beaton, *The Reform of Power: A Proposal for an International Security System* (London, 1972), pp. 204–11.

CHAPTER 10

1. See John H. Barton, "The Proscription of Nuclear Weapons: A Third Nuclear Regime," in David C. Gompert, ed., *Nuclear Weapons and World Politics: Alternatives for the Future* (New York, 1977), pp. 172–79.

2. For a brief discussion of the limits of such diplomacy, showing how the Concert of Europe failed under pressures deriving from domestic politics, see C. Wilfred Jenks, *The World Beyond the Charter* (London, 1969), pp. 39–41.

3. Alva Myrdal, "The International Control of Disarmament," *Scientific American*, 231 (Oct. 1974): 21.

4. Compare Jenks, *World*, pp. 51, 62.

Index

Index

ABM, *see* Antiballistic missile
Abrogation clauses, in treaties, 106
Absolutism, 47
Admiralty courts, 51
Afghanistan, Soviet invasion of
  (1979), 154, 165, 194, 243
Africa, 31, 35, 165, 169; southern,
  137, 231; arms control in, 192, 211
Aggression, instinctive, 1–5, 13, 45,
  235
Agreements, 78–79, 86, 90–91, 94,
  105–6, 168–74
Algeria, 13
Allegiance, limits, 6
Alliances, 211
Amorality, *see* Morality
Angola, 151
Animal behavior, 9
Annexationism, *see* Expansionism
Antarctica, 36, 99, 124; treaty on, 72
Antiballistic missile, 81, 88, 105, 124;
  strategy, 92f, 96, 149–50, 155–56
Antisubmarine warfare, 206
Arabs, 239
Argentina, 202
Armies, 13–14
Arms: and war, 31–32, 36; balance
  of, 89, 148–49; lobbies for, 92;
  embargo on, 136; transfers of,
  187–88, 203–4
Arms control, 43, 65–66, 112, 186–88,
  229–32, 245–46; effects of, 36–37,
  63, 68, 72–73, 123–26, 219; in
  1920's, 49, 92; agreements for, 54f,
  79, 107, 244; conditions for, 63–77,
  80–84, 89–90; patterns of, 71–73.
  See also Agreements
Arms Control and Disarmament
  Agency, 150

Arms race, 37, 91–95, 125, 243
Asia, South, 192
Authoritarianism, 8
Authority, obedience to, 3–5

B-1 bomber, 157
Balkan Wars, 26
Bargaining chips, 93, 125
Baruch Plan, 73, 89
Beaton, Leonard, 212f
Belgrade, 181
Berchtold, Count, 26
Berlin airlift (1948), 40
Bethmann-Hollweg, Theobald von,
  26
Biological Warfare Convention
  (1972), 108, 115f
Biological weapons, 63, 72, 143, 197
Bismarck, Otto von, 23f, 35
Bodin, Jean, 47
Brandt, Willy, 178
Brazil, 12, 69, 99, 198; and NPT,
  202
Brezhnev, Leonid I., 87, 152f, 180
Brown, John, 21
Buchanan, Pres. James, 21
Buffer zones, 37
Bureaucracy, 9–10, 12, 57–58, 116–17;
  and arms control, 75–76, 78; and
  treaties, 108–9, 243–44

Canada, 108, 121–22
Carter, Pres. Jimmy, 101, 152, 154,
  163, 173, 202f
Centralization, world, 222–27
Chemical Warfare Convention
  (1925), 100
Chemical weapons, 85
Chile, 12

China, 17, 56, 69, 212; and arms control, 79, 99, 204
Civil War (U.S.), 18–23, 28–32 passim, 241
Clay, Henry, 19f
Cold War, 30, 55, 128, 178
Colonialism, 24, 29
Comprehensive nuclear test ban, 209–10
Concert of Europe, 48, 223
Conference on Security and Cooperation in Europe (CSCE), 55, 179–84 passim
Congo, 142
Consultations, and arms control, 167, 184–85, 192–93, 228
Conventional weapons, and arms control, 202–4
Courts, and foreign policy, 58–59
Cruise missile, 151ff, 163–64, 214
Crusades, 9, 29f, 48, 50
Cuba, 40, 153, 244
Cuban missile crisis (1962), 39, 162, 185
Cyprus, 135, 142
Czechoslovakia, 41, 149, 198

De Gaulle, Charles, 132, 178
Denmark, 203
Détente, 82, 97, 151, 158, 178–79; and arms control, 70, 103, 243; and SALT, 90, 111, 158; collapse of, 165–66
Deterrence, theory of, 170n
Developing world, 8, 39, 65, 186–87; and international law, 45, 49; and technology, 71f, 110, 210
Diego Garcia, U.S. base on, 194
Diplomacy, 46, 120–21, 239–40; and war, 17, 32–43, 46; pre-First World War, 23–27; and arms control, 43, 172
Disarmament: after First World War, 68; general, 87, 126. See also Arms control
Dominican Republic, 198
Douglas, Stephen A., 20f
Dissidents, Eastern European, 180
Dred Scott decision, 20
Dulles, John Foster, 177

East Germany, 178

Economics, 8; and war, 15, 29; and arms control, 76, 81, 145, 214–16; and centralization, 229
Edward VII, 25
Egypt, 40, 96, 188, 202
Elites, international, 224
Embargo, arms, 127
Enforcement, see Sanctions
England, treaty with France (1303), 51
Entebbe raid (1976), 143
Environmental weapons, 63
Escalation, of diplomatic war, 37–39
Europe, 6–7; arms control in, 69, 95, 182f; nuclear arms in, 168, 205–6
European Economic Community (EEC), 10, 46, 143–44, 226f
Expansionism, 7f, 27, 29–30, 32, 186; and arms control, 219

Ferdinand, Archduke, 26
First World War, 23–28
Ford, Pres. Gerald R., 85, 151
Foreign policy, 8–11, 46, 58–59, 61
Fractional orbital systems (USSR), 107
France, 7, 11, 97–98, 99, 164, 203; and nuclear weapons, 72, 177–78, 206, 210; and arms control, 99, 108, 173, 203f

García Robles, Alfonso, 84
Genetic manipulation, 214
Geneva Protocol (1925), 85
Germany, 13, 23f, 79; and expansionism, 7f, 29–30, 32, 68f; and arms control, 88, 159, 201; post–Second World War, 177, 180
Government, and self-defense, 5f
"Gray areas," 164
Great Britain: and naval power, 71; and arms control, 77, 191–92
Greek-Turkish conflict, 184
Grey, Sir Edward, 25
Gromyko, Andrei, 181
Grotius, Hugo, 48
Guerrilla warfare, 35, 186, 189
Gunboat diplomacy, 35

Helsinki, 176; Final Act at (1975), 179–80
Hitler, Adolf, 13, 108, 129, 131

Hobbes, Thomas, 47
Horn of Africa, 151
Hot line (U.S.-USSR), 171
Human rights, 10–11, 62, 181–82

ICBM, *see* Intercontinental ballistic missile
India, 136, 198, 206; dynamism of, 69, 186; nuclear policy of, 72, 108, 121; and arms control, 99, 202
Indian Ocean, 37; and Zone of Peace, 194
Indonesia, 186
Intelligence, 36, 117, 217. *See also* Satellites
Intercontinental ballistic missile, 152
Intermediate-range missile, 206
International Atomic Energy Agency (IAEA), 118, 119–20, 200, 230
International Court of Justice, 60, 108, 144
International law, 41, 45–56, 61; historical development of, 46–50; and self-interest, 50–55, 87, 90; mechanisms of, 55–56; and arms control, 63
International Monetary Fund (IMF), 46
International parliament, proposed, 228–29
Iran hostage crisis, 153
Israel, 96, 132, 186, 202, 239; and nuclear arms, 207, 243

Jackson, Sen. Henry F., 85–86, 150
Jackson Amendment (1972), 90
Japan, 7, 29, 59, 68; and militarism, 11ff, 110; and dynamism, 32, 69; and nuclear arms, 168, 248

Kansas-Nebraska Act (1854), 20–21
Kellogg-Briand Pact (1928), 37, 48, 67
Kennedy, Pres. John F., 85, 121
Kissinger, Henry, 109, 121, 150, 158, 166
Korea, 128f, 136
Korean War, 69

Latin America, 13, 35, 137, 197–98, 203, 211
Latin American Nuclear Free Zone, 98, 101, 194–95, 197

Law, definition, 44
Legitimacy, and government, 6
Liège, 51
Limited Test Ban (LTB) treaty (1963), 54, 72, 79, 81, 85, 100, 201; and sanctions, 120; and nuclear testing, 124
Lincoln, Abraham, 22
"Linkage," 153
London Supplier's Group, 202
LTB, *see* Limited Test Ban treaty

McNamara, Robert S., 76
Madariaga, Salvador de, 87
Malta, 203
Marxism, 29, 49–50
Mexican Cession, 20
Mexican Revolution, 17
Middle East, 10, 23f, 31f, 35, 95ff, 184, 186; 1967 war in, 40; 1973 war in, 40, 183, 188; arms control in, 90, 169, 191f; sanctions in, 130, 134f; settlement in, 145, 185, 231
Military, 9–14; and foreign relations, 9–10, 35–36; and war, 11–14, 17; and arms control, 75–77, 133; and strategic doctrines, 82–83
Minuteman missile, 153
MIRV, *see* Multiple independently targetable reentry vehicle
Missiles, 160–64; deterrence by, 170n
Missions, controls on, 167
Missouri Compromise (1820), 19
Monroe Doctrine, 197–98
Morality: and war, 5, 16, 29; and foreign relations, 9–11, 45, 108
Multiple independently targetable reentry vehicle (MIRV), 81, 149, 151, 162, 165, 206, 214
Munich Pact (1938), 68–69
Mutual and Balanced Force Reductions (MBFR), 179–84 *passim*
M-X missile, 153
Myrdal, Alva, 84

Napoleon Bonaparte, army of, 236f
Napoleonic wars, 16, 29f
National self-interest, 45–46
Nationalism, 5–7, 8, 13, 16f, 33
Naval force negotiations: pre-First World War, 25, 34, 69, 71, 106f;

pre-Second World War, 79–80, 87–88, 97–98, 111
Nazis, 60
Negotiation, process of: of arms control, 39–41, 87–88; in multilateral situations, 97–101
Neutrality, 241; Swedish, 46; law of, 50–54; and arms control, 193–94
New International Economic Order, 49
Nixon, Pres. Richard M., 85, 87, 149ff, 157–58
Non-Proliferation Treaty (NPT), 73, 75, 102–10 passim, 118f, 159, 191–92, 200–212 passim
North Atlantic Treaty Organization (NATO), 176–81 passim; and arms control, 81, 130; and cruise missile, 154, 164
North-South arms control, 164
NPT, see Non-Proliferation Treaty
Nuclear arms, 10–11, 65, 90, 176f, 207; and war, 17, 37; testing of, 54, 57–58, 73, 98, 108; and arms control, 62, 82–83, 133, 143, 171–73, 201, 210–12; and deterrence, 128, 169–70, 206–8; proliferation of, 205–8 passim
Nuclear energy, 201–2, 210
Nuclear technology, 208–10
Nuremberg trials, 60–61, 142

Offensive force agreement, 150–51
Organization of African Unity (OAU), 196
Organization of American States (OAS), 196, 198
Organization of Petroleum Exporting Countries (OPEC), 10
Ostpolitik, 178
Outer Space Treaty (1967), 107

Pacifists, 74
Pakistan, 121, 202, 206, 208
Paris Accords (Vietnam War), 121
Patriotism, 2, 5–6
Peace movements, 30–31
Persia, 47
Persian Gulf, 186
Peru, 12, 76
Poison gas, 100f
Politics, 28, 30, 109, 221

Precision-guided weapons, 115, 133, 183, 187, 189
Prestige, 9, 29–30, 37–39, 203, 236, 239; and nuclear arms, 72, 100, 210–11
Propaganda, 87–88
Prussia, 11
Public opinion, 41, 129; and foreign policy, 46, 60–61; and arms control, 121, 130–31, 145, 220

Reformation, Protestant, 47, 223
Regional arms control, 175–85, 190–92, 227; non-European, 185–99; and consultations, 198, 211
Religious wars, 48
Republican Party (U.S.), 21f
Revolutions, 17
Rush-Bagot agreement (Great Lakes), 68

SALT, see Strategic Arms Limitation Talks
Sanctions, arms control, 119–23, 135–46; types of, 127; collective sanction, 128–34; economic sanctions, 244–45
Sarajevo, 26
Satellites: and arms control verification, 117–19, 217; and UN, 230
Saudi Arabia, 191
Schlieffen plan, 37, 40
Scientists, and arms control, 74, 144
Seabed Arms Control Treaty (1971), 99
Second World War, 13, 32–33, 53, 176, 241–42
Security Council (UN), sanctions by, 119–20
Self-determination, 45
Sharia (Muslim law), 47
Slavery (U.S.), 18–19, 20
South Africa, 10, 70, 186, 202
Southeast Asia, 186
Sovereignty, 45, 188–89
Soviet Union: and arms control, 77, 79, 147, 191–92; and ABM systems, 150; and West, 157, 181; internal politics of, 172f; and Eastern Europe, 184, 247; and Middle East, 188; China policy of, 157, 159, 179

Spain, 17
Spanish-American War, 29f
SS-20 (missile), 164, 181
Stalin, Joseph, 177
Standing Consultative Commission (SCC), 228
Stowell, Lord (British judge), 51
Strategic Arms Limitation Talks (SALT), 64, 72, 81, 88, 94, 166–67, 204–5, 220; motivations for, 83, 91ff, 156–58; violation of, 117, 121; and technology, 165, 231
—SALT I, 64, 85f, 108, 124, 178, 228; motivations for, 96, 154–60; terms of, 148–49, 243; and arms, 89, 92; effects of, 93, 106, 111, 116, 120
—SALT II, 96, 152, 160–67; motivations for, 89–91, 165
—SALT III, 164
Strategic planning, 34–35
Sweden, 136, 194, 203
Switzerland, 194
Syria, 96

Tactical nuclear weapons, 86, 181
Taiwan, 186
Technology: and war, 15, 16, 82, 94, 110, 189–90, 204; and arms control, 71f, 92, 167–68, 214–17
Tehran hostage crisis, 144
Terrorism, 30, 45, 144f, 189, 197, 209; nuclear, 37
Testing, nuclear, 95
Third World, see Developing world
Three Mile Island incident (1979), 208
Tirpitz, Admiral (Germany), 25
Tisza, Count (Hungary), 26
Totalitarianism, 8
Treaties, see Agreements
Trident submarine, 157
Triple Alliance, 24

United Nations: and arms control, 40, 60, 187, 209, 229f; verification by, 115, 173, 227–28, 230; sanctions by, 127–35 passim, 245; and nuclear arms, 173, 213–14; and regional arms control, 188–92 passim, 196, 227

United States, 17, 224; Constitution of, 19, 226; and arms control, 68, 84–86, 116, 117, 191–92; China policy of, 110; and relations with USSR, 158–59; nuclear arms policy of, 172, 177
U.S. Supreme Court, 58–59
U.S.-USSR Standing Consultative Commission, 122, 169, 213
USSR, see Soviet Union

Vattel, Emerich de, 47
Verification of arms control agreements, 79, 106, 112–19; and UN, 227–28
Versailles Treaty, 29, 32, 68, 102–8 passim, 116, 121, 123, 244
Vietnam War, 13, 68f, 85, 129, 179, 186
Vladivostok agreement (1974), 91, 151f

War: causes of, 3, 11–16 passim, 38–42 passim, 81; nature of, 3–8 passim, 15–18, 237; and popular ideology, 17, 28–33; prevention of, 32–33; declaration of, 45, 53; law of, 48, 53; of national liberation, 49; preemptive, 97; and arms control, 219, 239; legal definition of, 241
War of 1812, 68
War-fighting capability, 161ff
Wars, religious, 47
Warsaw Pact, 184
Washington Naval Treaty (1922), 110
Watergate scandal, 151
Weapons, see Arms
Webster, Daniel, 20
Weimar government (Germany), 106–7
Westphalia, Treaty of (1648), 32f, 47, 62, 223
William II (Germany), 25
Wilson, Woodrow, 9
World Wars, see First World War; Second World War

Yugoslavia, 184